Document No. 9.

IN THE ASSEMBLY.] [SESSION 1854.

REPORT

ON THE

GEOLOGY OF THE COAST MOUNTAINS,

AND PART OF THE

SIERRA NEVADA:

EMBRACING THEIR INDUSTRIAL

RESOURCES IN AGRICULTURE AND MINING,

BY DR. JOHN B. TRASK.

[B. B. REDDING, STATE PRINTER.

To His Excellency,

JOHN BIGLER,

Governor of the State of California.

Pursuant to resolution of Assembly, passed Feb. —, 1854, I have the honor herewith to submit the accompanying report on the Geology of that portion of the State, authorized by Joint Resolution of Senate and Assembly of the fourth session, all of which, with accompanying plates, is respectfully submitted.

Yours, &c.

JOHN B. TRASK.

TO THE SENATE AND ASSEMBLY

OF THE STATE OF CALIFORNIA.

Under the Joint Resolution, passed May 6. 1853, by the Senate and Assembly of the State of California, authorizing a farther Geological examination of some parts of the Sierra Nevada and Coast Mountains, and report the results of the same to the ensuing Legislature, I have the honor of submitting the following report in relation thereto, and in conformity to the above requisitions.

JOHN B. TRASK.

PREFACE.

The examinations authorized were entered upon soon after the passage of the resolution, and continued until the 28th of November, comprising a period in the field of about six months. The first five weeks were occupied in examinations of the more elevated and western portions of the Counties of Butte, Sierra, Yuba, Nevada and Placer, in determining, as far as possible, the position of an ancient water course in this section of the State, and its peculiarities—the description of which will be found in the body of this report.

On the 23d June, the southern portion of the tour was commenced, and carried on almost uninterruptedly for four months. The route south was carried through the Counties of San Francisco, Santa Clara, Santa Cruz, Monterey, and the north part of Luis Obispo; on the west, and returning on the east, (or through that range denominated the *Monte Diablo* Range) by the west part of Tulare County, Mariposa, Tuolumne, Alameda, Contra Costa and San Joaquin.

The range of country bounded on the north by the Straits Carquinez, and south by the Nacismiento, was divided into four sections, formed by lines running nearly east and west from the great valley to the coast. On the first of October, the country north of the Straits Carquinez was entered, and preliminary examinations only were made in the counties of Solano, Napa and Sonoma. From the County of Napa a section was carried across the basin of the Sacramento, and connected with examinations made two years previous on its eastern edge. A similar section was also made, passing eighteen miles south of Monte Diablo and continued across the San Joaquin.

The remainder of the months of October and November was employed in investigations of the middle mining sections of the County of Nevada and those intermediate between the former and the middle and western parts of Calaveras county. This range leads through that section in which the principal gold mines of the middle portions of the State are located, and was selected, with the view of conducting those examinations which will be found in the appendix of this report, under the head of Quartz Mining. As those mines have of late presented many interesting facts connected with their ultimate prospects, a set of sketches representing the positions of the views and investing rocks has been given for illustrating their present features.

Doing the tour in the agricultural sections of the State, the modifications of the soils in different sections has been noted, and the natural productions arising as resultants, where they seemed of a general character, and extending over any considerable area. The "Saline lands" have been observed, and the opportunities that were offered for their reclamation, whed at any time demanded. The extent of cropping and resultant crops in some parts of the State, are of peculiar interest, and the facts developed in this particular will prove of much value to our agricultural interests, being an exhibition of the capabilities of some our soils for the production of the necessaries of life, unexcelled in the history of the world.

The temperature of the mountainous and valley sections of both branches of the coast mountains, was noted as far as the nature of attending cir cumstances would permit, for the purpose of ascertaining as far as possible the peculiar adaptation of the different sections to the culture of exotic fruits and trees, and where no opportunity of personal examination offered, a careful inquiry of persons long resident in different sections, was made, by which many interesting facts have been obtained, relating to this subject.

This report will embrace the examination of a district of country, included within 120° 16′ and 122° 32′ west longitude, and from the thirty-fifth parallel to the thirty-ninth degree of north latitude, inclusive of the coast mountains and mineral districts.

The coast mountains are watered by thirty-two streams, the most of which are small, their names and the counties in which they are located will be found below.

COUNTY.	RIVER.
Sonoma.	Sonoma.—
Napa.	Napa.—
Contra Costa.	Merced.—
Alameda.	San Antonio.—
	San Leandro.—
	San Lorenzo.—
	Alameda.—
Santa Clara.	Coyote.—
	Aguagos.
	San Felipe.—
	Gaudalupe.—
	Los Gatos.—
	Camels.—
	Llagos.
	Carnadero.—
	Pescadero.—
	La Brae.—
Santa Cruz.	San Lorenzo.—
	Lougell.—
	Syante.—
	San Augustine.—

County.	River.
	Corallitos.
Monterey.	Pajaro.
	San Benito.
	Carmello.—
	Berjeles.—
	San Antonio.
	Saliñas.—
	Francisquito.—
San Luis Obispo.	Nacismiento.
San Francisco.	San Mateo.
	San Francisquito.—

There are twenty-three of these streams which furnish a sufficient quantity of water for milling purposes, and are marked with a dash, (—) the above list does not include many small arroyas that course through these sections.

REPORT.

The coast range of mountains, and its included valleys, which form the principle subject of this report, extend from the 42nd paralel north latitude to the southern boundary of the State. Their general features present much more diversity of character than is usually to be found in the eastern chain of mountains, which forms the Sierra Nevada; from the occurrence of a greater variety of rocks constituting their mass, and the much greater area of covered by the sedimentary formations, the principle of which are sandstones, interspersed occasionally with calcareous rocks, and more rarely slates; this latter class of rocks forming but a small proportion of the sedimentary formations, of which later extensive portions of the coast line of mountains is composed.

The eastern belt of the coast range presents a repulsive aspect to the traveller as he approaches it from either hand, from its naked and barren appearance, producing but little of forest growth in any part of it, while those portions of the coast line of hills proper, are covered to a great extent with forest trees, consisting principally of the redwood, pine, and spruce, with groves of oak near their base, all of which are well adapted to the wants of the settler and usually easy of access.

This peculiarity in the two principal ridges of this chain was general for near three hundred miles of their course, the eastern ridge presenting no traces of timber except here and there an isolated patch of the pine on some one of its higher points; and for miles in extent even low shrubs are almost entirely absent.

Notwithstanding the barren aspect of the eastern belt of the coast mountains, it is not to be inferred that their slopes or valleys are unproductive, for it is found to be otherwise, being covered with a luxuriant growth of native grains and grasses, with herbaceous plants, affording extensive pasturage for flocks and herds. The lower foothills of the range, and the immediate banks of the small streams that meander through them, afford a few scattering oaks and other trees, but not sufficient in extent to furnish more than a very small local demand, to so extensive a population as the valley sections at the base of these hills must in a few years require. The oak groves found on the plains are not adapted to any other uses than that of fencing and for fuel. The western or coast line of mountains must become the principal source of supply, in lumber for building purposes, except that which may be obtained by importation.

The coast range consists of two principal and distinct lines of ridges for a distance of nearly two hundred miles of their length; these are separated from each other by wide and long valleys that continue almost uninterrupted through their whole course, and should be considered as distinct ranges of one system both from their geographical position as relates to the mountains in which they are situated. The valleys have recieved different names, as the Santa Clara and Salinas; and these again are subdivided and recieve local names even on the same line of plain; they can be considered strictly but one valley, the lineo f continuity being broken by the interposition of a range of hills, not exceeding in altitude three hundred feet, and even below these figures.

This division of the Salinas from the Santa Clara is caused by a low spur putting in from the Gabilan range, in a direction nearly north-west. Across the northern part of this spur the Pajaro River, an inconsiderable stream, holds its course, discharging its waters into the Bay of Monterey. The extent and geographical position of these two valleys would seem to warrant a different arrangement than that at present existing in reference to the coast range; as they form a line as distinct and clear in the separation of the two principal ridges, as the valleys Sacramento and San Joaquin in the separation of the coast range on the west from the Sierra Nevada on the east.

The division of the coast range proposed will be bounded as follows: commencing at a point due east of Monte Diablo on the valley San Joaquin, the latter and the Tulare valley to form the east line to the intersection of both ranges with the San Bernardino Mountains, near the thirty-fifth degree north latitude, thence running west to a point that shall cut the west base of this range, and lying on the north-western border of the Salinas, thence north along the west border of the latter, and also the west border of the valley Santa Clara to the south-east terminus of the bay San Francisco, following the east coast of that bay to the point San Pablo. This range inclusive to be denominated the Monte Diabolo, and all mountains to the west of these lines to be still termed the "Coast Mountains." This division in the mountains now bearing the latter name, will become the more necessary when it is understood that much difficulty now exists in localizing phenomena and transactions that have from time to time occurred, as well also as another distinctive feature which marks them, viz: their relative age, the one being of comparative recent date to the other. The term "Coast Range" implies a line of mountains following the coast only, but which, as it is used at the present time, includes a chain whose eastern base is as far removed from the coast, as the foothills of the Sierra Nevada are from Bodega Bay on a line cutting through the City of Sacramento to the ocean. This chain, it will be seen, is separated by broad and long valleys, as distinct in their characteristics as the Sacramento and San Joaquin, while their length, including the bay San Francisco, equals the latter and has nearly half its average breadth. The geological and mineral characteristics of the two ranges are equally as marked and distinct as their geographical position and vegetable productions, while the courses which both pursue are widely variant, forming an angle of thirty-six degrees in ninety-one miles. For local convenience of description this division should be made, if for no other reason.

A division, or rather a new arrangement, is to be introduced in relation to the entire mountain chains that lie upon the west side of the continent, which will give more uniformity and a much better classification than that now existing. It is not proposed however to change local names in the arrangement, but to name those parts of the mountains, which, as yet, have received none, except "Sierras," as they are termed. Through Mr. Blake, of the U. S. R. R. Survey, I am informed that it is now proposed to term the entire chain of mountains, extending through to the northern part of Oregon, and running south into lower California, "Cordilleras or Western America," and all those portions south of the thirty-fifth parallel of north latitude, [which, as yet, have received no name,] are to be termed the "Peninsula range" in order to separate them from the coast mountains with which they are now often confounded, and again as often termed Sierra Nevada, by persons who have occasion to describe them, or any part of them.

The terms "Sierra Nevada," and "Cascade Range," will thus be retained as local names, with their boundaries the same as before. The coast mountains will comprise the entire chain lying to the west of the above, and which are found to have an age more recent than the tertiary rocks, which rest upon them, and such local changes as may be necessary will be applied, but so far only as will be required in order to elucidate any peculiar characteristics they may possess.

This arrangement is one much needed, and is founded on strictly scientific principles, and this proposition of Mr. Blake will meet the universal concurrence of the country, as it will reduce the mountain chains of the western part of the continent, to a more perfect system than they have heretofore possessed.

A more specific classification of these mountains has before been proposed by different persons, among them that of Lieut. Wilkes, who proposed the term of "California Range of the Cascades;" for the Sierra Nevada being but a continuation of the former, all of them heretofore have been objectionable on the ground that old and established names would be changed by the arrangement; notwithstanding those names conveyed erroneous impressions. No such objection can be urged against the present proposition of the gentleman above named, as it affords a convenience of arrangement not heretofore suggested or presented to the public for their consideration. With these remarks on this part of our subject, we will proceed to the examination of the chain termed the Monte Diabolo Range.

GEOLOGY OF THE MONTE DIABOLO RANGE.

This chain of mountains forms the south shore of the Straits Carquinez and part of the bay of Suissun. The rocks bordering the bay and straits are mostly a sandstone, which belongs to a similar range occurring on the opposite shore. On the western flank of this portion of these mountains, or on the east shores of the bay San Pablo, and north part of San Francisco, a range of sharp Peaks are seen; their slopes are abrupt from the summit for a considerable way down toward their base, and in the latter part of winter and through the spring are covered with wild oats and grasses.

For several miles these mountains are made up of trapean rocks, which have forced themselves through the sedimentary rocks, and are in all respects similar to the volcanic series that has protruded through the older and also more recent formations in the Sierra Nevada. These rocks are cut through and disturbed by a suite of igneous rocks of still more recent origin, causing material change in the structure of the rocks that preceded them, both sedimentary and plutonic. Among the latter we find the pitchstone and obsidian, showing conclusively that they belong to that class known as recent volcanic rocks. These rocks may be conveniently observed in some of the lower hills about two miles east of the house of Victor Castro, in the County of Alameda. The more recent volcanic rocks form the first summit of the high ridge east of the bay, and the frequently isolated conical peaks to which they give rise, and which are known among the native inhabitants as (Picaches) stretch to the north for six miles, when they are replaced by the older trap rocks, and followed by the softer sandstones, which form the smooth rounded summits of the hills to the Bay San Pablo and Straits of Carquinez.

The sandstones on the shores present many marks of disturbance and change, by the intrusion of the late igneous rocks, and it is not unfrequent to find fine threads of quartz ramifying through them in every direction; when this is the case, or when they are in contact with the more recent of the igneous group, their former structure is usually found materially changed, a conchoidal fracture in these rocks is often the result of this contact either in large or small masses.

There are considerable areas of the sandstone in these mountains, that present little or no traces of change, subsequent to their deposition, except that of uplift; thus proving that they must have been deposited on the trap rocks after the latter had become firm, and parted with their heat: but where the sedimentary rocks are found in close proximity with the later igneous rocks the change indeed in them is clear and decisive: thus demonstrating the fact that volcanic action has occurred at a date long subsequent to the period in which these rocks were deposited, and probably after their emergence above the surface of the sea, in which they had their origin. It was found, in examining the sandstones lying upon the older trapean rocks of this part of the range, that the fine threads of quartz before noticed, gradually increased in dimensions as they approximated the inferior strata of the sedimentary rocks, and where the igneous rocks were exposed to view beneath them, in favorable situations, they often exhibited true well and defined, though small veins of quartz passing through them.

These general characteristics continue south untill a point nearly east of the town of Oakland is obtained, and here the trapean group of rocks are interrupted to a certain extent. East of this town we find the primitive rocks occurring, and an outcrop of serpentine makes its appearance, together with some of its subordinate members, among which the Shales and some of the cherty rocks appear. These are flanked to the east with rocks of the trapean group, forming the high ridge in that direction, and are surmounted with the fossiliferous sandstones. The serpentine rocks of this district contain considerable quantities of chromic iron, but its extent is not accurately known. South of Oakland to San Antonio, the country is of the same character as that immediately preceding it. The mountains were not examined, but the creek was followed four or five miles, and its bed showed nothing to indicate a change in the structure of the country from which it has its rise, with the exception, perhaps, that the sandstone pebbles exhibited no marks of fossils.

These features were general for the entire distance to the San Leandro, being about eight miles: but after crossing this stream, the fossiliferous rocks become more fully developed and continue to gradually increase to the arroyo of the Alameda. The sedimentary rocks of this district rest on the older trap formations, with frequent small threads of quartz passing through them, but no material change of structure was observed in these at the points of contact. The sandstone of these hills is much coarser in its texture than that forming the shores of the Bay San Pablo and Straits Carquinez, and its fossils exceedingly fragile and imperfect.

Crossing the Alameda and entering the hills in which the Mission of San Jose is situated, a distance of four miles, no change in the general character of the rocks is noticeable, with the exception that the sedimentary rocks have suffered more from disintegration than at any point north of the arryo Alameda, and the contour of the country being such as to retain a large part of the detritus of these rocks, the result has been the production of a soil, throughout the hilly and rolling districts, of almost unequalled richness and fertility.

Following the west side of the Central Range we pass into the county Santa Clara, a short distance south of the Mission San Jose. The sedimentary rocks containing fossils continue to cap the summit of the ridge for the distance of twenty-five miles south of this point, all of which appear to be of the same age as those above described. South of the *Hot Springs* (a point defining the boundary between the counties Alameda and Santa Clara) the trachytes crop out in two or three localities, leaving but little room for doubt that the more recent of the volcanic rocks underlie this entire section. At the distance of sixteen miles south of the Spring, the chlorite slate flanks the west base of the ridge, and at short intervals along this distance fragments of these rocks are frequently met; on the Rancho del Palo this rock again occurs at a distance of three miles east of San Jose, here it crops out on the hills three hundred feet above the valley, and appears to have been much disturbed and broken up; immediately west of this an alluminous slate appears dipping southwest and corresponding to the inclination of the chlorites.

In the hills of this district there is considerable quantities of quartz, some of which has proved auriferous.

Traveling parallel with the ridge and south of the Pueblo San Jose, the fossiliferous rocks become less developed, and at the distance of thirteen miles very few sandstones containing fossils were to be seen. In the arroya Caoti the first specimens of scoriaceous lava were met with, this induced a more critical examination of the mountains to the east of the valley than would otherwise have been made. The hills were entered a short distance south of Laguna Seca, and followed thence southerly for eighteen miles. Small patches of fossiliferous rocks are sparingly distributed over the route, the predominating rocks being igneous and composed principally of trachytes and lavas; from Laguna Seca an almost continuous dike of the latter extends along the western base of the ridge for a distance of near twenty miles.

As you approach the Rancho Cantine it becomes more cellular than farther north at any point where it was observed. In the vicinity of Gilroy's it has been used for milling purposes, to which it seems admirably adapted, being unequalled in hardness to the best French Buhr. I saw at Gilroy's three sets of these stones which have been in use at that place for several years in flouring wheat. These stones are capable of being split out to the diameter of four feet and the requisite thickness that may be required for the uses of the mill.

The principal rocks forming the east ridge of the Monte Diablo range, and continuing southeasterly from Gilroy's, are composed of the more recent volcanic series, and are but a part of those above alluded to. At the distance of eight miles from this town, the ridge attains an elevation near three thousand feet, and shoots up into a series of jagged, conical peaks, which maintain this character for sixteen miles south of San Felipe; the pass known as "Pacheco Pass," leading from the Valley Santa Clara to the San Joaquin, is situated among these latter hills and near their northern terminus.

Nine miles northeast from San Filipe is the well known landmark known as "Pacheco's Peak;" it is visible for a long distance from the east, west and south, but not from the north owing to the hills between having a considerable altitude and their close proximity on the principle line of travel; it is formed of trachyte and scoriaceous lavas, and is evidently the remains of an extinct volcano.

The Santa Anna mountains stretch in a south-east direction from San Felipe a distance of twelve miles, and from this point sink gradually into an uneven ridge having an altitude varying from one thousand to fifteen hundred feet, but far more rugged than its equivalent north of the Alameda Creek. The section inclusive from the vicinity of Pacheco's to the extreme southeast part of the Santa Anna mountains, has been one of the grand centres of the more recent volcanic disturbances which has imparted to the mountains their present contour; the greatest amount of local disturbance is confined within a line of distance comprising about eight miles north and south, exerting a considerable elevatory force on the sedimentary rocks of recent date to the west and south-west.

The disturbance among the latter rocks is manifested in a striking manner on the south-east portion of the "Loma Muertas," (a range of hills extending from the south-east part of the Santa Clara Valley across its upper end, dividing this from the Valley San Juan) which extends also to the fossiliferous rocks near the Mission San Juan, they all have a dip to the west, which is continuous for miles.

The Rancho Tres Pinos, eight miles south-west of Santa Anna, may be said to be the southern terminus of the Valley Santa Clara, though south of the "Loma Muertas" it is called San Juan; at this point it narrows to a cañon and continues thus forty miles to the south-east; after passing the Tres Pinos it becomes rough and irregular, though attaining no great altitude for most of this distance, and from the appearance of the cañada beyond, obtained from an elevation of eight hundred feet, it is probably connected with the Tulare plain some forty miles south, and from its appearance the elevation must be very moderate, as no hills were visible along the axis of the cañon to obstruct the view to a horizon beyond.

The stream that courses this cañada is termed San Benito as far south as the Arroya los Muertas, and eight miles south of the Rancho Tres Pinos, after which it takes the name of San Juan; it discharges its waters into the Pajaro fourteen miles north of the Rancho Santa Anna; the latter river forming the boundary of the counties Santa Clara, Santa Cruz and Monterey.

The pass Santa Anna is situated in the Monte Diablo Range and enters these mountains from the west, two leagues south of the Tres Pinos, and from the cañada San Benito; it was extremely rocky so far as examined though attaining no great altitnde, the mean of its course was fifteen degrees north of east. This cañon appears to have formed the banks of an ancient stream, and it is not improbable that the San Joaquin might have flowed through this section, and discharged its waters into the bay of. Monterey; I did not pass through the entire length of the cañon and am therefore unable to form an opinion on this point that would be satisfactory in this particular. The features observed on which this supposition is founded, are that a series of outliers, or rather narrow terraces are traceable for nine or ten miles up the cañada, such as occur on streams whose beds have been drained from successive elevations from subterranean forces. These peculiar features are not uncommon in the more elevated portions of the Sierra Nevada or Coast Mountains, and in the middle and northern parts of the former they may be traced for long distances.

The Monte Diablo Range is connected with the line of mountains which separate the Tulare and Salinas Valleys; and constitute in fact but one range, having their terminus within the thirty-fourth parallel, when they are intercepted by the San Bernardino mountains, which it appears from the U. S. R. R. Survey, pursue a course nearly at right angles to the trend of the former; while the low mountains forming the east border of the Salinas from the Mission San Miguel on the south to the Pajaro River on the north, can be considered nothing but a spur of the Monte Diablo Range.

The principle part is of this spur of granitic and other primitive rocks, on which the tertiaries rest; the granite is first developed in and about the Cinega del Gabilan, this mountain being made up for the most part of these rocks; at the next highest peak twelve miles south of the above known as the Chupedero, the granite passes into a coarse sienite much disintegrated and loose on the surface; the sienite continues to the cañada Solza a distance of six miles, beyond which it was not examined for twenty miles. It is doubtful if the granite rocks extend to any considerable distance beyond this locality, as the general aspect of the country changes materially after passing this point, and the magnesian rocks begin to be gradually developed.

The mountains were again entered fourteen miles above the canada Solza, and followed for eleven miles, the magnesian rocks were met at short intervals throughout the entire distance. Chlorite and talcose slates with beds of impure serpentine occur, containing actinolite, and in the ravines fragments of chromic iron; at one locality this mineral was found in considerable quantities. No chromic iron was found in place in any of these rocks, but the detached masses in the ravines indicate deposits to a considerable extent.

The Panoches were visible from this point and distant about seven miles, bearing per compass south-east by east, and the entire range of hills intervening leads to the belief that the same class of rocks as those above alluded to, compose the principal rock of this section. This opinion was subsequently corroborated by the results of an exploring party from the Mission San Juan, who were out in search of what had been supposed an argentiferous vein, up the cañada of that San Juan, the ore brought in by this company proved to be an excellent quality of the chromic mineral, containing considerable quantities of the emerald nickel, which is far more valuable than the mineral with which it is associated.

A line from the cañada Solza carried east to the Arroya San Juan terminates at a point four miles north of a sandstone formation lying upon the east declivity of these mountains which contains marine fossils; those that were sufficiently firm for examination were found to be of present existing species of the Pacific Coast, consisting of Mytilus and Cytherea; in one part of these tertairy sandstones some fragments of Purpura were found, which are identical with those on the Arroya Pescadero, county of Santa Clara, and the litteral sea beaches on the Straits Carquinez. This was the only deposit of sedimentary rocks found on this spur of the Monte Diablo Range, and points to a period remote, when the waters of the ocean washed those shores, and furnishes corroborative testimony of the recession of the sea from those places by uplift from volcanic agencies below the surface.

On the west flank of the Gabilan (which is the most prominent peak on this spur) a bed of primitive limestone occurs, extending from the cañada Vergeles on the north nearly to the Sierra Chapadero on the south, a distance of twelve miles; it was observed on the lower hills of this part of these mountains only, and at no elevation exceeding five hundred feet above the level of the Salinas Plains.

At one locality these rocks have been cut through by two dikes of trap, and also a heavy dike of quartz is found on its eastern edge, which runs parallel with the course of the calcareous rocks; the quartz has cut both the granite and limestone, and *thrown* both to the west, it is heavily charged with iron, and contains in addition the blue and green carbonate of copper with a little gold. The limestone passes under the Salinas Valley and has a considerable inclination in contact with the intrusive veins above noted; it contains silver and lead (*Argentiferous Galena*) in small veins in several places. As the calcareous formation does not show itself on the opposite side of the valley, opposite this locality, the presumption is that it underlies the plain at a considerable depth, and should it carry those veins throughout which is found upon its surface it is not improbable that valuable deposits of ores may be found within it.

SALINAS VALLEY.

This extensive plain will follow as next in order, in the description of its general features, previous to the consideration of the Coast Mountains.

The valley is about ninety miles in length, and has a varying breadth from eight to fourteen miles; it is situated between the Coast Mountains and those denominated the Monte Diablo Range, and is bounded on the east by that spur of this range in which the Gabilan is situated.

The Salinas River flows through this plain from the Cadesal Pass in which it has its rise, to the bay of Monterey. The stream for fifty miles of its course follows the western margin of the valley, and crosses the plain for the first time eight miles south-east of the Mission Solidad, after which it becomes more irregular. Three observations were taken at different points, by which it was estimated that the river had a fall of eighteen inches in one and three-fourths of a mile for seventy miles of its course. The bed of the stream is composed of a loose micaceous sand, derived from the granite rocks to the east, and also from the tertiary rocks on its western border, the latter, however, do not enter largely into its composition.

The plain of the Salinas consists of three terraces running through nearly its entire length, thus making three different positions which the river has occupied since the formation of the valley, and its recession from the eastern to its western border where it at present holds its course. These terraces are very regular in their general outline, and impart to the mind an idea that the plain has a uniform grade for its entire breadth, when the point viewed is one or two miles distant. Commencing on the western side of the valley, the lower terrace is found to occupy a breadth of about four miles, and is composed of a rich alluvium; at this point the second terrace rises abruptly to the height of eleven feet, its average width being nearly that of the former; this is also composed of a similar soil as the first, though not in so fine a state of disintegration, or containing so large an amount of vegetable mould. Both terraces support a dense growth of indigenous grasses and plants, thus furnishing an abundant supply of pasturage for stock of all kinds.

The third and upper terrace rises nearly as abrupt as the second, and has a varying breadth from one to six miles, it is more irregular upon its surface than the two former, and attains a higher grading as it approaches the hills to the east; the irregularities of the surface are not sufficient to produce any sensible effect in destroying that uniformity which a view of four miles will give on any part of the plain, and would not be noticeable except in passing over it.

South of the Alisal Ranch, and situated on this upper terrace, are a series of little elevations that continue at intervals of half a mile or a mile through a distance of twenty-seven miles, on the eastern side of the valley. They are symmetrical in form and rise on every side to heights varying from six to ten feet above the level on which they stand; their surface is smooth and even, covering an area from fifty to one hundred yards square. They appear to be composed of the valley and neither rocks or small stones were to be found on any part of them. The first impression received by the traveler on coming up to them, is that they were the work of art, perhaps thrown up by the aborigines to secure themselves from inundation; but when we consider their extent and number, it will be found rather inconsistent with the habits of these people to erect works of this extent; there are no traditions among the Indians of this part of the country respecting the origin of these singularly formed hills.

The causes of their production must remain a secret which future time alone, and the art of man, will eventually unravel. Their irregular dispersion and general uniformity of character indicates an origin from natural causes than otherwise, though it must be confessed that the agents that are active in producing them are not very apparent.

The upper terrace or "Mesa" of the Salinas, exhibits more distinctly the sources from which the superficial covering of the plain has been derived; the soil is harsh and gravelly, and retains moisture but a short time after the rains cease; it much resembles the soils derived from the granitic rocks of some parts of the mining counties; but notwithstanding the sterile features of this "Mesa," it produces the wild oat in sufficient abundance to furnish extensive grazing land, and in the "Encinals" the natural crop is heavy.

The slopes of the hills on the eastern side produce the same grain, but here it is frequently replaced by the indigenious grasses; these latter do not become so general until after passing above the limestone range, and these rocks seem to favor in an eminent degree the growth of the cereal to that of the grasses in this section and south beyond the Chupedero; beyond this the grasses form the principle covering of the hills on the east side of the plain to the southern extremity of the range.

The Salinas has an inclination of eight degrees in twelve miles transversely to its course. The line was projected from the Chupedero and carried through the Carmel Mountains to the sea, and connected with another line which was carried through the Monte Diablo Range and cañada San Juan at a distance of two miles south of Los Muertas, thereby obtaining a sectional profile from the western edge of the San Joaquin to the ocean.

The section thus formed will give the following series, and the order in which they occur. First, alluvium of the San Joaquin, tertiary sandstone containing no fossils, and resting on trachytes; 1200 feet on east ridge, the trap rocks are found, same altitude on west ridge, porous and compact lavas, on the west slope 400 feet above the level of the Arroya San Juan, mountain limestone. Valley half a mile in breadth flanked by calcareous rocks, resting on granite, 1600 feet through to the Chupedero granitic and trapean rocks, 400 feet above Salinas Valley crystatine limestone, valley twelve miles in breadth, ascend one high plateau of sixty-four feet of gravelly alluvium, thence over a high ridge trapean rocks, which are followed by coarse granitic rocks to the sea. The highest ridge is the granitic mountains toward the ocean, and the highest point crossed 2900 feet.

FROM POINT PINOS TO THE NACISMIENTO RIVER.

The Coast Mountains extending from Point Pinos, Monterey, to the northern line of Luis Obispo are mostly primitive; the character of the rocks which form the principle basis of these mountains are best observed about Point Pinos and the town of Monterey; they are composed of a coarse-grained but apparently firm granite, having a bluish grey color where the solid masses have been recently fractured. In some places this granite contains imbedded translucent crystals of felspar, (Adularia) in others it is close grained, and contains but little mica, its disintegration forming a fine white sand but little discolored by iron, and from its brilliancy below the surface of the ocean, produces a most pleasing effect on its waters at considerable distance from the shore. The light-house at Point Pinos is constructed of this rock, and from the appearance of the stone when properly dressed, it is highly probable that if the ledges were properly opened, a good material for building purposes may be obtained and in sufficient quantities to supply all the local demands of this country.

The granite shows itself as an underlying rock for four miles into the interior, from the coast, where it becomes covered with the debris of the sedementary rocks resting upon it and alluvium, but there is but little difficulty in tracing its course for forty-five miles easterly of Monterey; it becomes more largely developed after crossing the Carmello and entering the mountains on its southern side.

The trend of the Coast Mountains south of Monterey for fifty miles is south 50 degrees east, while the strike of the granite rocks is at an angle of nearly 18 degrees to the line of trend, or in other words cutting the course of the ridge at an angle of eighteen degrees. The granite rocks at Point Pinos are of the same series as those occurring in the vicinity of the Rancho Piojo, and south of the Estella, thirty miles distant from the latter in a southerly direction; the texture of these rocks in these southern localities is more compact than in the vicinity of Monterey, and in some cases are hornblendic in their character. On the east the granite is flanked by an extensive group of the Serpentine formations, which continue south as far as the Mission San Antonio; they constitute the principle part of a ridge running parallel with the granite, and situated between the latter and the Salinas Valley. The country over which the magnesian rocks predominate is easily distinguished from that in which granitic or trapean group is found, by the vegetation incident to both—the serpentine hills being generally destitute of the larger forest trees, and covered with a thick "Chamisal" and stunted varieties of the oak; this peculiarity of these hills is very striking, and cannot fail to arrest the attention of the traveler, either among the Coast Mountains or Sierra Nevada, in passing over them. The talcose and chlorits slates of these mountains were found to be auriferous in several localities, and mining to a considerable extent was conducted in some parts of these mountains during the past summer.

The magnesian rocks cross the Nacismiento River fourteen miles above its junction with the Salinas; on the banks of this stream they appear in the form of massive Serpentine, but assume a schistose structure three miles beyond to the south, and at the distance of six miles the chlorite slates abound. These mountains were not followed beyond this point to the south, but it became evident that the trapean rocks prevailed at the distance of ten or twelve miles farther on, the sharp outline of the higher hills corresponding with those of a similar character observed in other localities.

To the south-east and south-west the mountains were less rugged in their appearance, a considerable extent of a white micaceous granite was found, on which detached masses of sandstone were met with, containing marine shells, also a conglomerate apparently of the same age. The fossiliferous rocks were much disintegrated, and their fossils very imperfect; the species observed were Pectinea and Terredina, and evidently were of the same age as those in the immediate vicinity of Monte Diablo; all the other shells were so imperfect that nothing reliable was to be obtained from their examination, being merely fragmentary in their character.

To return again to the northern part of this range of mountains, and in the vicinity of Monterey, we shall find that the fossiliferous sandstones of this district do not compare in any degree with those above noticed, but, to the contrary, all of the marine fossils of the northern part of the range are found to differ in their character and relative age. On the Carmello this interesting fact may be conveniently observed; the fossils are found in an argilaceous sandstone, about nine feet in thickness, and rests alike on both serpentine and granitic, and has a dip of seven degrees west. It is found at intervals through eleven miles of distance on a course east southeast, and for a breadth of about four miles; this formation, which must be regarded as the *Post Pliocene* of this country contains imbeded fossils of the genus cancer, with casts of Cytherea, mactra and tellina, all of living species in the adjoining Bay and Bay of Monterey.

From the delicacy of the preservation of these small animals, and the character of the rock in which they are imbeded, it appears evident that it must have been deposited in still water, and was probably an estero into which the tide ebbed and flowed regularly, with sufficient protection to break the violence of the surf upon the coast. After its deposition it had been gradually elevated above the surface of the waters, and subsequently tilted from its horizontal position by the intrusion of igneous rocks in its vicinity.

The cause of its disturbance and inclination is found in the intrusion of a trapean dike which has cut through the granite and clay state, which latter passes into a micaceous schist, and near the contact of the igneous intrusion small but imperfect garnets are found imbeded. The fossiliferous rocks are regularly stratified, and cleave easily in one direction; they are much twisted and contorted nearest the points at which the trapean mass broke through, but become much less curved as the distance increases from that centre. A clay of fine texture and creamy color is found resting on the argilaceous sandstone, and covers a large extent of country stretching to the east of Monterey as far as the Toro Hills; this clay is composed almost exclusively of *infusoria*, apparently of marine origin; five distinct species have been observed, four of which are discoid. It is probable that they have been described either by Professor Bayley, of West Point, or Ehrenberg, as both these gentlemen have had opportunities for the examination of the infusorial formations of this State—and until access may be had to their descriptions, it will be impossible to determine this fact. Specimens have been secured for the State collection, and will be described at the earliest opportunity.

My route next followed a northeast direction across the Toro Hills and Cañada; the first range of high hills on the north side of the Carmello, and which divide the Toro from the Carmel valley, have an altitude of about seven hundred feet; they are composed of a coarse sandstone, containing a few indistinct impressions of shells of marine species; an out-crop of trap was observed among the latter rocks, flanked by granite of the same specific character as that found at Point Pinos, and may be seen four miles southwest of the Toro Ranch. On the south side of the valley an extensive bed of calcareous travertine occurs, and also a brecia of the same character, they cover about one mile of area; no limestone rocks were found *in situ* in this vicinity; the travertine here observed, evidently had its origin from springs highly charged with calcareous matter, and which were undoubtedly formed in the limestone described on the east side of the Salinas valley, and which dip under the same as described in the preceding pages. From the intrusion of the more recent volcanic rocks in the immediate vicinity of those springs, it is probable they were diverted into another channel, and thus ceased to flow in places in which the calcareous tula is now found. Similar springs now exist a short distance from Santa Cruz, around which the calcareous deposits are very extensive.

Crossing the Toro Valley or Cañada, and following the course of the bay of Monterey, there is little else to be seen than the tertiary rocks for fifty miles, and extending easterly in elevated plateaus and hills for eighteen miles from the coast; among the Chamisal hills frequent intrusions of trapean rocks are met, and in nearly every case where this occurs the granite is also seen broken through by the same igneous intrusions. The sandstone is generally of a buff colour, and yellow-brown, having a greater or less abundance of fossils, in some instances, firm and compact, and again loose and friable; it is almost continuous in a northwest direction, being broken through only by small streams, and is found north of the mission of Santa Cruz, from whence it gradually narrows out, being found immediately on the coast at the base of the mountains.

Beyond this point the principal rocks on the coast are primitive and volcanic, forming sharp, high hills and low mountains with a bold coast line.

SANTA CRUZ MOUNTAINS.

These mountains approach the coast a short distance northwest of the Mission and town of Santa Cruz. They extend from the head of the Santa Clara Valley and Pajaro river to Mount Bruno and Presidio Point west of the city of San Francisco; they are separated from the mountain forming the coast line to the northern terminus of the State, by the Golden Gate or entrance to the bay of San Francisco. The greatest altitude attained in these mountains, is the Black Hill, (Loma Prieto or

Umhumin,) the latter being the original Indian name applied to this hill.

The entire range is composed, principally of the primitive rocks, among which the serpentine formations play an important part; this suite was traced from near the Rancho La Brae on both flanks of the mountains, to the Francisquito on the east side, and Anno Nuevo on the west, and belong to the same series as those occuring at Point Lobos and the Presidio. In several instances throughout the range, the trapean rocks have broken through, as detailed of the mountains south of Monterey.

On the west flank of these mountains, and in the central and northern parts of the County of Santa Cruz, there are views of quartz cutting through the serpentine and other rocks in other places; and is particularly observable on the upper portions of the arroyas Sogell, Syant, and Rio San Augustine. The general rule heretofore laid down respecting the contact of these two groups of rocks in this country is found good in the present case. "That when the two series are found in contact, either as dikes of great length, or smaller views, one, or both is *always* auriferous." And such has proved to be the fact in the case before us; from all appearances the quartz has been one of the most recent disturbing agents here, as well as elsewhere.

The mineral characteristics of these mountains will be noticed more in detail when speaking of that subject hereafter.

The south-east spur of these mountains terminates at the Pajaro River, thirty-six miles east of Santa Cruz, and fourteen from Watsonville. On the southern extremity are found extensive beds of fossils finely preserved. The arroyo Pescadero and la Brae cut their way through these hills, and their beds abound with boulders containing these organic remains. The fossil sandstone at this point rests on the Serpentine and trapean intrusions, being changed in its texture near the points of contact with the latter rocks. On these streams are to be found several bituminous springs, which discharge large quantities of the fluid bitumen, at times covering several acres of ground. The occurrence of these springs has led to the belief that bituminous coal existed in this section, such, I think, is not the fact in the present case, though it might be a tenable supposition in parts of the world where coal measures exist, or where any of the superior groups of the secondary rocks may be found.

The position of these springs, geologically considered, would render it impossible for coal to abound, as they make their appearance among a mass of rocks having an igneous origin, where not even a lignite is likely to exist. There is but a possibility that the tertiary rocks in the vicinity may overlie some members of the secondary group, from which these springs have their origin, but no outcrop or other indications are to be found which will warrant such a conclusion. There is every evidence that the tertiaries above rest on the primitive and volcanic rocks with no intermediate series between them. The origin of bituminous springs is but little understood; in the present state of our knowledge they are found to arise from the newer as well as the older formations, and alone are not reliable evidences of the existence of coal, except when found among the carbouiferous rocks.

Following the east flank of the Santa Cruz mountains, we find small patches of the tertiary sandstones among the lower portions of the hills, from La Brae to the Llagos Creek; after which they are not again seen for several miles. Near the last named creek, the more recent volcanic rocks make their appearance and continue, at short intervals, for sixteen miles, when we again pass into the primitive formations, which become more metaliferous and particularly in the region about New Almaden in the county of Santa Clara.

North of Almaden, and near the Los Gatos Creek, a bed of recent conglomerate, loose and friable in texture, is found occupying an elevation of four hundred feet above the level of the valley, and having a thickness of about seventy feet, it occurs on both sides of the Los Gatos, and is found, at short intervals, for ten miles, crossing Camels Creek and following its banks for two or three miles; it has been considerably disturbed and large masses have been thrown down. West of McCartyville the mountain limestone occurs in large masses and is continuous for several miles to the west, north and north-west. Extensive operations are now conducted in the manufacture of lime for the market, for which purpose it is admirably adapted. This group of calcareous rocks cannot be less than thirty miles in length from east to west, and has a strike transverse to the line of the mountain range, appearing on the coast at Santa Cruz, at this point it is highly crystaline. These rocks extend north of Camel's Creek about four miles; and a calcareous rock of an amorphous character is found as far north as Sanchez Ranch, in the County of San Francisco. The west flank of the mountains, lying between the San Mateo and a point nearly west of Mission Dolores, was not examined personally, but from the specimens of rocks from that section, which I have seen, their geological characters appear identical with the rocks at the Presidio, which are mostly serpentine.

On Presidio point are to be found beds of a Jaspery rock having a riband-like appearance, and colors from a greenish hue through red-brown to red and yellow; this rock has been considered by Mr. Dana as a variety of the Prasoid rocks, and as he says—"the graduation of prase into jaspery rocks exhibits a close relation of both." These transitions were met with in other parts of the country over which he had travelled. In relation to this subject he further says—"From the transitions that occur, it also appears that the jasper and prase rocks are closely connected with the talcose series, and that the translucent jasper and bloodstones of this section are only different varieties of its condition." The jaspery rocks of San Francisco are worthy of description; the green, red and yellow varieties occur in the same vicinity, they form a series of layers averaging two inches in thickness, and varying from half an inch to four inches; the layers are distinct and separted by open seams, and on the front of bluffs or ledges the rock has a riband-like appearance, the layers coalesce and sub-divide without regularity though uniformly parallel, they are often twisted, and thus change at short intervals from a vertical position to a dip of twenty degrees."

The colors red and yellow are often mingled and sometimes appear as parallel bands; in some instances, the surface is red while the rock is yellow beneath, this may have resulted from the burning of a tree on the spot, for by heat the yellow varieties readily change to red; a small specimen had an agate-like structure as though formed from an aqueous solution.

An impure talcose rock occurs at Point Lobos, which extends east for one and a half miles. The works of the "Mountain Lake Water Company" have been carried through a portion of these rocks, and the masses of serpentine that have been elevated to the surface from the depth of one hundred and sixty feet have exhibited an interesting feature in the history of these rocks. It was found, on examination, that the strong odor given off from these stones was composed of free Bromine and Iodine; it is very persistent, and specimens which have been exposed to the air for nearly three months have not lost their odor.

From the Presidio on the bluffs near the bay, slates and sandstones are found in a much disturbed condition from intrusions of trap; the strata are much contorted and twisted, and tilted in every direction, the inclination varying fron five degrees to verticality in very short distances. These rocks, as yet, have presented no fossils in the immediate vicinity of the city, but pass into tertiary sandstone, containing organinc remains one mile west of Montgomery Street, San Francisco, where they may be found forming the west point of the North Beach.

South of the city and near Rincon Point, the trachytes appear with small veins of quartz running through them and the adjoining slates; the latter having suffered considerable change in structure near the point of contact with the igneous rocks. Traces of carbonate of copper are observable in this vicinity.

Crossing the Bay of San Francisco from Presidio Point, the rocks on the Saucelito side correspond with the primitive formations above described. The serpentine series continue for several miles up the bay, varying in its mineral characters at short distances. At San Quentin the rocks are schistose, and half a mile beyond, again passes into a massive form, and contains actinolite in fan-like groups of crystals; a mile beyond this, the rock becomes hornblendic, and thence gradually passes into a trap formation, containing well defined crystals of the latter mineral.

On reaching the northern shores of the Bay San Pablo the hills to the north appeared rugged and conical, indicating a preponderance of the volcanic rocks.

The route traveled next, lay through the Counties of Solano and Napa. It has been before remarked that the sand-stone on one side of the Straits Carquinez was identical with that on the other, and the line of dip in both will be found to correspond. These rocks are permeated by minute threads of quartz, and contain considerable quantities of magnetic sand; in some cases the quartz viens acquire a thickness of one or two inches, and have in several instances been found to contain gold, while the sand-stone itself possesses this character in a limited degree; it is contained mechanically in these latter rocks, and in general will be found as a local deposit only. Small quantities of this metal have been found in the stone used for building in San Francisco, which were taken from the quarries in the vicinity of Benecia. It is doubtful whether these rocks would ever warrant mining explorations, except in those locations where the quartz has intruded to a considerable extent. In this case they would prove of sufficient value probably, for mining in the rocks below the sand-stone, and would be governed by the same natural laws that are found to prevail in other parts of the country in relation to auriferous veins.

These sand-stones are found to extend into the interior in a northwest direction, a distance of about eight miles, when they are succeeded by volcanic rocks of recent date for thirty miles in the same direction; the points of contact in the igneous and sedimentary rocks exhibit distinct and striking marks of change in structure among the latter in many places, and it is not uncommon to find trachytic injections into the sand-stone along the line of coast on the bay and straits.

Where these veins are large, the sandstone in contact is often nearly as hard as the trepan rock itself, a true conchodial fracture, having quite sharp or roughened edges, with a semi-earthy surface, is the result of this metamorphosis. Above this sandstone and resting directly upon it, is a littoral sea-beach, having an elevation of about thirty feet above high tides, and extending for several miles along the coast of the bay. It is composed of fragmentary and entire shells, mixed with a little sand and clay; its thickness varies from one to three feet. Its position is immediately below the alluvium.

It forms a distant white line along the bay coast of San Pablo on its north side for eight miles, and may be seen at the town of Benicia in the vicinity of the sandstone quarries at that place. The shells of which this beach is composed consist of a small species of ostrea, purpura, and other small shells now inhabiting these waters. The elevation of this beach points to a period comparatively recent, when subterranean forces were in operation in elevating the lands adjoining the coasts and bays, which part of our subject will be considered more in detail when reviewing the geological changes which have occurred in the different portions of the coast-line followed.

Among the sandstones of this region is a bed of limestone having an average thickness of two feet; it is found one mile north of the town. This limestone was traced in a northeast direction for two miles, and is probably the same range as observed by Mr. Tyson on the east side of the hills on Suisun Bay.

The foot of the ridge lying between Suisun and Napa Valleys, was followed for twenty miles. At this distance from the bays it attains an altitude of about twelve hundred feet. The rocks composing this ridge are mostly volcanic, with sandstone on their eastern flanks dipping east towards the Sacramento Valley; a few very imperfect casts of marine shells were observed, but none sufficiently perfect for preservation.

The ridge on the west border of Napa Valley presents much the same characteristics as those on the east. These two ridges unite about eighteen miles north of Napa City, at which place they become extremely rugged and elevated.

The highest and most conspicuous peak in this range is Mount Helen; its sharply defined outline and truncated summit shows most conclusively its volcanic origin. A section cutting Napa Valley nine miles south of the town was made, and carried across the Sacramento Valley to the foot-hills on its eastern side, by which the grade of both valleys and the altitude of the hills were obtained.

Before reviewing the geological changes that have occurred in the Sierra Nevada, Monte Diablo and Coast Mountains, a view of that part of the great basin separating the Coast Mountains from the Sierras will be given; and in speaking of the Sacramento Valley, that of the San Joaquin will also be included, and the physical characters of both briefly explained.

STRUCTURE OF THE VALLEYS OF SACRAMENTO AND SAN JOAQUIN.

These valleys form a "single geographical formation,"* stretching from the terminal spurs of the Cascade Mountains at the north, to the junction of the Sierra Nevada with the southern terminus of the Monte Diablo range with the thirty-fourth parallel of north latitude. The length of the valley is about three hundred and eighty miles in length on an air line, with a breadth of fifty miles at its widest point.

The general appearance of the valley is that of an extended plain composed of alluvium, and this opinion would obtain in the mind of any person whose line of travel should lead him over the lower terraces of the plain, or what is denominated its bottom lands. It is only by making a transverse section of this plain that we should be able to arrive at any correct conclusions of its structure, and peculiarities of its formation; by pursuing this course, very distinctive and marked features are observable of different periods of elevation to which this portion of the country has been subjected subsequent to its emergence above the level of the sea.

To arrive at a correct understanding of the formation of the "California Basin,"† we must first observe the rocks which form its borders, their character, position and relative age; and in doing this it will be necessary to pass beyond either of its margins to ascertain the facts on which an opinion may be founded.

On the east side of the basin and at the distance of fourteen miles from its border, we find the first out-crop of the primitive rocks, (granite) on hills attaining an elevation of about one thousand feet above the sea. Resting upon this, we find detached masses of sand-stone, which increase to a well defined formation a few miles to the west; immediately below the latter a bed of slate makes its appearance, having a dip varying from thirty degrees to nearly a vertical position, but as the lower hills are approached, the inclination of these rocks become much less. Below the slate, a conglomerate having an argelaceous cement is found, firm in its texture, with a dip corresponding to the other rocks with which it is associated; the pebbles composing the conglomerate are quartz, jasper, granite and trap; at times this rock is highly ferruginous. The components of the rock are made up from rocks found in the mountains to the east, and must have been formed subsequent to the appearance of the older trapean formations of this part of the country.

Succeeding the conglomerate,‡ which by way of distinction, we will denominate *Eocene*, another bed of fissile clay slate and aluminous clay

* Col. J. C. Fremont.

† Being similar to the London and Paris Basins, this name will be adopted.

‡ This suite of rocks are often confounded with another group, of the same character which appear of more recent date, and are found south of Consumnes river only.

occurs, having a thickness of about one hundred feet; these rocks comport in position with the other sedimentary rocks above them, and are found resting directly on the granite, and other igneous rocks far into the interior; in the lower hills their structure is fissile, cleaving with ease over considerable surfaces, while in the eastern parts of the mountains they have often acquired a crystaline structure from contact with other and more recent volcanic rocks, and such as have broken through and disturbed the primitive formation.

On the western side of the valley or basin, the series do not follow in precisely the same order as occurs on the east; the sandstone and slate of the same age is found, but the conglomerate is wanting; if it exists, it is completely obscured from view, except on the west slope of the coast mountains towards the sea, and its occurrence there is a reason for the supposition that it does exist below the other stratified rocks on their eastern slope. Above all the others, the miocene rocks are found disturbed and cut through by the recent volcanic intrusions of that period.

The following then will be the arrangement of the rocks from below upward:

EAST OF THE SACRAMENTO RIVER.		WEST OF THE SACRAMENTO RIVER.	
Primary Rocks.	*Granite.*	*Primary Rocks.*	*Granite.*
	Slates.		Slates.
	Conglomerate.	Uncertain.	Conglomerate.
Sedimentary.	Slates.	*Sedimentary.*	Sandstone, Eocene.
	Sandstone.		*Sandstone Miocene.*
		Recent volcanic	cuting the latter.

With this arrangement of the stratified rocks which pass under the California Basin, it is obvious, that the waters flowing at the line of junction between the sandstone and the slate-rocks below them, muss pass under the sides and central parts of the valley, varying in depth at the distance from either of its borders increases.

It must be remembered that the dip of the sedimentary rocks on which the alluvium of the valley reposes, will increase or diminish the distance that may be necessary to bore for obtaining water, as the inclination of these rocks is greater or less; and with the view to demonstrate if possible, (or at least approximately) the depth that it might be necessary to sink in order to obtain a plentiful supply of water for agriculture or other purposes, an examination of both borders of the basin was made of fifty miles in length, and the mean of all the dips taken.

It was found by measurement that the surface of the basin rises at the average rate of six feet per mile from the river to either of its borders. Taking the grade of the surface with the lowest average dip of the rocks where they pass under it, (being equal to twelve degrees,) and assuming that the sedimentary rocks decrease in inclination, as the distance increases, which is probably the case, it will be found necessary to reach the depth of 775 feet at the City of Sacramento, in order to obtain a permanent supply of water.

This presumytion is based upon the fact that a constant source does not exist above the conglomerate, and this point is selected more for the purpose of exhibiting the greatest probable depth at which a permanent supply of water wiuld be found; the probabilities of obtaining water at much less depths is strong, and amounts to almost a certainty, that water would be found immediately below the sandstone, and above the first slates; in that case the depth would be diminished about two hundred and fifty feet.

If a correct idea of the inclination of the sedimentary rocks is presented in the diagram, we shall have the following depths at different distances from the centre of the basin, on both sides.

ON THE WEST SIDE OF THE RIVER.	ON THE EAST SIDE OF THE RIVER.
11 miles,............700 feet.	Sacramento City,........775 feet.
15 " ....650 "	12 miles,............700 "
22 " ....550 "	17 " ....650 "
	20 " ....625 "

At the distance of twenty miles the rolling hills are entered in which springs usually abound.

The rocks on both sides of the valley are arranged in the order in which they occur, as observed by the outcrop.

Sandstone, EOCENE,	Sandstones and upper Slates,
Slates,	Conglomerate, EOCENE.
Fosil Sandstone,	Lower clay Slates.
Trap,	
Granite,	Granite.

These rocks included within the Eocene lines are classed by Mr. Dana, as the early sandstone, slates, and conglomerates, to distinguish them from the more recent tertiaries among the Coast Mountains.

The geological structure of this basin was noticed by Mr. Tyson in 1849. He examined it with a view to ascertain whether a deposit of coal might not exist below the surface; and also whether its structure would indicate the means of supplying water for agricultural and mechanical purposes.

In regard to the first question he says: "The first query is answered by the fact of finding the comparatively recent strata of a formation, not older than the eocene and miocene periods, resting immediately on the metamorphic or hypogene rocks of ancient origin, the remaining members with all the sedimentary rocks of older date being entirely wanting, and the the coal formation, which belongs to the lower of the secondary series." A coal formation under the basin is therefore out of the question, unless deeply seated, and entirely covered, edges and all, by the sedimentary rocks above noticed.

The character of the soil in many parts of this valley will render it of little importance as an agricultural district, unless water in ample quantities for irrigation can be obtained. (These remarks apply particularly to the upper terrace of the valley on each side of the river.) And we hope that attention may be called to this very important subject of making the extensive areas of the arid districts of the basin available for market and agricultural purposes."

Experience has demonstrated the almost certainty of obtaining water and in sufficient quantities for agricultural and other purposes, in all valleys resting upon sedimentary formations and having a basin-shaped structure, and where the different beds have a degree of uniformity or regularity in their position, and are of a texture that will admit the free percolation of water through the superior beds and sufficiently firm to prevent its escape in those below.

These conditions are all fulfilled in the basin of the Sacramento, and from the united testimony of different observers, we have ample evidence that the sedimentary formations of one side are the same as those upon the other, with the exception, perhaps, of the conglomerate.

The absence of the conglomerate on the west side of the basin, will not affect the result of obtaining water by the means proposed. The clays and clay-slate, below the sandstone, appear on both sides and are sufficiently impervious and firm to prevent the escape of any water that may rest upon them.*

REVIEW OF THE GEOLOGICAL CHANGES IN THE COAST MOUNTAINS AND MONTE DIABLO RANGE.

Having briefly detailed the more general characteristics of the geology of the above mountains, it will become necessary to review in a measure the geological changes that have been instrumental in producing the peculiar features noticed in the preceeding pages; in doing this the same lines will be followed as in the outset.

Starting from the Straits of Carquinez, it has been stated that the rocks forming the borders of those Straits and part of the adjoining bays, were composed of a recent sandstone; in following up these in a southerly direction for a few miles, we find the sedimentary rocks thinning out, and are succeeded by high hills and low mountains of volcanic rocks, composed of trochytes and other intrusive rocks of recent date. These are followed by the primitive rocks, composed of the older trap, and in the vicinity of Oakland, consist in a great measure of serpentine.

The latter rocks form the western side of this part of the Monte

*Since October last, there have been three Artesian borings, carried to depths within one hundred feet, on the valley of Santa Clara, and in the vicinity of San Jose. The result of each has been successful, and a head of water from four to nine feet has been obtained. These indications of water so near the surface and in such quantities, will much enhance the value ot agricultural land throughout this valley and render available much that would otherwise have laid unocupied and unimproved for years.

Diablo Range for thirty-five miles, where a district of the recent volcanic rocks is again entered, which continue to the head of the Cañada San Benito and San Juan, for a distance of about eighty miles.

Returning on the Gabilan spur of these mountains, and which form the eastern boundary of the Salinas Plains, the primitive rocks are met with for twenty-eight miles, flanked on the east by the recent igneous rocks of the same age as those appearing at the Santa Anna peaks, twelve miles to the east; (during one of the convulsions that agitated this part of the country, about four hundred feet of the Galiban Peak, on its northeast side, was fractured and thrown down into a deep ravine at its base,) intrusive dikes have had the effect to change the sedimentary rocks when found in contact with the same.

In the Coast Mountains to the west, the granite and serpentine series are predominant, and on these rest the sedimentary rocks, of early and recent date, unchanged generally, except in local position.

Crossing the Pajaro Valley and entering the Santa Cruz Mountains, the main ridge is composed of the granite and serpentine rocks on which rest the fossiliferous formations as those above mentioned. The primitive series extend north into the County of San Francisco, but unlike the formations in the County of Santa Cruz; no tertiaries, containing fossils, are to be found, except in the sandstone forming the point to the west of the North Beach, and here the Pholas and some other shells of present existing species are found. South of the city the trachytes have intruded through the slates, producing considerable disturbance both by uplift and change of structure in the latter; on the north side of the city, similar features are to be seen, but on a more extensive scale; among the deep excavations which have been made about Clark's Point, it is found that the stratified rocks have been tilted from the horizontal position, and in some cases twisted and contorted into every conceivable position; at one time presenting a wave-like form, and in the distance of a few yards, passing from this to high angles or verticality.

Northwest of the Telegraph Hill the active causes of this diversity in the appearance of the rocks is seen. Nearly on a line with Dupont street, and fronting the bay, is a dike of the trap rock, passing up through the sedimentary rocks above. A change of structure in the sandstone in contact with the dike is observed.

This class of rocks (the volcanic) occur at frequent intervals along the bay coast on the west side, and thence into the valley of the Santa Clara. At the distance of four miles south of San Jose they form the low hills that protrude into this valley from the western side, and which are continued at intervals to the arroga Llagos, a distance of thirty miles beyond.

In none of the lower hills on this side of the valley are the volcanic rocks found in contact with the sedimentary formations, until after passing the above arroya, and then only after first breaking through fissures in the primitive rocks after reaching the Pescadero.

The intrusion of these rocks among the primitive series is marked by a discoloration of the rock through which the dike has passed, sometimes of several inches in breadth on each side of the volcanic vein; this is more particularly observable where the disturbed rock is of the granite class; in that case it usually presents a brown, or reddish brown color, and is decidedly more given to decomposition than at a short distance from the intrusive material. The slates and sandstones when thus acted upon assume either a sub-crystaline or completely metamorphosed structure, and comport themselves in this particular much in the same manner as similar formations on the west slope of the Sierra Nevada.

The area covered by the metamorphic rocks in the Coast Mountains is not as extensive as those of the mining sections, but the changes, when they do occur, are equally as perfect and complete. The most extensive change of this character noticed among these mountains was that on the Alameda Creek in Sunol Valley, eight miles north-east of the Mission San Jose, and again after crossing this valley on the road to Livermore's. The slates on the creek were changed into a hard, compact rock, for the distance of one mile, and three-fourths of a mile beyond they had assumed a porphyritic character.

Following this series to the right of the road, among the hills which divide Sunol's from Livermore's Valley, the greenstone-trap became largely developed, with basaltic fragments among the drift of the arroyas. On the east side of Livermore's valley the fossiliferous rocks again made their appearance, and continued south for eight miles, beyond which to the south the mountains were not examined.

The classification of the rocks in these mountains according to their relative ages will follow as next in order.

CLASSIFICATION OF THE ROCKS OF THE COAST MOUNTAINS AND MONTE DIABLO RANGE.

Our most northern point in this case will be Bodega Head and a line forty-three miles north of Napa City, and in this case shall avail myself of that part of Mr. Tyson's report on this part of the country, and which is contained in Senate Doc. No 47, 1st Sess. 31st Cong., this being the most northern geological section yet made.

By reference to his section, we find that the primitive rocks occur as far north in the Coast Mountains as the above locality named, and that the rocks of sedimentary origin are found to rest directly on the primitive rocks for a considerable distance east from the coast line.

After reaching eight or nine miles from the coast, the recent volcanic group succeeds the primitive, when the latter is again replaced in the hills bordering the western edge of the basin; from this view of the case it appears that all the rocks of this section are similar in their positions with those detailed farther south.

Commencing with the lowest in order we find:

First.—The granite series and serpentines; on these rest the older sedimentary rocks.

Second.—The more recent volcanic rocks. These are more largely distributed through the Monte Diablo Range. They consist of trachytes and lavas, and have protruded through all other formations that preceded them. These rocks form at least three-fourths of the mountain range extending from Point San Pablo to the head of the Cañada San Juan, beyond which the primitive rocks again occur, and continue to the extreme southern point visited.

THIRD.—THE TERTIARIES. These complete the formations found in these mountains. For convenience of description, this class will be sub-divided into the different periods to which they belong. They will occur as follows:

PERIOD.	GROUP.	WHERE FOUND.
Eocene.	Middle.	Calaveras County, at Murphy's, and other localities. Bones of extinct animals, &c.
Miocene.		North and south of San Francisco in the Coast and Monte Diablo Mountains. Consisting of marine shells with most of the species extinct.
Pliocene.	Lower.	Coast Mountains and Gabilan Spur. Also in cavern deposits in Calaveras County.
Post Pliocene.		Southwest of Monterey. Marine shells, all of existing species.

POSITION AND RELATION OF THE VOLCANIC ROCKS TO THE TERTIARIES.

Before entering upon a description of the relations of the recent volcanic group with the primitive rocks, it is thought best to examine their positions and effects, among the sedimentary formations, both ancient and modern; in order to elucidate more distinctly the difference in age, of another group of the volcanic series, which have been described as having been cotemporaneous with those under consideration, and of which there is some question.

The examination of the Coast Mountains has shown us the fact, that those forces on the west side of the basin, which have been instrumental in elevating the range, have had the effect to produce a series of continuous and nearly parallel ridges, throughout the greatest portion of their length; this peculiarity will force itself upon the observation of the traveler if they are crossed at almost any point transversely to their course.

In many parts of this range, the ridges are narrow, and the declivities steep, and the higher isolated peaks are conical. On the summits of these ridges, there are often to be found nothing but bare volcanic rocks which are mostly of a trachytic character; on the sides of some of the hills, which are less abrupt, are to be met beds of sandstones and at times a few slates which from their nature modify and soften the rugged contour of the surrounding country, by their easy disintegration from natural causes.

The sedimentary rocks, as far as observed in this part of the State, are, without exception, of marine origin—the fossils they contain being of that character exclusively.* In some parts of the country they form beds of considerable thickness, and are rich in organic remains. In some parts of the mountains, the shells are of present existing species, not found upon the coast at the present time; these consist of three or four species of the Arca, and one or two of the Pectinea; these rocks are commonly found resting upon the primitive series, though at times on some of the more recent igneous intrusions. It is considered very doubtful by our conchologists in this part of the world, whether the living shells of the above species now inhabit these waters; and yet these imbeded remains are found in abundance on the summits of our hills, removed many miles inland from the element they formerly inhabited.

The fossils of this part of the Coast Mountains, and which now appear to be extinct, consist of three species of the gryphae, two at least, of Pectinea, Astarte and Cytherea, the species of which will be noticed more in detail in another part of this report.

The position of the miocene rocks in the northern part of these mountains, appears to be directly succeeding the primitive; yet it is found often that they rest upon the trachytes; in all cases that have met my observation, the latter rocks when thus found in contact with the sedimentary group of this period, have broken through fissures in the primitive formations, subsequent to the elevations which occurred during the miocene and middle pliocene periods, or perhaps during the deposition of the latter. The trachytic rocks north of Napa, where they leave the sedimentary group, gradually pass into vesicular lavas, and in these sections considerable quantities of obsidian are to be met with; the Indians in the vicinity of Clear Lake use it for the manufacture of their arrow-heads.

Again, on the shores of Suisun and San Pablo bays, and on the Straits Carquinez, these igneous rocks are found injected into the seams of the sandstone, contorting the strata to a considerable degree. West of those bays the primitive rocks occur at intervals for several miles, and the fossiliferous rocks are found holding the same position as those further north. These alternate intrusions of the trachytic rocks continue south among the mountains on the east side of the Bay San Francisco, and for thirty-five miles beyond its southern extremity; after this they pass into porus lava, and compact masses, ceasing to present any traces of fossiliferous deposits resting upon them for forty miles on this western ridge; after this they again (the fossiliferous) make their appearance in small detached masses, which gradually increase to a well defined formation beyond.

These rocks in many instances are found to rest upon the recent volcanic series direct, and in these cases we find, as may be expected, a corresponding change in their structure, often to an extent that has obliterated every trace of organic remains; while in other cases, where the fossiliferous group has been protected from the more direct influence of the later igneous series by the intervention of any of the primitive

* The lacustrine deposits discovered during the past summer by Mr. W. P. Blake, on the desesrt of the Colorado are the first fresh-water formations found in this country.

formation, the fossils remain very entire and no change in structure is observable, except where the trachitic masses have broken through both.

Among the hills south of Monterey, other evidences of recent elevation from the intrusion of recent igneous rocks are found; and these occur among that group of sedimentary formations which have been denominated as the *post Pliocene;* (see Table,) these are found on the Carmello Creek, three miles above Meadow's Ranch, where the fine grained sandstone, containing impressions of existing crustacea are found resting upon the granite, but tilted from their former horizontal position by intrusion of recent trap rocks from beneath. This same feature is noticeable north of Monterey, and into the Santa Cruz Mountains, where the marine formations of the Pliocene period are found elevated to different heights above the sea, for miles interior from the present coast line. With these facts before us, it will be impossible to arrive at any other conclusion than that the volcanic series of which we have been speaking, has been continued into a period comparatively recent, and was the active agent in producing those disturbances so manifest through-throughout those portions of these mountains under our consideration.

An interesting feature in the geology of the eastern part of the Monte Diablo range has been developed during the past season, by the officers of the United States Land Survey, which is worthy of note, as illustrating the mutations which have been going on in different parts of the country, and has served also to fix the age of districts hundreds of miles remote from each other; the marine shells brought into the Survey office by Mr. Von Schmidtz, from the hills bordering the west side of the Tulare Lake are found to be indentical with those obtained from the Buttes on the Sacramento Valley; among the fossils are found the Arca, of which there are three species, with two species of Cardium, differing from any found in our waters at the present time.

The surveys of the United States Rail Road Exploring Expedition, under command of Lieutenant Stoneman and Williamson, on the desert of the Colorado has been the means of eliciting much valuable information of that almost unknown and desert waste. The personal and attentive examinations of Mr. W. P. Blake, geologist of the exploring party has opened a new field for investigation in addition to those already existing in other parts of the State. The old water line of the Gulf of California has been traced with unerring certainty for a long distance into the interior, and the fossil remains of marine animals and shells are found promiscuously mingled with those of fresh-water origin, which subsequently occupied the place where the waters of the Pacific formerly held undisputed sway. The discovery and demonstrations of those interesting changes in the elevation of the interior of this part of the State above the level of the sea, with its recession from natural causes, reflects much credit on the discrimination, and careful judgment of Mr. Blake, and must be regarded as a great acquisition to our very limited stock of knowledge respecting the absolute condition of that extensive portion of the interior. Among all those who have preceded him in crossing this "Jornada" at different points, not a word of information has been elicited from which not even a probability of its true condition could be gleaned; until the present time it was a blank in the geological history of this part of our continent; how far beyond the line of travel to the east, of where this expedition left it, it may extend, is equally as uncertain as was that portion of the ancient sea-beach, and bottom, over which the United States exploring party traveled the past season. The facts which have been gleaned from this interesting region will appear in the forthcoming report of the expedition, and from what little is now known of their operations, the parties in charge of its several departments have manifested a determination of purpose and assiduity in collating reliable testimony of this hitherto unexplored and unknown waste.

Our present information of this remote section of the State, exhibits in a still stronger light, the mutations to which the surface of the country has been subjected, and which are probably persistent at the present time; to what period the changes of this district are particularly referable will not be known probably until the following year, but enough has already been developed which leads to the inference that the sea has receded since the commencement of the tertiary era.

VOLCANIC ROCKS PRECEDING THE TERTIARY ERA.

On a preceding page it was observed that a suite of rocks which are often confounded with the recent volcanic group, existed in the Coast Mountains, these rocks and their peculiar position will be noticed at the present time.

Following the west side of the Valley of Santa Clara, from the arroya Francisquito in a southerly direction, a range of low hills, generally barren in their appearance, is found, which protrude themselves into the valley nearly at right angles to its course. The range of hills were examined for the distance of forty miles, and in no instance, I believe, was there a trace of any one of the sedimentary formations to be found upon them. In this particular they differ much from the other volcanic series, either north or south of them, with the exception of those of the Santa Anna range.

Their naked and rugged aspect on the west side of these hills with their peculiar local position leaves but little room for doubt, but that they are the remains of the summit of ancient craters, elevated above the surface of the then existing sea, prior to the deposition of the marine formations which occur in other parts of the mountain range.

This suite of rocks have evidently found their way to the surface through the primitive rocks of this district, as it is found that they cut the latter in several places in the form of dikes, while the debris of both are found to enter largely into the components of the valley in which they are situated. Another evidence, which lends confirmation to this belief, is the fact, that had the emergence occurred at any time subsequent to the tertiary era, we should have seen *some* traces of such a fact in the elevation of those rocks of aqueous origin. The gradiency of the entire northern portion of the valley Santa Clara will also be found incommensurate with such an extensive series of disturbance as must have occurred at the period when these hills were elevated above the surface. The narrow limits within which they are situated, would have received an inclination much greater than that which the surface now presents, had their intrusion corresponded with those of a similar character found among the sedimentary rocks on every side of them. Our evidence that these rocks hold an age anterior to the tertiaries, rests in part on this fact; that if the change of position, which the latter rocks have suffered in adjoining districts bear any testimony of the maximum of disturbance among them, we should find *some* corresponding changes of similar character had this volcanic group been of the same age.

In all other parts of the coast mountains, wherever volcanic rocks occur, in masses or dikes, cutting either sedimentary or primitive groups, the evidences of uplift are conspicuous, and either a high uniform grade, distinct undulations, or a terraced form of the valley sections, mark the extent and character of the forces exerted over such areas; while in the case before us, we find the valley adjoining these igneous outbursts maintaining its level to the very base of these volcanic hills. Were there any differences observable in the inclination of the surface of the plain, taken from its northern to its extreme southern point, there would be some reason to suppose that the group under consideration was more recent than the tertiary era.

Passing to the west of these hills, we find the same undisturbed condition of the surface, extending to the base of the Santa Cruz, and you meet with nothing that would in the least indicate any subsequent alteration in the general level until you reach their eastern base; and here, for the first time, a narrow terrace is found, its face rising rather abruptly for twelve feet, and then very gradually for eight feet more, being nearly level from thence to the mountains, a distance of one-fourth of a mile. So little disturbance is manifest in the half formed conglomerate, of which it is formed, that it must be looked upon as having been gradually elevated by forces that have acted equally, and at the same time, on both the older igneous, and recent formations of this section, and the forces that thus gradually operated in producing these phenomena are unquestionably persistent at the present time.

MOST RECENT VOLCANIC ROCKS OF THE COAST MOUNTAINS.

Under this head, a brief description of a class of rocks differing essentially in relative position, lithological character, and general effects on the surrounding country in which they are situated, from those noticed in the preceding chapter, will be given. The section of the country though which they may be observed, has been stated to extend through about forty miles in length of the Monte Diablo Range, and make their appearance in the Santa Anna Picaches, on the south-east border of the Santa Clara valley.

In examining this group it was found, that they consisted principally of compact and vessicular lavas, having different degrees of firmness and texture.

A conspicuous and striking feature of these rocks is found in their connection with other formations, both igneous and sedimentary, and in the case of the latter class they are seen to have acted directly upon them, elevating the same to different altitudes above the sea level. The former rocks form the principal ridge, separating the Pass of Pacheco from that of Santa Anna Pass, (or Cañada Las Muertas), and present a very rugged and conical outline at a short distance. They were probably the grand centre of those recent volcanic disturbances that were in action during the elevation of this part of that mountain range. The higher peaks are composed of trachytic masses, while the lower hills contain immense quantities of the vesicular lavas above noted; from the position which the latter occupy to the former, it appears that during the later periods, when these fires were in action, fissures had been formed in the sides of the two principal craters, through which has flowed large quantities of the fluid masses: one of these dikes cannot be less than eight miles in length and ran in a northerly direction.

At the Santa Anna peaks, the principal crater has, apparently, fallen in during some period of its eruption, and subsequent to this, a large fissure has been formed, probably from the effects of an eaarthquake, and, perhaps, at the time when the north side of the Gabilan was precipitated into the deep ravine at its base.

North of the latter mountains at the distance of eight or nine miles, is the elevated peak known as "Pacheco Peak," which is a true volcanic cone, and in the ravines to the north of this crater, the Indians of this section of the country obtain absidian for the manufacture of their arrow heads; to the north-east of the mountain a large dike of lava, similar to that noticed above is found, which appears to have flowed through a fissure very nearly down to the base.

South of the Santa Anna, the tertiary sandstones of recent date appear, resting directly on this class of volcanic rocks, and bear every evidence of having suffered their principal disturbance from these agencies; the almost complete metamorphosis of the sedimentary group is a proof of this; and the evidences of comparative recent action is found in the fact, that the organic remains found imbedded in these rocks contain a large per centage of present existing species on the coast.

It will be apparent that a difference in the age of that group found in the preceding chapter, and the one under consideration will be manifest, from the fact that in the present case the most recent of the aqueous rocks have been disturbed and elevated since their formation, while in the former group of igneous origin, no features of this character are observable. The vesicular character of the group under consideration and the trapean character of the others, is also a distinctive point that would place each in a different period as regards their age; the older group have every appearance of what has been termed the "primitive trapean rocks" found in some parts of the Sierra Nevada, and which could not have held an age but little posterior to the older rocks of the Eocene, as they are found not to have disturbed the middle group of that period.

The tertiary groups of the Coast Mountains consist of the miocene, pliocene, and post-pliocene periods; the eocene rocks being entirely absent as far as yet examined; it is also found that the miocene rocks do not extend on the coast line beyond a point sixteen miles north of Santa Cruz, and that south of this point the pliocene series predominate. This fact then once established affords a clue by which we are able to determine to a certain extent the age of the volcanic series which has disturbed them, and fixes that age posterior to the formation of the latest of the groups.

CHANGES OF LEVEL AND RIVER TERRACES.

The valley sections of this State present a general uniformity of character in their superficial structure, wherever found; their surfaces are distinctly marked by a regular series of minor elevations, which give them the terraced form so peculiar to those sections. The face of these terraces are of different heights, and the surface of each is found to have a gentle inclination toward the streams that flow through them. In some parts of the "great valley" there are to be seen a range of hills having flat summits, which on examination are proved to have been the shores of an inland sea; these usually arise from the higher portions of the upper terraces, and where they are found near the borders of the plain, they present often trifling evidences of excessive subterranean action. These "tables" when found on the immediate borders of the plains, do not appear to have participated in the more violent disturbing forces found in the interior; they are usually from four to five hundred feet in height, while those farther to the east attain an altitude frequently of more than two thousand.

Immediately succeeding these, the first terraces of the valleys appear, and from the observations of different travelers, we learn that they are continuous into the Territory of Oregon, and probably beyond that point; while south of California their existence is known to the northern boundary of the Province of Sinaloa in the Republic of Mexico. In these we see the evidences of gradual and probably persistent elevation over an extent of country nearly two thousand miles in length, and in the present state of our knowledge, must be regarded as part of one of those great continental elevations that has occurred during the comparatively recent history of the world. This State is situated nearly in the centre of this line, and from its position must partake to a greater or less extent in all the general changes of level that may occur on either side of it; and all observations which have been made within the last ten years have only tended to confirm this fact.

Mr. Dana who has given more attention to the formations of the valley sections of the Pacific Coast, and who probably had better opportunities for observation from San Francisco to the north, in speaking of them, says: "We traced these terraces from the Cowlitz to the mouth of the Sacramento, along many of the smaller streams as well as the rivers. There appears to be but two ways of accounting for these terraces, either lakes have existed along the rivers, which have burst their barriers, or the rivers have excavated the country in consequence of an elevation. The existence of lakes throughout a whole country, connected with all its rivers, is highly improbable, and requires for its proof the strongest evidence. Rivers cut out their channels by a gradual process, as a country is raised above the ocean, forming with few exception a complete drainage for the land. Lakes could not exist, therefore, to the universal extent implied by the facts, except, perhaps, as a sudden rise of the land from the ocean.

"The formation of such lakes by an abrupt elevation in a region having the ranges of heights parallel with the coast, is certainly a possibility. But the water to make the alluvial accumulations, must be running water, and be in operation in its channels a long period. And how long would such lakes exist after an elevation? If the violence attending a change of level did not open for them at once a passage, the accumulation of water during a single flood would break a passage through such soft sandstone beds as occur at the mouth of the Sacramento."

These terraces occur on the Sacramento to the distance of one hundred and fifty miles from the sea and at this point they were as high above the level of the river as at any point lower down, and have nearly the same elevation in all parts examined above the existing level of the stream.

The flats are several miles in width, and until reaching Carquinez Straits, no other place for a barrier could have existed. In this place a permanent barrier of at least four hundred feet in height would have been required, to set the water back so as to cover the upper terrace one hundred and fifty miles above the mouth of the river, and in the second place, the lake should have a surface slope like the present bed of the river, for this is the fact with the land of the terrace—of course an impossibility. Wherever the bed of the stream was four hundred feet above the level of the sea, there the terrace should disappear; in place of which they attain an altitude of seven hundred feet at the distance of two hundred and twelve miles from the head of Suisun Bay.*

It is therefore impossible that one or many lakes should accomplish the results we have before us; it is the proper effect of river floods, and the terraces must be received as indicating a change of level in the country.

Was this change of level an abrupt one, or was it slow and gradual? This seems at first, a question easily answered. We may best understand it by considering the changes that would take place during the elevation of a region of alluvial flats. If a country rise abruptly, the river will commence to work itself to a lower level, and proceed with rapidity, ending finally the very gradual slope of ordinary rivers, having a descent of one or two feet per mile. At the same time, in the season of floods the river would wear into the former alluvium (now its banks) and widen its surface; and this widening would go on at each succeeding freshet till the river had a new lower plain on its borders.

But would not the effect be the same during a gradual rise. As the country rose slowly, the excavation of the rivers bed, and latteral widening during freshets would go on gradually with the same results, producing a deeper bed and a new lower flat, both of which would change as the change of level progressed, and in case the lower flat resisted removal in any part, the portion left standing would form a subordinate

*I have in my possession at this time, specimens from this highest terrace, which is found on Weaver Creek, Trinity County. They were taken from different depths of a shaft which has been sunk through the alluvial deposit *eight hundred feet;* the different strata found though are composed of clay, gravel and sand, in nearly all of which, gold has been found throughout.

terrace between the upper level, or that of the plain before the rise began.

A terrace slope may thus be formed by a gradual elevation, and also without any intermission in the process, there might be intermediate terraces in some parts of the same region. A river terrace then, in an alluvial district cannot be considered an evidence of abrupt elevation of country in which it is found, the more especially if a uniform slope is found upon its surface.

The district south of San Francisco in which extensive valleys are to be found comport themselves in all general features with those found on the Sacramento and thence into Oregon. On the south part of the Santa Clara Valley, beyond the ranch of Cruz Cervantes, the terraced form of the valley is clear and distinct; in this place there were but two of these flats observable—that through which the San Benito flowed, had a rise of nine feet above the level of the creek, while the higher terrace to the east rose very abruptly eighty-five feet above the former. The surface level had an inclination of twelve degrees from the base of the Santa Anna Mountains towards the west; the river flowed upon the western side of the valley entirely.

Two successive terraces were found on the Pajaro, the upper one still retains the marks of tide water upon its surface.

The Salinas Valley exhibits the terraced form in a marked degree, and its inclination of surface from the east toward the west corresponds very closely with that just noticed as occurring on the south part of the Santa Clara and San Juan. The number of terraces on this valley are three, and have a varying width of three to five miles, the slope of each surface is gentle and smooth throughout the entire length of the plain. It differs from the Sacramento or San Joaquin in having but one line of inclination or dip, the others have a dip from each border toward their centre, thus giving them their basin-shaped structure. The slope of the Salinas appears to have been acquired from the recent volcanic agency that formed the Santa Anna Mountains, and those to the north as far as Pacheco's Peak; on examination it is found that the dip of all the sedimentary or stratified rocks of this part of the country correspond in direction, and that the dip decreases as the distance from that centre increases. The Post Pliocene rocks of the Carmello were disturbed at this time, and the entire range of sedimentary rocks of recent date, throughout the Coast Mountains in this section of the country have suffered in a similar manner, and undoubtedly from the same cause.

From the peculiar features manifested in the formation composing the Coast Mountains, as noted in the preceding pages, and the more recent causes of disturbance which have acted in this part of the range, as is found in the modifications of level extending through the valleys above noted, and the intervening mountains between these valleys; it will appear very doubtful that any formation containing mineral coal will be found. The forces that have acted on this part of the country and have elevated the different rocks found on the mountain sides, have as yet developed no member of the secondary series, in which the coal formations are found; but like the mountains to the north, both in the Sierra Nevada and Coast Mountains, nothing above the primitive is to be seen, except the tertiaries, in which no coal beds of extent have yet been discovered.

From a careful examination of this part of the country, with this object in view, I feel no hesitation in saying that coal will not be found in any part of the Coast Mountains south of the thirty-fifth parallel of north latitude; what there may be south of this point, I know nothing having never visited it.

It is not unfrequent in passing over the country to hear of *beds of mineral coal;* during the past season I have visited four such localities, and, as was anticipated, each of them proved to be merely small beds of lignite, and two of them hardly deserving that name. One of these deposits proved to be but a bed of leaves, having a thickness of about three inches, resting upon a tertiary sandstone containing marine shells, and covered with twelve feet of a sandy alluvium. This is one of those coal beds which has figured so largely in the public prints of the State during the past year, and has induced several gentlemen to pay the locality a visit, and to return as deeply disappointed as their previous anticipations were elevated.

The report of coal veins in the Coast Mountains must be received with many grains of allowance, and at the best, none but tertiary deposits will be found, and these, even should they exist, would be capable of supplying but a limited demand, and that usually of an inferior quality.

SOILS OF THE VALLEY SANTA CLARA AND SHORES OF THE BAY SAN FRANCISCO.

The character of mountains on the borders of valleys, afford a good criterion to judge of the capabilities of the soils found at their base. It is therefore not difficult to form a correct opinion of the constituents of a soil, once knowing the nature of the rocks in adjoining sections, and consequently their adaptation to the various purposes of agriculture.

The more rapid disintegration of some classes of rocks compared to others, will form a striking feature in the productiveness of the soil with which they enter as a component part, their chemical constituents, adapting them to agricultural employment, or rendering them totally unfit for these purposes, without the addition of some agent not found as an integral of their composition. It is therefore not surprising that in passing over a range of valley, or mountainous district, to find so many and diversified features presenting themselves often in adjoining localities; it is not unfrequent to find a perfect transition in the indigenous productions of the soil, occurring in the distance of a few hundred yards.

These peculiar features are best exhibited among the native grains and grasses, and occur alike, on the valley bottoms or on ascending a hill-side. Thus, on ascending a hill, at whose base may be found a calcareous rock, resting on any one of the plutonic series, the native product at the base, and within the direct range of the limestone, may be the wild oat, almost as soon as these rocks are passed, and you enter the granite or trapean group, the cereal ceases to grow, and is replaced by the native grasses in some of their varieties, or if the rocks succeeding the former, should belong to the serpentine group, a useless shrub will often be the resulting growth.

Equally as perfect and marked are the phases presented on the valley bottoms alone; passing through the same transitions as above, and on an examination of the sources from which the soil has been derived, it will be found that the mineral constituents of both sections presenting those changes, will differ in a material degree. Take the upper terrace of any one of our large valleys, and by following this to a lower terrace, the first principal change occurring will be found near the junction of the former, with the latter, and this as it recedes from the former, will be found productive of a widely different and greater variety of plants than the hill-side or upper terrace preceding it, and the native productions of these, not unfrequently disappear entirely.

Another feature equally interesting and instructive, is found in transitions of the varieties of production on the same line of valley, which has derived its soils from the same suite of rocks, this might easily be mistaken for a change in the mineral constituents of such soil, which is not the case, but the modification of growths in this instance are attributable to the more uniform and equal distribution and communication of the material composing the soil, thus rendering its chemical constituents better adapted to assimilation, and the consequent production of variety as well as quality and quantity.

The soils on the Bay San Francisco differ much on its eastern and western sides; both borders of the Bay present the tertiary series, but both do not present the trapean rocks to the same degree of development; this, then, of course, will cause a distinctive and marked difference in the productive capabilities of either shore. It will be found that in all the soils which have been derived, in whole, or in part, from rocks more recent than the tertiary group, that a more extensive and varied adaptation to agricultural purposes will be present; this will be particularly manifest in those sections where the tertiaries, containing organic remains, enter somewhat largely into the components of the soil produced from such sources.

We often meet an extensive and even tract of country lying at the base of a range of hills of the character named above, which are found not to possess so high a degree of fertility as an adjoining section, yet both have derived their soil from the same sources; it becomes not only interesting but important to ascertain the cause of such a discrepancy, and an attentive examination will often point out a natural obstruction of a mechanical nature which has thus been the cause of the impoverishment which may be present. In this case a barrier will often be found among the foothills which has prevented the uniform distribution of the disintegrated rocks above, rendering the plain within its line less productive, rather than the introduction of any new agent, except, perhaps, that derived from the rocks forming that barrier, the amount of which would be inconsiderable, compared to the mass of alluvium beyond.

In illustration of this a single case only will be mentioned. On the Valley Santa Clara a few miles east of San Jose, the mountains are capped with fossiliferous sandstone for miles in extent, north and south.—On examining the slopes of these hills and the broad ravines among them, a rich and deep soil was found to cover the whole, and the vegetation growing upon them bore a just relation to the character of the ground on which they flourished. Passing to the westward toward the valley it was found that the same character of soil continued to the first hills rising from the plain, these bearing an altitude of one hundred feet above its level. On reaching the summit of these hills, the rich, mellow soil to the east instantly gave out, and in its place a heavy, clayey covering was found upon the surface for a considerable distance into the valley; this transition occurred within so short a distance that I was led to examine more particularly the cause producing it, and accordingly followed the line of these hills until an outcrop of these rocks were found; they consisted of aluminous and chloritic slates, having a high inclination and dipping to the west; from their position they presented a perfect barrier to the passage of the richer soil of the hills passing on to the valley in any other junction than north and south. As far as this line of slates extended, the valley beyond partook, in a greater or less degree, of the character that would be produced by their disintegration, and ill adapted generally to purposes of agriculture unless by artificial application of reclaiming agents and tillage. As soon as the slates began to disappear in the foothills, the character of the soil on the plain beyond assumed a different appearance, and a marked and corresponding change in its vegetable productions.

A mechanical impediment simply is the cause of unproductiveness in such cases, and in instances of this kind, the remedy usually abounds in abundant quantities and at short distances from the points where it may be required.

On the south-east shores of the Bay San Francisco, there are large areas of land that at the present time are considered useless for agricultural purposes, from their low position and semi-argilaceous character; they have often been denominated "mud flats," and heretofore have been considered unadapted even to grazing for sheep. These flats generally extend (toward the bay) one or two miles from what are considered available and good agricultural lands. Their general appearance to the passer-by is such as would not be likely to impress a person very strongly in their favor, as lands retaining much fertility, but from their superficial appearance would be regarded as a poor representation only of a salt meadow, productive of little else than the common samphire. But such is not the fact and if experience and experiment have any value or weight, they will be thrown in the balance to the favor of those lands; experiments have been made during the past season on these sections, which cannot fail to convince us of the fact, that the opinions heretofore entertained respecting the available character of a large portion of these districts, are entirely erroneous. A single experiment illustrating their capacity for production if properly tilled, will be given.

Near Uniontown, in the County of Alameda, several acres of land, producing the *samphire* on their flats, was broken up and planted to corn; in one case it was sowed in drills; the corn continued to flourish until September which was the last time I saw it; and at this time the stalk of that in the drills had acquired an average heighth of about nine feet. On the south side of the arroya Alameda another field was planted in hills, which was equal, if not superior in heighth. The soil, when broken up, is rich and highly productive in other grains, notwithstanding the meagre appearance it presents prior to tillage, and will in a few years be as successfully and largely cultivated as any other of the valley sections. The *saline lands* of the interior sections are also of the same character, to a certain extent, and if properly tilled are equally productive. Near the rancho San Felipe, Santa Clara County, a similar circumstance was met with; the corn grown upon these lands was being harvested in September and produced a full and well-formed ear, proving not only adaptation of soil, but climate—for the production of this staple in California. The latter case, the lands were 225 feet above the sea, and the field on every side except the south-east was covered with a thick growth of the salt grasses and other kindred plants (samphire) and when free from water the lands were covered with a saline incrustation.

Under a proper course of treatment these lands will be made available for the purposes of the agriculturalist, and our already large domain of arable lands thus much increased. The situation of these lands in the interior is such, that they may be easily reclaimed should they ever fall within the jurisdiction of the State, which undoubtedly they will under the law regulating "saline lands." In the counties of San Francisco, Santa Clara and Alameda the wet land that may be made available by drainage is about seventy square miles, exclusive of the "saline lands" at the southern part of the County of Santa Clara.

Most of the valley sections of this range of country is arable land, and that which is not can easily be made so when required; the agents for bringing this about being found in the adjoining hills to the east.—The character of the soil and climate adapts it to all the productions of temperate climates, and where local position modifies the climate of any section, it is found capable of producing plants of the tropical latitudes.

The extreme south-eastern part of this valley would be adapted to the growth of foreign fruits and other products, but it must be beyond the influence of the cold sea-wind that passes inland across the range of lower hills which divide the Salinas, Pajaro, and Santa Clara Valleys, the effect of which would be to blight the fruit, though the plant or tree might continue to thrive.

The low hills that flank the east side of the valley contain all the elements required for the culture of tropical plants and fruits; the climate and soil will be found adapted, and the only agent that appears in the least to be wanting is water sufficient to supply the demands of those plants. From the appearance of small lagoons and rivulets at different elevations it is presumable that a sufficient quantity of this agent may be found a short distance below the surface.

As a general rule the mountains lying upon the east border of the valley Santa Clara are covered with a soil superior to that of the plains, and of much greater depth. I have measured the depths of these soils in many places, and where it is well developed have found it varying from four to eleven feet for miles continuous; its extreme fertility produces heavy crops of the native grains and grasses which annually contribute to its increase by their decomposition.

Although these lands are situated within the reach of the sea-breeze from the Bay of San Francisco, they are protected from its cold by the slope of the hills and the modifications of its temperature acquired in its passage down the bay before reaching the northern portion of the valley. So much is the temperature increased that an addition of ten degrees is often acquired in its transit from San Francisco to the head of the valley, a distance little rising fifty miles. This increase of temperature in the air is accompanied with an increase in its capacity for moisture, hence it is usual to find a slight aqueous haze, which results from the condensation of its moisture, hanging about this entire range of hills during the summer months, and is usually seen early in the morning.

At this time and for a short time after sun-rise the leaves of plants in these hills are covered with moisture, when no trace of this deposit is observable on the plains. The foreign horticulturist seems to have siezed upon the natural advantages which these mountains present for the culture of the vine and other fruits, prefering these elevated situations to the lower plain lands, the climate and soil being more congenial to their growth. The altitude at which the first qualities of the grape will flourish in these mountains (Monte Diablo Range) is seventeen hundred feet above the sea, the fruit produced equals that grown in lower situations; the temperature at this elevation through the night is higher than on the plains at their base and sufficiently comfortable to sleep without shelter.

But a very few years will elapse before these "barren" mountains will yield a handsome income to the planter, and a large revenue to the State, from the taxable property that will be found in these mountains, arising from the prodution of the vine alone; some idea of the extent to which it is now being propagated may be obtained when it is stated that nearly two hundred thousand sets have been put into the ground during the past year, and on one ranch alone over twelve thousand new sets were placed in the ground last season, in addition to those already in bearing condition on the same farm.

The absence of timber in these mountains is one of the most serious objections to the settler, if this objection can be removed there is no reason to doubt but that large tracts of this fertile district would command a population that would soon approximate that on the plains. It would not be difficult to produce a forest growth of trees upon these mountains, one that would prove useful as well as ornamental, conducing to health, comfort and luxury, as well as profit. The history of the Guava furnishes us with some facts on this point that are well worthy of notice; the tree is of rapid growth, spreading itself over large districts in a very few years. In Mexico it attains a height of forty feet, and grows at elevations of five thousand feet; its wood is used for fuel and many other purposes, and from its fruit the guava jelly is manufactured, and forms an extensive article of commerce.

Fifty years ago this tree was introduced at the Sandwich and Society Islands; it has in that short period of time formed one of the principal forest trees of those islands, and reaches the summit of their highest hills. A tree of this kind introduced into our timberless hills would in a short time render the barren aspect they now present, more pleasing and profitable as well as useful. There can be but little doubt that this tree will flourish in this country, as it is found so to do in a climate equally cool as that in which it would be required here. Other varieties of fruit bearing trees of foreign climates will flourish in these mountain; among them may be mentioned the date, prune and fig, and in this country we possess an advantage in the preparation of the two latter fruits for the market, which is seldom found even in countries where they flourish best, viz: a clear, dry air, or containing but a small degree of moisture, a most essential requisite in forming a good commercial article. Often the entire fruit crop is ruined in the drying process in countries where these fruits abound, (and where all conditions for their propagation are not more fully developed than in this country,) from the presence of too great a quantity of moisture in the air, a circumstance that cannot exist in this country south of the county of San Francisco.

We have the most ample proofs of the capabilities of our soils in the interior, in the production of the foreign fruits. In addition to the above, the olive and the almond flourish and produce plentifully, and though the latter is not indigenous, the luxuriance with which it grows and its plentiful production of fruit, must be received only as another evidence of the fact above stated. The value of these fruits as regards their quality, suffers no deterioration from having been naturalized to our climate, but in the case of the latter named fruit, it is found to be materially benefitted by the change, for as it loses none of its flavor it becomes the more valuable from its increase of size, being nearly double that of the ordinary fruit of the market.

Respecting the main body of lands on the valley and shores of the bay, but very little of which is not adapted to agricultural purposes, it may be said to cover an area little short of six hundred square miles, nearly all of which is well adapted to the cultivation of the cereals and root crops. The higher table of the valley produces excellent corn, and the season though dry permits this crop to mature well. I observed several corn fields on the high terrace of the valley last season, flourishing well at altitudes of three hundred and sixty to four hundred and ten feet, and in localities where it would hardly be supposed from its external appearance, that moisture sufficient to rear a blade of grass could be found. The cause of this productivness in these localities, is in a great measure attributable to the existence of a small quantity of sulphate of lime in these apparently dry soils, derived from a limestone formation in these mountains, and which extends south beyond the Almaden district. The detritus of this rock is found mingled with fragments of other rocks containing ferruginous pyrites in a decomposing state, hence the key to its appearance in this locality, and in the case before it serves the purpose of an absorbent of moisture, thus materially facilitating the growth of crops in these sections.

VALLEY OF THE SALINAS.

This valley is situated south of the Pajaro River, and is separated from the Santa Clara by a spur of the Monte Diablo Range which sink into a range of low hills forming a divide between the former and the Pajaro Valley also. The length of the Salinas is about ninety-five miles. The main course of the valley is about south-east by east; and is coursed by one river (the Salinas) for its entire length. The stream is situated on the west side of the valley for the first fifty miles of its course, after which it crosses the valley a short distance above the Soledad Mission, at an angle of forty degrees to the main axis of the plain. The physical appearance of this large plain differs much from that of the Santa Clara or the Pajaro; when viewed from its centre it has a gentle slope from the east toward the west; but more minute examination exhibits a terraced form to the plain, similar to those observed on the Sacramento, and are three in number, and each possessing a soil of different degrees of fertility and value. The river has a fall of about two feet to the mile, and has acquired its present position within a very recent period, running as it does amongst the most recent tertiary rocks, and alluvium in its more northern portions. Near its sources there are several small streams putting into it, which furnish water throughout the year. The bed of the stream is composed of a fine whitish quicksand, which renders it dangerous to ford at times, and it is seldom attempted, except at localities which are used for this purpose. A large portion of the valley, within eight or ten miles of the coast, and on its south-east border and centre, is made up of low wet lands, covered with willows and tule, these terminate in lagoons and sloughs as they approach the coast, and contain a sufficient depth of water to float a medium sized vessel to the Bay of Monterey. The only obstacle that renders these waters innavigable for some distance into the interior of the valley, are the bars of drift sand which are thrown up by the surf on the coast: a good and substantial breakwater, constructed at some one of these points, would render navigation safe, and materially enhance the value of the public and private property of this section of country, and be the means of affording not only much needed facilities of transportation in the productions of the interior to market, but afford iuducements for the permanent settlement of this immense tract of country (now almost, it might be said, uninhabited and unimproved,) which this, or some other equally efficient measure would be the means of consummating in a short period of time. The extent of land in the interior that would be affected by a measure of this kind would be very great; it being not less than one hundred and fifty miles in length, and possessing capacities for agricultural production equal to any in the State. This will appear the more evident and necessary, when we find that the lower bottoms above the Salinas Valley are capable of producing a wheat crop, (at thirty-two bushels per acre) sufficient to meet the demands of a population numbering three times that of the present within this State:—say nine hundred thousand.

A district of our State presenting capacity and advantages of this character, and crippled as it is for the means of transporting its productions to our markets, should command some attention, and such, at least, as would have a tendency to induce an early and permanent settlement of such lands, if nothing more; and this the more especially as a considerable area of the over-flowed and saline lands of these plains must ultimately fall within the jurisdiction of the State.

SOILS OF THE SALINAS.

The soils of this valley have been derived from the primitive formations on both sides of the plains: that derived from the granite series on the coast side is coarse and easily permeable to water; this obtains more particularly in the vicinity of the Gabilan mountains, and this variety of soil does not extend beyond the high "mesa" on the eastern side. The trapean rocks and limestone of this range exert an important influence in modifying the sterility usually attendant on soils derived from the detritus of the granites, and in this case they exist in sufficient quantities to render those soils productive on the upper terrace of the valley. The productions of each of these terraces differs in a material degree, arising principally from two immediate causes; the first moisture, the second, the finer disintegration of the material composing the soils; to these may be added a third, which sometimes exerts a wide influence on the lower bottom. The upper terrace produces the native wild oat for the most part, or a wiry tough grass; the oat flourishes to the exclusion of the latter on a brown red soil composed of loam mixed with the harsher material derived from the granite, and wherever this loamy matter is found to diminish in quantity, a corresponding increase in the native wire grass is found. This rule was found to hold good in the entire length of the plain on its eastern border.

Passing to the second terrace, plants of a different character are found. The oat is found to a considerable extent on some parts of this, but is usually succeeded by another variety of grass which seems much better adapted for feed to animals, and usually grows very thick and matted; among this the common bargrass, which increases in quantity as the lower terrace is approached, and which animals are extremely fond of eating, in preference to the oat when placed side by side; on the western edge of the second terrace, the wild mustard abounds, covering thousands of acres, and growing to the height of ten to fourteen feet, forming an impenetrable jungle to man or beast for miles in extent; wherever the settler has succeeded in eradicating this article from the soil, it has been found to produce abundant crops of grains or roots, and if anything superior in some cases to the lands of the lower bottom. The lower part of the terrace on which the mustard is usually found in greatest quantities. is sufficiently moist for the propagation of any crops that may be necessary to be placed upon them. Water is obtainable within a few feet of the surface on any part of it.

Passing to the lower terrace, we find the principal native productions to be the burgrass and a variety of the rumex, mingled with a much greater variety of others than is to be found on any other part of these bottoms. On the higher positions the mustard also abounds in considerable quantities. Some parts of this terrace are arenaceous, being covered to the depth of two feet with a loose, fine sand, usually the result of a heavy freshet, and not otherwise. In this is found a third cause for the varieties which these bottoms produce. An interesting exhibition of this occurred from the freshet of last winter, on the Castro Ranch, adjoining the Wacional. At this place about three hundred acres were covered with this sand to the depth of two and a-half feet; on a portion of it a fine field of corn had been raised the previous year, also wheat and barley. The land formerly produced a heavy growth of mustard, but was reclaimed from this in part by tillage. The effect of the overflow was to destroy every vestige of former vegetation, and in its place a thick growth of willows had sprung up that were equally impenetrable with the mustard on the plains. At the time I visited them they had attained a height of about four feet. This immense deposit of sand on the arable land of this part the lower bottom is covered by the obstructions on the beach of the coast to the free egress of the waters from the interior during freshets, and until they shall be removed, some of the best lands of this valley will be constantly subjected to this ruinous result in all coming time.

The amount of land liable to be thus buried beneath this arenaceous deposit is great, and as it comprises a large part of the most valuable property in this section of country, it demands consideration.

The quantity of arable lands contained within the Salina Plains, is estimated at about seven hundred and eighty square miles, this being comprised in the lower terraces only ; the upper terrace cannot strictly be considered as available for agriculture, but it more properly a grazing country with very few exceptions. The above quantities are divided as follows: the lower terrace or river bottom contains three hundred, twenty miles, and the second terrace about four hundred and sixty, and enjoying a climate in its different sections which will be found adapted to the growths of the extremes of temperate zones.

PAJARO VALLEY.

This valley is situated on the coast, and is bounded on the north and east by the southern part of the Santa Cruz Mountains, and on the south by the low hills forming spur of the Gabilan Range, and which divide it from the Salinas Plains. The valley is about eight miles in length, and about four in breadth on an average, exclusive of the foot hills, or low, table hills, on its west border; the Pajaro River forming the boundary of the counties Monterey, Santa Cruz, Santa Clara, has its rise near San Felipe, and flows in a westerly direction through the low hills at the base of the mountains, thence along the northwest border of the valley for about two miles, where crosses the latter within about a quarter of a mile of the town of Watsonville, and reaches the sea at a point south ten degrees west of the latter locality, four miles distant.

This plain is of comparatively recent formation, and formerly was a well-sheltered bay of the sea; the sandstone formation in the hills to the north and east are of the same age as that now forming the coast line between it and the town of Santa Cruz, the fossils of which of present existing species; the forces that were instrumental in elevating this section have been gradual, as is evinced in the highly disturbed position of the sedimentary rocks along the coast for thirty-five miles; in these localities, it is difficult, in some instances to detect any inclination of the strata whatever, and it is only in the mountain sections that this disturbance becomes markedly manifest; the uplift of this entire section has taken place since the rocks on which the tertiaries rest assumed

assumed the solid state, as no instance of change in the structure of any of these rocks is apparent at the points of contact. The under-lying rock is primitive and of the granite class, and this continues for eighteen miles north of Santa Cruz. In this valley and also in the vicinity of Santa Cruz the soils are made up of a mixture of the primitive and sedimentary formations, thus rendering them fertile and easily tilled. In the lower lands the soils are much better developed, yet the hilly lands are capable of producing abundant root crops and grains. The cause that render these hill-sides adapted to agriculture is the same as that found on the high terrace of the Santa Clara, viz.: a quantity of sulphate of lime acting as an absorbent, and retaining sufficient moisture to support a healthy nutrition in the plant.

The entire range of hills lying between the Pajaro and south part of the Santa Clara, and also a large portion of that range between the Salinas and Pajaro are well adapted to cropping, particularly for winter grains, and in some instances they are preferable to the valley lands, and would, if brought under cultivation, produce better crops than the plains; they are also much better adapted to the culture of fruit-trees than valley sections, possessing all the elements of which the valleys are composed, and which render them fertile, they possess the advantage of sheltering the young tree from the effects of the strong winds that pass over these sections from the sea, and also its chilling effects on the young blossoms and fruit.

There is no part of this State that I have visited, which possesses the same natural advantages for fruit culture as are to be found in the district above alluded to; while artificial irrigation is necessary in other parts of the State, in order to sustain the vitality of the tree; this is furnished regularly each night by aqueous exhalation from the ocean, and extending some thirty miles into the interior; during the months of July and August, last summer, an opportunity to observe this part was offered, and I found that over this entire section a sufficient amount of moisture was deposited each night to wet the leaves of plants very sensibly, and during the heavier fogs, a quantity sufficient to keep the ground wet under medium sized trees until near mid-day; a person entering this section of country in the morning would suppose from the appearance of the ground that a light rain had occurred during the night, and it was not unfrequent that I was obliged to dry my blankets in the morning previous to saddling my horse.

The soil is equally adapted to their propagation being of texture that will permit the expansion of the roots below the surface without the necessity of sinking deep into the earth, as is the case in many parts o fthe country, where even the most hardy indigenous trees are found to send their roots to great depths in order to obtain nourishment and support for the trunk. It is surprising that with the advantages presented for the cultivation of American fruit-trees in this section of the State, that so little attention has been given to this subject in this vicinity; heavy losses have been sustained by individuals in attempting to rear trees in many parts of the country, and this has, in a great measure, prevented others from embarking in this enterprize; but in most of those cases where failures have followed the attempt, it has been from a soil ill-adapted to their propagation, or in localities where floods have had the effect to destroy them.

These injurious influences are absent here, and there is every thing that can be desired to invite the pomologist in this ornamental and useful enterprize.

Fruit culture is to form an important branch in the industrial pursuits of this country ; the lands best adapted these purposes in other localities than those mentioned, are to be found in the south and middle portions of the County San Francisco, from the San Mateo to the Francisquito and toward the foot of the mountains to the west. North of San Francisco, the upper portions of Napa Valley and Sonoma are equally as good as those of some parts of the county of Santa Cruz, affording much the same general characteristics as those of the latter county.

LIVERMORE VALLEY.

This valley is situated in the central portion of mountains lying east of the bay San Francisco and valley Santa Clara ; it divides these mountains into two distinct lines of ridges, and runs rather obtusely to their course. The different names that are applied to this valley convey the idea that there are as many distinct valleys, but such is not the case, as no hills intervene to destroy the general level throughout its entire extent. From its extreme north to its extreme southern terminus the valley is about sixteen miles in length and from five to seven in breadth. On the north it is bounded by Monte Diablo and its adjoining hills, separating it from Pacheco Valley; on the east by a single high ridge separating it from the plains of the San Joaquin; on the south by the hills near the northern part of the Cañada Corall, and on the west by the high ridge separating it from the Bay San Francisco. A large portion of the northern centre of this valley is occupied by a lagoon filled with tule, and the latter extend for a considerable distance from its borders.

The soil of the valley is generally good on the borders, but toward tho centre it is either wet and heavy and withal somewhat saline, on the higher parts dry and gravelly. The entire district appears much better adapted to grazing lands than to agriculture, unless water for irrigation is obtained through artesian borings, and from the appearance of the valley there is but little question that an abundant supply is obtainable from these sources. The altitude of the valley is four hundred and thirty feet above the sea; and derives the principal portion of its sup: plies of water from the slopes connecting with Monte Diablo. On the south and southwest sides, among the hills, considerable masses of the metamorphic rocks are to be seen, and the appearance of quartz veins is more frequent in this vicinity than in any other section of these mountains that were observed.

On all the hills that surround this basin, are to be found fossiliferous sondstones, and among the alluvium, in some localities, are to be found considerable quantities of fragmentary shells, among which a large Gryphea has heretofore existed in considerable quantities. Some specimens of the latter fossil are to be found in the office of the U. S. Land Survey, but none that were sufficiently perfect for cabinet specimens could be obtained at the time I visited the locality from which the above specimens were taken. These monstrous bivalves retain the animal in a petrified state most perfectly preserved, and it is evident from their distribution and appearance that they must have been elevated above the surface of the waters during life; the evidence of this exists in the fact that nearly every shell contains the animal, which if they had been raised above the surface after life had been destroyed the probabilities are that very few animals would be found.

The route from this valley to the San Joaquin plains lays through a narrow pass emerging from the southwestern side of the valley. The pass retains the name of the valley into which it enters, and is about sixteen miles (inclusive of that part of the valley through which it passes,) in length: at this point you enter the San Joaquin Valley at a point known as the Elk Horn. The house at this place is two hundred and twenty feet above the sea. A gentle rise of the land occurs here for about half a mile, and then the valley slopes gently towards the river. The road to the river follows the course of the tule bottoms for about twelve miles, and then enters an Encinal of oaks, which continue to the river.

One of the chief points of interest in this vicinity is the extensive area covered by tule; they commence near the junction of the river and Suisun bay, and extend to a point about eighteen miles south of Castoria on the west side of the river; having an average breadth of about twelve miles. From the appearance of the country in which they are situated, I had formed an opinion that a large proportion of these lands might be easily reclaimed, and if so, they must ultimately become valuable property. With this view the altitude above the sea was taken in several places, on my return to the mountains to the west, and the average of those results gave the sum of eighty feet above tide level. Should it prove that this level is maintained to any considerable distance and the general character of those lands favor this presumtion, or should there be a depression to the amount of twenty-five feet from their border to their centre, which is rather improbable, there will still remain fifty-five feet fall to reclaim them by drainage.

If properly drained, these lands could be applied to the culture of rice or other vegetable productions, and judging from the character of the soils immediately about them, they would prove highly prolific. And here in passing I will mention one incident in relation to the capacity of the soil for production, that may prove not only interesting but useful, in illustration of erroneous opinions heretofore expressed relative to lands on the San Joaquin Valley, and which perhaps has exerted as great an influence in preventing the permanent settlement of these plains as perhaps anything that has been urged against them. Toward the foot-hills of the mountains to the west, is a low table of the valley apparently destitute of water, either for the support of vegetation or animal life, in some parts this land has a slight gravelly appearance, but this is not general; on one ranch situated on this plateau there has been two full crops of barley harvested from the same piece of ground, and when I visited this place in October the third crop was then being harrowed in; the whole having occurred within the term of *two hundr d and seventy-three days.*

As soon as this fact became known, settlers were soon found to be on their way thither, and at that time there was not a farm to be found vacant for a considerable distance around. There is no reason for the supposition that land on the west side of the river and toward the mountains is unsuited for cultivation, for the fact before us is a sufficient proof to the contrary.

Having noticed the more general characteristics of the geology of that part of the country embraced in the examinations of the past season, and also their more general adaptation to the industrial departments of agriculture, it now remains to speak of their resources and the uses to which they may be applied.

MINERAL RESOURCES OF THE COAST MOUNTAINS.

The minerals of these mountains are widely dispersed throughout their entire extent; they consist principally of copper, iron, lead, silver, gold, mickel, and antimony, with agates, calcedony, and many others too numerous to mention here, but will be found under their proper head.

The metallic minerals are widely distributed; the ores of copper are found in the form of carbonate, sulphuret, and silicate, among the Santa Cruz Mountains; in the vicinity of Rincon Point, south of San Francisco, it is found sparingly disseminated among the trap and metamorphosed rocks of that section. In the mountains, south of Monterey, it is also found over a limited area, and again in the lower hills on the east side of the Salinas Valley, near the Rancho Alisal. At this locality it occurs in an extensive quartz dike that has forced its way through all the other rocks both igneous and sedimentary; the forms in which it appears are the blue and green carbonate, in crystals, the sulphuret, the latter found in small masses detached from the gangue. In the same rocks is to be found considerable quantities of iron pyrites, generally disseminated and containing a small quantity of gold. The above ores of copper are often met with in these mountains, their occurrence over so wide a range and the trapean rocks with which they are so often associated leads to the belief that at a future day they may be found in sufficient quantity to be profitably worked.

Silver.—In the county Monterey, this metal occurs in the form of argentiferous galena (or lead and silver) this mineral is found in the primitive and transition limestone abounding in this section; it is found in small veins and disseminated; the range in which it occurs, extends from the Gabilan Peak to the Chapedero on the south, a distance of twelve miles inclusive. The limestone in which it is found, and the granitic rocks adjoining have been disturbed by the intrusion of trapean rocks to the east, and from the opportunity that was offered for its examination it dips under the valley of the west at a considerable angle. A cross-cut has been driven from the west side of the hill for the purpose of intersecting the line of the view, but was abandoned before reaching the limestone. A shaft has also been sunk on the vein to the depth of fifty-five feet, and at the bottom the granite had been reached, an opportunity was presented in the level from the bottom of the shaft to make an examination on its line of strike, and from all that could be seen, (as there had been much caving in of the walls) it is evident that the metallic vein is confined to the calcareous rock, as no vestige of it was to be found in any part of the granite below it.

At one point the decomposed vein showed a power of four or five inches for two feet in depth, this was followed down to the granite, and at its junction all traces of the vein ceased to exist. It is not improbable that a well defined sett may be found under the valley, but it will require much exploration and expenditure of capital to determine that point, as mining operations cannot be entered upon with small means and ultimate prospects of success.

Traces of this mineral are to be met with for several miles north and south of this locality, and its distribution over so wide a range of country induces a belief that a profitable vien may yet be found in these mountains.

IRON.—This metal is found in almost every variety of form, from one end of the Coast Mountains to the other, the prevailing mineral however, is the peroxide and protoxide of this metal; the latter is often found in the form of hydrate, and when occuring in proximity to serpentine rocks often found to be more or less auriferous. This mineral is largely developed in some parts of the auriferous district of Mariposa county, and from one of the most valuable receptacles of gold among the gold-bearing rocks of that section.

SULPHATE IRON.—This article known in commerce under the name of "Copperas," is found native in large quantities near the town of Santa Cruz. Its principle had occurred a short distance west of the house of Mr. Medor in a gulch running from the mountains through the low hills to the coast. I followed the course of the ravine from where it enters the high hill near the crossing of the road north-west of the town to near the sea, the average depth of its banks varies from fifteen to thirty feet, its length from the hill to the coast being about two miles.

The copperas formed an efflorescence on the sides and bottom of the ravine covering entirely the earth and stones, on which a great quantity had crystalized; it was not difficult to scoop up a pound or more, at any one of these places; the banks of the ravine above the water were covered with the effloresced salt to such a thickness that a white and green color was given for several yards in length, the ground being entirely obscured. The depth of the earth that was thoroughly impregnated with the salt, would average ten feet for the whole length of the ravine the depth to which this descends below the surface is unknown, but it is probably considerable; the rocks at the bottom are a micaceous schist and were broken into for two or three feet and at that depth seemed as strongly charged with the ferruginous salt as at the surface. A small stream of water runs through the gulch which is permanent throughout the year, and carries a sufficient quantity to answer all the purposes of an extensive manufacture of this article for commerce. It would be difficult to find a loccality that combines the same advantages that this does for the manufacture of sulphate of iron; all that is necessary to be done has been performed by nature, and to extract the salt it is only necessary to erect vats upon the coast and shovel the earth, to be leached, directly into them. An area of several square miles is highly charged with the mineral and the day is not far distant when Santa Cruz will become as celebrated for the manufacture of this article as it has been heretofore for its vegetable productions.

MAGNETIC IRON.—At the distance of two miles north-west of the above locality, an extensive bed of magnetic iron occurs, running down to the coast, at which point it crops out and exhibits a depth of several feet. Toward the mountains I have been informed that it again shows itself above the surface in several places; there is every reason to believe that it underlies an extensive district, as much difficulty has been experienced in obtaining correct courses by the compass; in one instance the needle was deflected to thirty-one degrees on approaching its southern edge.

GYPSUM.—Sulphate of lime is reported to abound in the northern part of Santa Cruz, and in the vicinity of the Palo de los Yeska, some six miles from the Mission; it was frequently spoken of by the inhabitants of this place but I was unable to learn its precise locality. It is not improbable that it does abound in this vicinity, as ample material for its formation exists in this section of country. An extensive bed of mountain limestone occurs in close proximity to the native sulphate of iron alluded to in the former paragraph.

CINNABAR—Has also been reported to have occurred in this vicinity. I found one small piece east of the San Lorenzo on the side of a hill, but it is not impossible that it might have been carried there by human means, as no other mineral of the same character was observed; the occurrence of small detached pieces of cinnabar in these places is not sufficient evidence to found a belief that it occurs in situ, or that a deposit may occur there.

NIKEL.—The ores of this metal are found from Contra Costa on the north to the utmost southern limit reached in the Coast Mountains. It occurs in the primitive rocks, associated with chronic iron in almost every case where the latter may be obtained. It appears as a bright green mineral on the fractured surface of the other ores, and is known in technical language as "nicked green." The scarcity of this metal renders the discovery of its ores in this country an object of some importance, and its wide distribution leads to the belief that it exists in sufficient quantities to warrant investment for its extraction from other ores, at no distant day. It is extensively used in the manufacture of German Silver for wares and household utensils. When reduced, the metal is white, much resembling silver in in its general appearance, and for which it has been mistaken in this country. The principal localities where it has been observed this season are at Contra Costa, in the serpentine rocks south of Tulecita and near San Antonia in the county Monterey, among the large beds of chronic iron from the San Benito, and the Panoches, of the Gabilan range. These localities afford the largest amounts yet found in this State, and it is to be hoped that those explorations which are now in progress in this part of the country may result in the development of this mineral to a much greater extent than yet known.

GOLD.—This metal has been found in the Coast Mountains, from the County San Francisco on the north to Luis Obispo on the south. The slates and serpentine formations which have been noticed in the preceding pages of this report are found to be receptacles of gold here as in the Sierra Nevada; these rocks are extensive in the Coast Mountains, often comprising an entire ridge for miles, they are usually flanked by the granite. During the past summer, the placers in the County Santa Cruz were much worked; the gold found here was principally on the San Lorenzo and its tributaries; it was fine, and much resembled that found in the Caoti Hill, near Nevada; under the glass it had all the appearance of having suffered but little from attrition by water, the surface of the grains being rough, as though just detached from their original matrix. The slates and serpentine rocks occur on both sides of this creek, with small veins of quartz running through them, and from what we know of auriferous districts of this and other countries, the presumption that gold in *situ* exists here, amounts nearly to a certainty.

On the upper portions of the Carmello, in the county Montery, gold is also found, in the immediate vicinity of the Rancho Tulecita. Farther to the southeast, near the head waters of the creek, it is also found on the tributaries of the main stream, that flow from the western ridge of these mountains. On the Francisquito, a tributary of the Carmello, coming from the southwest, and twelve miles from the coast it is also found near the house of Barondo. Three or four Mexicans were working with the battaya at the time I passed that ranche. The serpentine rocks are largely developed on the east flanks of the granite ridges, and from their course they may be considered as forming the northern part of a series which occurs at the Mission San Antonio fifty miles south.

I was informed by Mr. Meadows, who has traversed the interior of these mountains probably more than any other man in this part of the country, that the same class of rocks are found throughout the distance inclusive between the Carmello and the above Mission. Near San Antonio there were several persons at work during the past summer, in the placers in this vicinity. This was no new discovery, for the existence of gold at this locality has been known since 1850. Those at work at this place were mostly Mexicans, and while traveling on the Salinas I frequently met companies of five or six, with their camp material and tools, wending their way to this section.

On the Pescadero Creek, a tributary of the Pajaro River, gold was found during the past summer; it was first observed a short distance above the bituminous springs lying on the north bank of this stream; the serpentine rocks abound in this vicinity, and also some of its subordinate members; at this place the Magnesian Group of the Santa Cruz Mountains, which run north into San Francisco, have their southern terminus.

On the Rancho La Brue, near the Pescadero, and into the very edge of the Valley Santa Clara the talcose series and gold is found; on crossing the Pajaro, these rocks and with them the gold closes; not a trace of this metal, or rock that would indicate its existence was to be found in any of the hills east of the Gabilan.

The district of country in the Coast Mountains in which the auriferous deposits are now known to occur is about eighty miles in length, and thus far is confined to the counties of Santa Clara, Monterey and the north part of Luis Obispo. This is a material addition to the already known area in which this metal is found, and its location in what has heretofore been considered the agricultural districts of the State, will in time exert a beneficial influence in the permanent settlement of those sections.

Antimony.—The common sulphuret of this metal is very abundant in the Monte Diablo Range; at Mount Oso it is found in large masses, also at various other points throughout these mountains; it occurs in considerable quantities in some parts of the County of Santa Barbara. This mineral is deserving of attention as it often contains a notable quantity of silver, though as yet no specimens which have been found in this country contain a large per centage of this metal. That variety of the antimonial ores which is argentiferous, has a lively steel-gray color, cuts easily with the knife and is brittle, while the common gray antimony, which is the principal yet found, has a lead-gray color, its fractured surface, easily tarnishes and scales of the mineral are slightly flexible.

Bitumen.—Bituminous springs abound through the Coast Mountains, and in some places is much used in the construction of buildings, and walks in front of buildings; for the latter purposes it is admirably adapted in situations where the sun will not have too powerful an effect upon it, as in such cases it is apt to become soft. In the counties of Santa Clara, Santa Cruz and Monterey, several of these springs occur, and further south are found more abundant. Information has been received of an extensive deposit of bitumen in Contra Costa, some six miles from the shores of the bay, but at what point I have as yet been unable to learn. This article has been used of late in the manufacture of gas, for illumination, and it possesses some advantages over the common oil or resin gas in general use; a sufficient quantity for the illumination of the country may be easily obtained and at low rates when required for this purpose.

Cinnabar.—This mineral is well known, and the principal mine now opened in this country is at New Almaden in the County of Santa Clara and situated twelve miles from San José. The town of Almaden is situated four hundred and eighty feet above the sea and the mine is eight hundred and sixty feet above the town, making the elevation of the mine thirteen hundred forty-five above tide level. The ore at this mine is found in bunches or deposits in a clay highly charged with peroxide iron. The cinnabar contains considerable arsenic generally disseminated through the ore, small veins of calcareous spar are found running through the mineral giving it at times a fanciful appearance. The magnesian rocks are largely developed in this section, both at the mine and in the mountains to the south-west. The rocks in the immediate vicinity of the mine are talcose in their character, much decomposed and broken up; at the base of the hill on which the mine is located there is to be found native magnesia on the surfaces of the rocks.

The deposit of ore at this locality is very large, and will require many years to exhaust it. As the mine consists of deposits simply, there is uo certainty of its continuance beyond the surface that may be exposed: it has been supposed generally that the ores of this mine occurred in the form of veins, but such is not the fact, and so far as I could learn from the superintendents at the mine, no well defined vein had been found since its opening. The principal adit of the mine is one thousand feet in length, and at the end of this a body of ore fifteen feet square had been exposed in one place; other similar masses, and even larger ones, were laid bare in different parts of the mine. An inclined winze had been driven to the depth of about one hundred feet below the level of the adit, at the bottom of which immense bodies of ore had been found. From the quantity of ore on hand, and that exposed in the mine, the prospects of the company are highly flattering for a handsome return for the heavy outlays of capital which have heretofore been made. At the date of my visit, the company were erecting twelve new furnaces in addition to those already in operation, having a capacity for working of twelve thousand pounds per week each, with an abundance of ore in the hacienda for their supply. The construction of their adit and the interior of the mine, with their reduction works, are of a character for permanency, workmanship and scientific skill to be found only among large mining operations. The ease and regularity with which everything connected with the mine argues well for its administrador, and exhibits a thorough understanding of the requisites necessary to insure success in extensive operations.

A better regulated, or more systematic method of mining, is not to be found in this or any other country, and is well worthy a visit from any who may wish to obtain an idea of what practical mining is in a large way. At the distance of three miles, another mine of the same character has been opened, but is not in operation at present, this latter is called the Gaudulupe; it has not proved extensive up to the present time.

In the lists of minerals, appended to this report, will be found more specific detail respecting their distribution among the rocks of the coast mountains. A description of the fossils will also accompany the latter, as far as the nature of circumstances will permit. The scarcity of books of reference in this country, at the present time, will render it impossible to define all the species that have been secured the past season; the genera will be nearly complete, and in the course of the ensuing season, the species of those genera will be described, as ample works for that purpose will be at hand within that time: there appears to be many that are undescribed in any of the works on hand at present.

MINERAL DISTRICT.

After completing the examination of the coast mountains within the parallels alluded to, a visit was made to the mineral districts, embracing parts of the counties Nevada, Placer, El Dorado, and Calaveras, the object of which, was to connect a line of travel commenced in May and June last, in the counties of Butte, Yuba, and Sierra; and to obtain, if possible, some information respecting the general character of placer and quartz mining at the present time, compared with its earlier prospects.

Two years having elapsed since I had visited this section of the country, and having in my possession the original notes of travel and maps made at that time, with a general acquaintance of their former condition, it was deemed advisable to make this particular examination, in order to form some estimate on their future prospects.

With this view, the more central portions of the mining districts were selected, as these may be considered a fair example of the extremes, and from the lateness of the season and distance were more accessible.

PLACER MINING.

The extensive excavations, which have been made within the last two years, in this branch of mining has afforded an opportunity of examining the different mountain formations not heretofore obtained, and has been the means of eliciting much valuable and interesting information, relative to the early condition and mutations, which have taken place in the superficial coverings of our hills. The rapid progress of advancement in the methods of conducting mining operations in this branch particularly, has opened a door for scientific research, which it seems impossible to have accomplished in so short a period as that in which they have been occupied; they have the appearance of having been in operation for half a century rather than the short space of *four years.*

It is now ascertained to a certainty that the placer ranges extend to the east, within ten or fifteen miles of the "summit ridge" so called of the Sierra Nevada; and the condition in which it is found at these points are similar in all respects to that in the older or more western sections, with perhaps one exception, and that the relative age of both. There are evidences which clearly indicate a deposit of gold older than the diluvial drift of the lower or western diggings, (which latter is often confounded with the drift deposits of the tertiary periods in this country) the character of which differs in almost every respect from any other deposit yet observed in this country, except in this particular range.*

Its direction has been traced for about seventy miles, and is found to extend through the counties of Butte, the eastern part of Yuba, Sierra, Nevada, Placer, and El Dorado; it appears to have an average breadth

* This deposit appears to hold a position and age below the tertiaries, and may be considered intermediate between the latter and the primative formations in this State, its fossils differ from any thus far found, in any formation within the State, and I am disposed to refer it to the Brandan group of Vermont, discovered by Prof. Hichcock, vide Sillman's Journal of Science.

of about four miles, with an elevation of four thousand feet above the sea for the greatest part of its length.

From the examinations that were made upon this range, there are abundant evidences that an ancient stream flowed through this section of the country, and in a direction parallel with its then existing mountain ridges, and the extensive mining operations conducted in the south-east part of Sierra county on this range, has been the means of demonstrating this fact, which had heretofore been strongly suspected only. The outliers of its banks are very definitely marked throughout the entire length of the formation under consideration, and its former bed filled in many places with a volcanic sand and ashes, which probably accompanied its displacement.

In the county Sierra these peculiarities are best observed; in the vicinity, and for ten miles west of Downieville, the hills are covered with a volcanic brecia and tufa, which may be conveniently studied between the Negro Tent and Galloway's Ranch, also on all the hills and ravines surrounding Yumanna on Oregon Creek. On the creek the tufaceous deposit is found to the depth of sixty feet.

The exact point from which these immense quantities of volcanic materials were ejected, is somewhat obscure; yet there are reasons for the supposition that they had their origin in the truncated cones which lie a few miles to the north-east, and of which the Pilot Peak forms one of the principal points or centres of this rugged and forbidding district. This presumption is based on the grounds that between Pilot Peak and Yumana there are ample evidences of a direct connection with these larger centres of disturbance; an extensive dike of black scoriaceous and vesicular lava is traceable throughout the entire distance between Yumana and the Pilot Peak, passing through the hill north-west of Downieville, and within two hundred yards of the town, it crosses the river at this point and appears at Durgan's Flat on the opposite side of the stream, from thence it is again met near Galloway's Ranch, and continues from there to the high bluff which overhangs the town of Yumana, on Oregon Creek. There are no other true volcanic cones in this section that would seem commensurate with so large a scale of operations, except those above noted, though the minor peaks undoubtedly added much to the general result.

The displacement of this ancient stream and the subsequent filling of its bed has opened a new and rich field for scientific research in this State, but its more direct and economical bearings are that it affords an equally new and extensive field for the operations of the placer miner, and that thus far has proved itself equal to that of any range yet discovered in this country. Besides being equally abundant in its produce of gold as far as opened, with the best placers of the State, it possesses the advantage of being the most extensive of any one system which has yet been found. The peculiarities which characterize this formation and which distinguishes it from all others in the State, are the following:—the boulders found throughout its entire extent are very uniform in their characters, and are composed of quartz exclusively, (or nearly so) this has a bluish-watery color in the mass, highly translucent and vitreous when fractured, constituting ninety-seven per cent. of all the stones found in the deeper diggings, they are invested by a dull but deep blue earthy material highly charged with pyrites, which in most cases is as firm as the rocks themselves, making it extremely laborious and difficult in driving shafts or adits. The gold is contained in this matrix for a distance of six or eight feet above the "bed-rock," and resting directly on the latter, it is coarse and generally rough, and its external appearance is that of a poor quality, though it assays high and brings the first prices; its pale and dirty appearance is due to a small quantity of arsenical pyrites which adheres to its surface and which is found in considerable quantities in the matrix containing the gold.

The underlying rocks are serpentine and talcose slates; on Oregon Creek they are found to contain small veins of mundic (arsenical pyrites) one or two inches in thickness, this has a clear and lively grayish-white color, when recently fractured, but soon tarnishes on exposure, becoming a dirty lead gray, and even quite dark; this mineral is rich in gold, it is difficult to find a small piece that does not present this metal to the naked eye on some part of its surface.

The mineral was first observed in the Johnson Shaft, half a mile north of the town of Yumanna, and occurs at a depth of fifty feet below the level of the creek, at the edge of which the shaft was driven, the strike of these veins was north-west by west, and is found on both sides of the stream on that line. There were four other shafts in this vicinity in which the mundic was found under the same circumstances; and there can be scarcely a question but that it exists in true veins among the serpentine rocks throughout this part of the country. These veins have been found to penetrate the rocks in which they occur to the depth of six feet from the surface, and should it ultimately be found that the area is in any way considerable through which they run, they offer sufficient inducement to erect works for the reduction of this ore.

The blue color of the drift in this range has been found to pervade all parts of this peculiar deposit wherever it occurs, its boulders maintain their character and per centage, its extent over so large a district, its dissimilarity in these respects with all other placers yet known, has suggested the propriety of adopting a name which shall at once seperate it from other sections, in order to designate more particularly its course and extent in the future; by this means we shall in a short time be able to acquire additional information relative to its extent that we do not now possess, and as its developements at the present time are of so flattering a nature, that any information of its present undiscovered boundaries, would add but another link to the great chain of our mineral resources, equally as important and productive as the best now known.

I would, therefore, suggest, that the term "*Eastern Blue Range*," be applied to this district; this will separate it from those lower down having the same color, but not possessing any one of its other peculiarities.

To define more particularly the position of this formation, both geographically and geologically, we will follow more particularly the outline of the ancient stream, and some few of the localities now situated upon it. On the south fork of Feather River, opposite to Sailor Bar, and east of this locality for three miles it is found in the form of small flats on the sides of hills declining to the east; passing to the south, it is met with a short distance from Goodyear's Bar, again at Yumanna, on Oregon Creek, still farther south at Minesota, at Chipseg's, Smith's and

Kanaka Flats; crossing the Middle Yuba, it is found at Orleans Flat, Moore's Flat, New Flats, thence across the south Yuba, by the towns of Eureka, Washington, and Poor Man's Creek, and at Mule Springs. This vicinity has presented an area of nine miles in which this formation has been found. Crossing Bear River, it is again met at each side of the American Forks, and is particularly well developed in the vicinity of Sarahsville, extending from thence to Georgetown. South of this, but very little is known of its location.

Within the extremes of north and south named above, the banks of an ancient stream are distinctly marked out, and can be as easily traced as if the waters were still flowing in their original bed. It must have existed at a date when the adjacent country maintained a much less elevation than that now existing; this is proven from the fact that, even at this time a terraced form is observable in many places, in each of which the same peculiarities abound. The organic matters deposited are perfect in their forms, the most delicate parts of leaves are truthfully preserved to nature; the material in which they are imbedded is that usually found suspended in waters that were but slightly disturbed, and when disintegrated yields an almost impalpable powder—not a pebble, nor even coarse sand is to be found in any part of it. In fact every feature that would indicate a quiet state of waters is fulfilled in the section under consideration. Had it been otherwise, the leaves and other tender parts of plants would have exhibited a different appearance from that they now present.

The remains of plants found in these localities are extinct on this part of the coast at the present date, the fruit, leaf, and structure of the sap-vessels, differ from those of every other section of the country, either fossil or living. I have been enabled to obtain six varieties of leaves, and two varieties of fruits, which will be described as soon as opportunity shall offer. The depth at which these specimens were obtained from the surface was one hundred seventy feet, and near the end of an adit whose length was five hundred eighty feet, the principal bed was found in the Arcana Tunnel, at the town of Minesota.

The position of this formation has been stated in the preceding pages, to be below the tertiary groups and diluvial drift of the other placers. It will be unnecessary to roam over the entire State to illustrate or prove this point, as we have an adjacent district where both may be studied with ease and facility in an hour's ride between them. This locality is found at Chipseg's and Smith's Flats, about midway between Minesota and Oregon Creek. The different formations will be given as they occur at Smith's Flat and Minesota, which will fully illustrate the existing differences.

At Minesota we find the following in the descending order: First, volcanic tufa; second, diluvial drift, containing no gold and having a depth of seventy feet; below this is found a bed of clay and imperfectly formed slates beneath which a boulder formation of thirty-eight feet composed almost exclusively of quartz; succeeding this the formation in question, containing the silicified woods, and leaves and fruits, the latter in the form of lignites, and in abundance. Following a direct line from this locality to Smith's Flat and at the distance of half a mile from the latter we meet an outcrop of the slates, above these slates the drift and gold of this latter locality is found, and contains petrifactions of present existing species of plants and trees, which still flourish in the adjoining neighborhood ; among these the pine and oak are very prominent. The structure of these silicified woods are as perfectly delineated as in the trees of similar character growing above them. The drift deposit at this locality is composed of every variety of rock found in the adjoining countries, being composed of trap, granite, porphyries and quartz, forming no well defined order of position.

The drift deposit of Minesota being almost exclusively of quartz, such as has been described as occuring at Yumanna, forms a wide contrast with the above, and beneath the boulder formation the lignites, consisting of six species none of which are identical with any living species, or with the deposits of the section north of this locality. It will be seen from the peculiarities thus briefly enumerated in relation to the main features of both deposits, the widely dissimilar character of the minerals composing both, their relative position, and the difference in the organic deposits found in both, there is sufficient reason for assigning to each a different age.

How correct this conclusion may be, it yet remains to be proved, if additional testimony is required; and this can only be known when this particular section shall have been more fully explored. Certain it is, however, that its present appearance favors this classification; and should it prove as productive in its auriferous deposits as the partial explorations upon it now indicate, the amount of gold which it capable of producing would be unequalled in any district heretofore or at present known. There is not an instance known, where the lead in this range has been found, but that large sums of gold have been the result; this might be saying more, perhaps, than prudence would dictate, but such are the facts in the case, let opinion be what they may.

QUARTZ MINING.

For two years past this branch of industry has engrossed much of public attention, and speculation on the future success and prospects of these mines has been as diversified and fluctuating as upon any subject ever presented to public consideration; this has resulted from an incorrect appreciation of their intrinsic value, and want of information respecting their position, geologically considered, coupled with disappointments resulting in too high anticipations of abundant products from these sources in too short periods of time; the hasty and inconsiderate manner in which persons entered into these speculations in the country heretofore, and the natural results which must necessarily flow from such a course of action, has had the effect to cast a shadow of doubt for the time being, on the future prospects of these sources of wealth, while the pecuniary losses that followed in the the train of these causes were construed by alarmists abroad as indexes of certain failure, and thus rendered the doubt that existed an *apparent* certainty.

All this however, has had a beneficial effect in its ultimate results, by checking that abnormal cause of action incident to the first outbreak of all speculative movements of this kind. Had that cool discretion and judgment which has marked the subsequent career of these undertakings—that firm determination to surmount all natural obstacles and test the truth or falsity of the claim advanced of the value of these veins, been practiced in the earlier stages of quartz mining, we should have been spared the disagreeable task of chronicling adversity and *pseudo-failures* in a legitimate and profitable branch of employment, thus saving this one of the grand levers of our commercial prosperity the odium that has heretofore attached to it and is still persistent in the minds of some abroad.

Aided by the discrepant and in many cases malicious reports from our own hills, the *savans* of the Atlantic States and Europe reiterated the howl, and the public of those distant shores were nightly harrangued in the lecture-room, and popular assemblies, on the utter *impossibility of the auriferous veins of this country proving to be more than a mere ephemeral show*, and unworthy the confidence of reflecting minds. Their gratuitous expressions and unfavorable opinions, are now proved from the subsequent explorations which have been conducted on these veins, to be equally unfounded as were the arguments made use of by these men to convince their listening audiences of the *supposed facts* they so learnedly put forth; and our citizens engaged in these pursuits of industry have labored on, temporarily affected only by the confusion of opinions and anathemas issued from the portals of science, against this great interest of the State, and have borne the testimony triumphantly to the world that science unattended by personal experience will render him who uses it far more notorious than popular or reliable.

Notwitstanding the disadvantages of a manufactured public opinion with which this branch of industry has been obliged to contend, and the serious obstacles which have thus been presented to its progress, it has now become one of the permanent employments of the State, and should it meet with no other impediments than those which are the resultants of nature, it will obtain a position second to none, within the next two years.

The permanency of their character would scarcely have been demonstrated in the short period of time in which it has occurred, in any other country or State except this, and is in true keeping with the firmness of purpose manifested in every great undertaking by the citizens of this State, and is but another mark of that indomitable perseverance in overcoming difficulties either natural or artificial, that stand in the path of their advancement, for which they have become peculiarly characterized and proverbial.

The popular belief that the gold mines of this State, and the operations conducted upon them heretofore has been suspended, with the exception perhaps of a few isolated cases scattered through the country, and that they hold but a forced existence for speculative puposes, designed ultimately to be the means of conducting swindling operations on a large scale abroad, is as base as it is unfounded; those feelings and ideas find a haven in the breasts of a few only, who from their position commercially have been the means of propagating this erroneous and unjust opinion in relation to this subject. The embittered feelings of such persons, which have had their origin in disappointed hopes arising from too hasty conclusions respecting the productiveness of those operations in which they were individually interested, and which in nearly every case was caused by inadequacy of means and mismanagement of their operations, is no criterion whereby to form an opinion that would be just or reasonable, with reference to these metallic veins, and those in this country who would still propagate those opinions, do so in the face of every evidence to the contrary which reason or sober judgment would demand or can be found in this or any other country.

With these preliminary remarks on the general impressions at home and abroad, respecting their *theoretic* value, founded as they are on presumption rather than evidence, we shall proceed to consider the geological position which the quartz veins of this State hold to the rocks with which they are found in connection, hoping thereby to elucidate more clearly their present as well as prospective value.

QUARTZ VEINS AND THEIR RELATIVE AGES IN CALIFORNIA.

The quartz veins of this State are found distributed in nearly parallel lines throughout the west flank of the Sierra Nevada, and consist of three distinct lines separated by intervals ranging from four to eleven miles; as these divisions are found in nature they constitute what may be denominated the principal or main ranges. Between these are to be found smaller lines of these rocks at times running parallel with the former, at others having strikes more or less oblique, and even at right angles in some instances with the principal veins.

From the peculiar distribution of these rocks, as relates to their connection and position with the formations in which they are found, it would be difficult to refer them all to the same age; this would be manifest only by observing the different sections in which they occur. They will therefore be designated in this report as the *Older* and *Recent* groups, in order to better describe the peculiarities that may be found in both, and with reference also to the age of the rocks which they have been the apparent cause of disturbing.

OLDER GROUP.

The eastern and also a part of what may be termed the central line of dikes are included under this head. This group is found to have intruded itself through the primitive formations only, or through the trapean rocks which immediately succeed the primitive. The principal rocks which appear to have suffered the greatest amount of local disturbance and dislocation from these quartz veins, have been the granite serpentine and the earlier trapean rocks, which appear to under-lie both the former. The veins or dikes that occur in the primitive series are usually much more massive than those of a later period, and are not distributed over so wide an area, or possess so great a number of lateral veins, or cross-courses incident to the more recent group of these rocks.

The mineral characteristics of the Older Group are more uniform and regular so far as known, and are found to possess a firmness of texture, where they enter the greenstone, much greater than those of recent date. It is seldom found that this suite of veins has cut through or in any way disturbed the slates which rest on the granite, even when the latter are in the immediate neighborhood; less rare is it to find them cut through by the older group ; that in a line of travel over two hundred miles in length that I have seen but two instances in the eastern range of veins, and it is even questionable whether this dike belonged strictly to the older group.

The effect of these veins on the rocks which they pass through, has been to disorganize their structure to a considerable extent, which has rendered the decomposition of both more rapid and complete, hence it frequently happens that rich deposits of metal are found in such places, and usually occur near the point of contact of both series of rocks. The older group is found to extend from near the summit ridge of the mountains to a distance of about forty miles toward the west, and constitute nearly six-eights (6-8) of all the veins found within this line of distance, and on these are located the greatest proportion of all the mines at present in operation.

In that portion of the country lying north of the Cosumnes River and ranging thirty miles east of the Valley Sacramento, the central line of dikes belonging to the older group, are found, their western edge passes through the counties of El Dorado, Placer, Nevada, Butte and Shasta, and as far north as the Mt. Shata hills to the east of the peak. It is well developed in the counties of El Dorado, Placer and Nevada, and in one locality in the county of Yuba, a short distance above Scott's Ferry. In these latter counties the more recent group is also found, and in the county of Nevada it is seen to have disturbed the older groups in some localities, and in Placer county, where both have features in common which will be noticed more particularly when treating of the Recent group.

To localize the upper and older group of these veins, a few localities will be given for the purpose of familiarizing their geographical positions; in Nevada county it is met with at the National vein, also at German Bar, at the Ariel Mine in Sierra county, and the Jamison Creek mines in Butte county; on the American forks at the Volcano mine, El Dorado county; Leake Vein, Calaveras county; Big Oak Flat, and Marble Springs, Tuolumne county.

These localities are situated far into the mountains, and are situated on the eastern part of this line of dikes, and upon those parts of it where it is most largely developed, becoming an extended and well defined continuous range.

Returning to the middle or central range of dikes, at the distance of thirty miles from the valley, and travelling south we find that immediately after crossing the Consumnes, the granitic rocks that have heretofore been found associated with this range of veins further north begin to disappear in a gradual manner, and the prevailing rocks are talcose, to the exclusion of almost every other of the primitive series; for a distance of about fifty miles, the quartz is found associated with this or some of its subordinate members, the granitic rocks lying far to the east. The quartz vein found among the talcose series and which appear of the same age as those occurring in the granite, are equally uniform in the general characteristics they present, so far as relates to their mineral constituents, but there is one remarkable feature attending them here (as also to the north in a few instances,) which is not common to the granitic associations of these rocks, viz: the depth to which the vein is decomposed from the surface down, will not exceed more than one-fourth that which will be found where the inverting rock is of the granitic series. This peculiar feature is very striking in passing from a "sett" situated in the latter to one located in the former, and will be found to hold good even in the same neighborhood.

One other feature is equally apparent, and at the same time important in connection with this, which is, that while those veins present the contrast above noted, the "setts" occuring in the serpentive series which have been unaffected by the cause producing such extensive decomposition as is found among the granite rocks, do not possess a texture so firm and coherent as the veins found in the northern sections, such veins will be worked with a less amount of labor and capital producing an equal amount of ore.

There is nothing to distinguish the veins of this section from being of the same age with those at the north, and running through a similar range of country, like the veing of the granitic series they do not appear to have disturbed the more recent formation of the tertiaries, but are confined exclusively to the primitive rocks. Following a line west toward the valleys, the occurrence of a more recent group becomes manifest, and is unquestionably the equivalent of that alluded to as occurring throughout the northern counties.

RECENT GROUP.

This group of these rocks is found extending from the lowest foot-hills on the east border of the valley, where the first outcrop of the slates are met, to a distance of about eighteen miles to the east, and after is found running into the western edge of the older group; their intrusion appears to have formed one of the principal and later disturbing agents that has been in action in those periods of development of that part of this country, immediately preceding, and continuing into the middle Eocene and Miocene periods of the tertiary era.

Their altitude above the sea is variable, from one hundred to fifteen hundred feet, and some few localities reach the height of two thousand. One of the features, which this group presents, and which distinguuishes it from those of the older group is, that they have cut through and disturbed not only the primitive formations, but every other formation found resting upon them, this occurs in almost every case in which these rocks are found. A dike of this age is often found protruding through the granite or some other member of the primitive series, and may be traced frequently for one or two miles before any member of the sedimentry rocks are met with; in this case, the latter rocks will be found more or less disturbed at the point of contact with the vein, and it will often be found that its passage from the granite beneath into the slates above is perfect, traversing the overlying rock through a great part of its length, and sending out cross courses in every direction. A di-s turbed position is not the only change observable in these cases; structural change is as often the result of the intrusion among the slates as the appearance of the veins themselves. The above peculiarities in relation to these views are observable in every part of the lower mining districts, and an erroneous opinion in regard to the age of the dike under examination may easily occur as the part under our observation may be situated either in the primitive or sedimentary rocks.

A dike of this character occurs in the town of Centreville, Placer County, and extends in a northerly direction for one and a half miles through granite, when it enters the slates, passing entirely through their length and again appearing in granite at their northern extremity; another instance of a similar character is met with on Deer Creek, two miles below Nevada; here the dike passes through the trap, granite and slate, and also at Newtown in the same county. Still further north, in the County of Yuba, a vein cuts both the granite and slate, as in the vicinity of Brown's Valley, and again on Dry Creek; in many other localities throughout this range of country, the same features are to be found, and our opinion on the comparative ages of these veins, can be correctly founded only by a careful examination of the entire length of the vein.

On the same range of hills, this group is continued south as far as the Tuolumne River, and includes the district on which some of the principal companies of the southern counties are located. It frequently happens that the veins of this group are composed of a perfect *net-work* of small threads and veins, varying in power from one inch to one foot. This peculiarity is admirably exemplified at Angel's Camp in Calaveras County, at this locality and for miles around these small "*hilos*," constitute a large part of the rich veins of this section, while at the distance of four miles to the south, it again appears as a mammoth dike, popularly known as the "Great Carson Hill Vein," which extends southerly to the Stanislaus River.

From this point a line of large dikes interrupted at intervals continue in a southeast direction for sixty miles, passing through Campo Seco, Coulterville, Bear Valley, and thence to Mt. Ophir; throughout this entire distance they are found to cut through all other volcanic rocks, with perhaps one or two exceptions; the lasaltic rocks in some parts of the southern counties bear evidence of displacement by these intrusions, and I know of but two cases in which the latter intrusions have *thrown* these veins, and in these cases it is not yet fully determined whether this be the fact. It is on the west flanks of the hills in which the dikes of the recent group of quartz appears, that the features which mark their age are more particularly noticeable; here the slates (and in the foothills, the sandstone) present all the varied changes of position and structure, noticed by different writers on the physical features incident to the mountain districts of California—at one time dipping east at another west, and again half inverted, in the multifarious disturbances to which they have been subjected.

The greatest amount of displacement in the sedimentary rocks is always found in the closest proximity to the veins in their immediate vicinity, and although a vertical position only may be given in many instances, yet this is found to become less as you recede from the vein on either hand transversely to its line of strike; it is not unfrequent that the high angle of dip in the first instance will assume a nearly horizontal position in the distance of a mile from the point of uplift, but the next ridge will present a re-enactment of the first case if the rocks composing it are of the same character.

The vertical position of the slates is one of those peculiar features which attracts the attention of almost every person passing to or from the interior, from their appearance resembling an old church-yard they have been termed the *grave-stone slates*, and this distinctive feature is found to pervail to the lower range of foot-hills toward the valley, as well as in the more elevated parts of the mountains; this verticality among the lower hills has been urged as an objection to the point that the intrusion of the quartz of either group, was not the immediate cause of that uplift, but that the present inclination has been given by causes of a a similar character which have acted subsequent to the intrusion of the quartzose veins.

This proposition seems invalid for this reason: if any such agency as that proposed had been the immediate cause of producing the effects which are observable among the slates of this section and sufficiently powerful to have forced them into the position they now occupy; it seems but reasonable to suppose that some portions of the intrusive materials should make their appearance among them; but this is not the case,nor is it necessary to introduce such a complication in order to explain the physical features which are apparent in these rocks, as we find an agent distributed largely among them, which is fully adequate to induce all the changes of position or structure noticeable.

That we do not find massive outcrops of these dikes among the slates at the edge of the valley, is equally invalid as an objection against their agency in producing the disturbances which are clearly attributable to their intrusion a few miles farther to the east, for an examination will convince the unprejudiced mind that the causes which have been instrumental in tilting the slates from their former position in the interior has extended to the eastern edge of valleys and produced the ruptures we there witness.

In favorable situations for observing the intrusive character of the recent group, as in the canoñs through which flow many of our streams it is there found that the porphiries which lie superior to the primitive rocks, and have had their origin from contact with igneous rocks in an incanderescent state, as well also as the trapean rocks adjoining, are broken through the sedimentary rocks above them which are still unchanged.

Another fact of interest, and having an important bearing on this part of our subject is found on the west borders of the great valleys and in the Coast Mountains. From all the testimony in our possession at the present time relative to the sedimentary rocks which dip under the valleys of the Sacramento and San Joaquin, we are induced to believe that those which occur on the east border are of an age cotemporaneous with those on the west, and in addition thereto a group is found which evidently belong to a still later period. We have in these mountains then, a corroborative evidence that the disturbances produced by the intrusion of igneous rocks with which the quartz is found in connection has occurred during a comparatively recent period.

As these rocks have forced their way to the surface through all the species that lie above them, they can be considered in no other light than having an age posterior to most of the tertiary rocks within the State, or the northern and middle parts of it; and cotemporaneous at least with the lower portion of the miocene period. Under these circumstances it is not to be wondered at that gold may be found in San Francisco or Contra Costa, as the geological formations which have developed it east of the great rivers, are found also in the mountains to the west, though not to the same extent.

The disturbance of the recent sedimentary rocks of the Coast Mountains, and the character of some of the intruded masses that has produced the tilting and dislocations, their identity with the stratified rocks on the eastern border of the great valleys, leads us to the conclusion that the causes of uplift which have been found among the latter, were continued partially to the coast in the same period. With respect to the agents that played an important part in these turbulent periods, there can be but little trouble in their discrimination, and ample testimony is found to identify them with the recent group of igneous rocks under consideration, and if these conclusions are correct, the character for permanency of these viens is beyond all cavil or doubt.

Future investigation may disprove this position, but until it is made evident that the veins of the recent group have been disturbed by other and more recent vnlcanic agents on either side of the great rivers, we can regard them in no other view than being among the last of an extensive series of disturbances which have operated principally through a large portion of the west flank of the Sierra Nevada at a comparatively recent period in the geological history of this part of the continent.

The metalliferous character of this group is in no way inferior to that of the older ranges of these rocks; the proof of this rests in the fact, that some of the best placers yet found in this country are included within its boundaries among the alluvium and drift deposits of the tertiary epoch. The gold generally found in these placers is of that character known among the miners as "rough or recent gold," having suffered but little from attrition by water; but it is not unfrequent to find the recent metal associated with that which has been much worn by attrition, and the two qualities thus appearing in the same placer range, can be regarded only as having different orrigins and ages. It would scarcely appear reasonable to suppose that two pieces of metal driven from the same source and subjected to the same action, should present smooth and rounded surface in the one, while its fellow beside it shall retain all its angularities as though just detached from its original matrix.

With reference to the older group of these veins there are features manifest which are both interesting and important, when we consider the immediate position of the recent group, to those of the older where both are found in contact. It has been remarked in the preceding pages that the veins of the older series have disturbed the greenstone below and the granite above only; a casual examination of the district in which these veins occur, would convey to the observer an idea that a discrepency in the statements must exist, from the fact that veins which pierce the granite are found to cut the stites also in the same section. As in the case of the Centreville veins, these will be found to belong to the more recent intrusions of these rocks, and wherever those features occur the recent group will be found playing the part of a disturbing agent on the primitive veins themselves and their investing rocks; so far as our experience goes in judging of the effects produced by these recent intrusions, their influence is not an injurious one, for the recent dike has thus far proved equally metalliferous with the primitive setts.

CHARACTER AND POSITIONS OF THE OLDER VEINS BELOW THE SURFACE.

Under this head will be concluded all that we have to say upon the subject of gold mining in this State at the present time, and as the largest proportion of the mines of the State are situated on the older group of the quartz, the remarks that follow will be confined principally to that serries.

In the northern part of the State,* the granite rocks in which these veins are situated upon the surface, have been found to be underlied with another class of igneous rocks, which, from their nature and *presumed* age, it was feared might have so disturbed the "setts" as to render the successful prosecution of mining a doubtful project, and injurious speculation from this fact, have been indulged in to an extent that at one time threatened to destroy the well merited confidence which the discovery of these veins had induced from the outset; and for this reason no little degree of interest has been manifested both at home and abroad in relation to their future prospects.

Had those speculations which have been founded on presumptive evidence only, been confined to the sphere to which it legitimately belonged, and divested of the over-anxious fears expressed and manifested from abroad, the parties most directly interested would have suffered less inconvenience by loss of confidence and credit, which the voluntary con servators of our good in distant lands have been the means of inducing, and the public mind would have been unbiassed but for the opinions of men who should have had more discretion than to have hazarded their reputation on such premature evidences as they must have been possessed of at that time.

It is scarcely a supposable case, that men thousands of miles distant should be found adequate to judge correctly of the value of metaliferous districts, having never seen the sections alluded to, or even before the veins were known by the parties engaged in opening them. Elaborate discussions based upon presumptive analogy, may subserve the purpose of pleasing popular assemblies, but they will be found untenable and useless often, when applied to practiacal and systematic operations.

Mining exploration within the past eighteen months, has added much to our information relative to the position of metallic veins of the State, and the rocks with which they are associated. The granite series has

* North of the Consumnes River.

been closely investigated, and in several of the mines the workings have been carried entirely through this rock, and contrary to the anticipations of the incredulous, the *setts* have not been *thrown* at the point of contact with the inferior rocks. Thus far the depth of the granite series has not been found to exceed a depth of but little more than one hundred feet, and in almost every case where shafts have been driven, either on the vein or beside it, the rock has been found in a highly decomposed state, thus presenting but little difficulty in passing through it. There are, in some localities, many small veins running out at different angles from the principal "setts," into the surrounding granite, and when thus appearing in the inverting rocks, marks of dislocation are observable. These interesting features define most clearly the energy and extent of the supporting and injecting forces from below, at the date of the intrusion of the veins, and the angles which the small cross-courses make with the main "setts" from which they emanate, shows most conclusively that the fracture of the superincumbent rocks must have been extensive. Another and a striking feature is also to be observed in this particular, which is, that the small threads found in the granite have a greater power when they enter the greenstone below ; thus indicating that the intrusive dikes spent themselves principally in the superior granite above.

The entire mass of the granitic rocks in the vicinity of the quartz, is of a loose and incoherent texture, from the surface to the lowest point yet reached, and when brought from the greatest depths the same general characteristics are found to prevail throughout. It presents a crumbling, reddish and purple hue, at times faintly spotted with white, its felspathic constituent thus imparting a porphyritic appearance to considerable quantities. When damp it is somewhat clayey, in the dry state, after exposure to the air, it is easilly crushed in the hand, giving the greasy feeling of some of the talcose minerals. These peculiar features may be best examined in and about the towns of Nevada and Grass Valley ; for here they extend over several miles, and the extent to which mining operations have been carried in these sections, renders an examination of all the different phases that are presented in this class of veins, both easy and convenient.

Immediately below the granite, the greenstone is found underlying this entire section of country, in every instance in which the granite has been perforated, this rock has been found beneath, and when first met with in descending is much broken up, and the fissures filled with foreign infiltrations from above. The trap rock has a blueish-gray and greenish color, often highly charged with pyrites; the veins on entering this rock change their color from the deep reddish-brown, which they maintain in the granite above, and the cavities filled with the peroxide of iron which has resulted from the decomposition of the pyrites it originally contained, to a clear, white or semi-translucent mineral, holding considerable quantities of cubic and rhombic crystals of pyrites, which are more or less auriferous. In some of the trapean rocks arsenical pyrites is met with, but this latter is much more common in the southern districts, and on the forks of the American River.

In every mine throughout the northern districts, in which the greenstone has been reached, *the veins have penetrated this rock*, and in no one instance thus far is it found that the vein has either been *pinched or faulted*, but the reverse is true, *that every sett has increased in power the deeper they descend.* Of six companies now in successful operation in Grass Valley, all of them are obtaining their ores from the greenstone, in larger quantiry and better quality than was found to be the average in the granite above: on Deer Creek it is the same, and but two mines in this district still continue in the granite, viz:—the Illinois and Gold Tunnel mines, the lower gallery of the latter is within nine feet of the greenstone, with an increasing power in the "sett" at the point of working. In the counties of Butte and Shasta, the same fact prevails, and in each of those mines, which have entered the trap there has been no diminution in the power of the vein or qualities of the ore.

The depth to which some of these veins are found to enter the greenstone has been fifty-five feet, at the present time, and at this depth into this rock they bear all the reasonable evidence of continuing to an unlimited depth, and being of more recent date than their investing series. The greenstone in close proximity to the dikes is found much shattered and disturbed, exhibiting evidences of displacement subsequent to fracture, the inclination of the disturbed masses corresponding to the dip of the vein, the line of fracture form angles of fifty to seventy degrees to the dip of the "sett," and as high as forty in some cases with the horizon; this gives a stratified appearance to these rocks; this peculiar feature is obserable at the Osborn Hill Mine, and is indicated by the heavy lines in the sketch of its transverse section. At this mine may also be observed the other peculiarities before noticed, the highly decomposed and broken character of the upper part of the greenstone of seventeen feet below; at the Lafayette and Helvetia Mine, similar features are to be observed of the semi-stratified appearance of the greenstone, caused by the intrusion of the quartz dike through it; the entire length of the adit level of this mine is driven entirely through this rock a distance of about eleven hundred feet.

On Deer Creek, five miles north of Green Valley, we find a material change in the relative position of the metallic veins to the investing rocks, at the Gold Tunnel, as before remarked, the "sett" is exclusively in granite, while at the Wyoming Mine, one and a half miles below, the "sett" is situated in the greenstone inferiorly and the slate above, while in the adjacent mine above the Wyoming, slate and granite in the middle and greenstone below is the order of arrangement. At this mine may be observed one of those interesting features noticed in the concluding paragraphs of the Recent Group, and when we compare the accompanying sketches of the Osborn Hill and Wyoming, a sufficient illustration of the relative ages of the group will appear. The present working "sett" of the latter mine is protruded through the primitive rocks, and also through the slate above them, and from its dip it must pass through older veins at a depth probably not exceeding four hundred feet below their present level. The slate which lies superior in this mine is evidently of the same age as that occurring among the foot-hills toward the valley, and as the sketch of this mine illustrates, the vein passes entirely through them; the dip of this vein is forty-three degrees east, while those of the adjacent mine above varies from thirty-two to thirty-eight degrees. It is not surprising that a recent "sett" in passing through the cross-course of an older vein, or through a part of a primitive vein, should produce valuable deposits of metal which has taken place in this mine in several instances, and it serves for an illustration of the principle advanced in the preceeding pages, that the recent veins were equally metalliferous with those of the primitive series, wherever and whenever found in this State.

From the facts thus far presented to your consideration respecting the known position of these rocks in the northern part of the State, some evidence at least exists, that those veins thus far opened are now proved to have cut through that suite of igneous rocks which heretofore have been supposed would destroy their continuity to any considerable depth below the surface. Already has the establishment of this point exerted an influence which is beginning to be strongly felt, and is restoring that confidence in gold mining which it long since lost. More capital has been invested within the preceding four months in this branch of employment, than in the entire time which has elapsed since the general suspension of these operations. From the developments which have been made relating to the permanency of their character within the past year, individuals are fast becoming satisfied that the metallic veins of this State merit that confidence which is fast returning. If other testimony is required than that already cited of the almost certainty of their continuation to unlimited depths, it will become necessary to search out some other formations than those acknowledged to be the foundation on which rest the superstructure of this teraqueous sphere, for it is evident if facts have any weight, that they have disturbed the lowest of all known rocks.

It may be argued that the shallow depth, fifty feet into the greenstone, is not positive, but that these veins may be faulted by more recent volcanic intrusions below this point. This is possibly true, but at the same time, is there any good reason for such a supposition when no evidence of such disturbances are observable above the surface in their vicinity, and when those intrusive rocks are not to be found to depths of two or three thousand feet below the summits of those ridges on which these mines are located in many instances. There are many deep gorges among our mountains which exhibit the character of the rocks composing them to the depths above named, and on examination of their structure will convince an unbiassed observer of their primitive character. Among these gorges it is not unfrequent to find the quartz veins extending from their bottom to various hights, ranging as high as six hundred feet in every instance in which these veins are met among the rocks in situ. They possess their *greatest power at their lowest point.* In one instance I well remember having traced a dike of this rock from the river to the highth of thirteen hundred feet, a drawing of which is still in my possession; the "sitt" thinned out to small threads at this hight, with a diminishing power from the base of the hill to the summit; this vein passes through greenstone and porphyry, granite and slate, successively, until it finally spent itself among the latter. If intrusive dikes are found to increase in power as their distance below the surface increases, we may reasonably conclude that they may continue to a depth below, equal to that which may be found above, in a case like the last one cited, provided the rocks beneath the lowest point at which it is observable continue of the same character.

Abundant examples of this character are to be met with throughout our mountains, and with such evidence before us, the character of these metallic veins for permanency must be placed beyond suspicion or doubt, and our testimony on this point extends much beyond any that has, as yet, been adduced. In the County of Calaveras, an extensive dike, two miles in length, has been laid open in such a manner that a vertical depth of eight hundred feet of the vein is now exposed to view. The dike cuts through two ridges, which separate two streams of water, and the companies located on these streams have sunk their shafts to the depth of over one hundred feet, directly under the beds of the creeks, and have driven their gallerys each way untill within a few feet of each other: the vein in one shaft has a power of thirty-seven feet, but in no point on the "sett" is it less than five, in each of the five mines located on this vein, the power of the "sett" has uniformly increased the deeper they have descended. In this case we have a thorough examination of one, at least, of our metallic veins, which will compare with some of the operations in other countries. and we may deduce some safe conclusions respecting their probable stability, if depth below the snrface becomes an essential requisite to establiso that point.

The rocks through which these veins pass are principally of the talcose series, with greenstone, hornblende schists, and syenite, in the immediate vicinity; the dikes have cut through all of them in succession without having suffered any deflection from that parallelism which must have ensued, if any of the rocks with which they are found in contact, had an age posterior to the dikes themselves. This district is particularly noticed in connection with this part of our subject, for the purpose of exhibiting the stronger probability of permanency in the quartz veins of this country, for the reason that if disturbance in their position is likely to ensue in any part of this State, it would be likely to occur in these sections, as the effects of recent volcanic action is more prominent throughout the southern portions of the mining districts than any other part of the west flank of the Sierra Nevada.

From what testimony we have in our possession relative to these veins, it seems but reasonable to conclude that their integrity is perfect, or as nearly so as can be reasonably expected considering the short period which has been employed in developing their true character, and that the confidence which they formerly possessed was well grounded; all subsequent examinations have only tended to confirm this belief in the minds of those who have carefully and diligently studied this subject. The present condition of our gold mines, their flourishing state and prospective value, based on facts as now developed, most clearly indicate their importance, as an industrial pursuit and one destined ere long to form one of the leading interests in the economy of the State; and as such it would seem that all prudent measures to develop farther their extent and value, and place them upon that footing before the world which that value and importance demands should be used, either through the State or General Government, and through them promote such measures as will prove an inducement to more extensive and permanent operations than has yet been done.

In concluding this part of the report, and in connection with the magnitude and importance of perhaps a somewhat exciting principle in relation to it, I would beg leave to call your attention to a point on which there has heretofore existed much diversity of opinion, which not unfrequently has engendered angry discussion and beligerent feeling in a large proportion of our mining population. The experience of the last three years has elucidated the fact most clearly that the two mining interests of this State cannot be governed by the same rule of law in all cases, and prove alike advantageous to both; it is therefore suggested whether some method more congenial to this interest may not be adopted, that will favor the occupancy and improvement of the metallic veins of this State, giving at the same time widest scope and protection to all at present engaged, and those who may wish hereafter to enter upon those pursuits.

PRESENT GOVERNMENT OF METALLIC VEINS.

Before entering upon this part of our subject I will state, that throughout every part of the mining counties, which it has been my fortune to visit, in my examinations of previous years, and up to the present time, the subject of needful protection to capital investment and labor in this branch of mining, has been fully and unequivocally expressed by those engaged and interested in it, and by a large portion of those engaged in placer mining, having no direct connection with the former. And it is at the solicitation of nearly *every individual* engaged in the pursuit of mining on veins, that the subject is presented to your consideration at the present time. A wish has long since been expressed, and urged through all the various channels of communication, that the present tenure by which this species of property is holden and conveyd may be changed in such manner as may render available capital investments, which must be largely employed in order to develop those sources of wealth and insure their occupancy.

It is perhaps a questionable point whether the State government is vested witb the power to cede and convey title in fee to lands containing the precious metals, even were that title absolutely required from the nature of existing circumstances; but whether her jurisdiction in the case be sovereign or not, she legitimately possesses a conservative jurisdiction over such lands, and through that power, as a member of the great confederacy, may exert an influence to obtain such modifications of existing laws of the general government, as would conflict with the common interests of her citizens, or of those rules and regulations temporarily instituted by the State, which by their present action, have a tendency to cripple and reduce her otherwise available means of revenue.

Under this form of the question it becomes a matter of some importance to consider, whether the entire interests of the State would not be materially and beneficially affected, by placing such lands as are under its conservative influence in a position that would be likely to yield a revenue from their occupancy, and which at the same time would yield an adequate security for the investment of capital to be employed in their developement. A system of law that would induce a more extensive occupancy than that now existing must insure, as a resultant, a corresponding increase of revenue, thereby reducing taxation on the great mass, render less burdensome the support of the State government.

A course of action that would accomplish this end, and at the same time prevent that result which it has been the careful study of the representatives of the people to guard against, and whose every effort has been directed to preserve to the people the most liberal policy in the acquirement of wealth from the varied and prolific sources presented in no other country than this, must be unobjectionable either to the miner or merchant.

A strong objection has been urged against the sale of mineral lands, and justly too, as in this case the title must pass into the hands of private parties, which in most countries has proved objectionable in many particulars, and a course of this kind could never meet the approbation of a large majority of our population, in the present state of our information. In all other countries as in our own, the title to mineral lands is vested in the crown, or general government, (with the exception of Great Britain,) and the title or permission to use or occupy can emanate only from that source, where it properly belongs. In all countries where mines of the precious metals have been found, different policies for their government have been pursued, but as yet that policy which has been the most liberal, and at the same time protective of private rights, is found to have exerted the widest and most beneficial influence in their developement and occupancy; under such a system it is impossible for it to do otherwise than prosper, and the experience of nearly three centuries have gone to substantiate that fact.

There can be no possible objection to the *general principles* on which our present system is founded, it is the same that made Spain and Mexico what they were and are, and one that with these countries has stood the tests of time, the best proof of its utility and univeral applications. Throughout all the political changes that have convulsed and shattered the civil codes of these governments, no change or alteration of a restrictive tendency has been made in the Ordinances des Mineria. For the last fifty years no change that in the least has affected its vital features, except to render them more liberal and congenial; its dictates with them are as sacred as their holy creed, and to molest or change its principles would be regarded as equally sacreligeous.

Under that system individual rights in mines are scrupulously respected, and strict non compliance with its requisitions are followed by a reversion of party rights to the crown, from which only can a similar title be obtained by others wishing to occupy and improve.

The history of mining proper throughout the world, has taught us that it is impossible to pursue that business to advantage without heavy outlays of capital; this applies equally to mining for silver or gold; the great amount of labor and expense attendent in opening a mine is the cause of this, that branch alone often being the work of years, before the reduction of any of its metals take place whereby any return of profits can be realized. We are not wanting in illustrations of this kind, they are as wide-spread as the mining operations of the world; and if more deffinite examples of this fact is required than the general history of this branch of industry, we need but to refer to the superficial operations of our own State heretofore, to show that limited means cannot succeed in gold mining, though the veins producing the metal may be (as they frequently are in this country,) exceedingly productive.

Our citizens embarked in this delusive speculation in a most inconsiderate manner. The results that followed from their earlier operations are too well known : the capital at their command, being small, was expended even before their veins were opened, and this great lever of success in these operations being thus early suspended, prevented the prosecution of the enterprise to a successful termination, which would have ended in profit in place of loss.

The fault, "if fault there be," lay at the door of misguided apprehensions, induced by flattering reports of results which had flowed from hasty examinations, but not in the veins themselves ; as these were dumb, and unable to speak for themselves, until men of larger means developed their capabilities, the cause of failure was attributed to a want of metal in the lodes ; hence the distrust which has up to the present time attached itself to this branch of mining, and has resulted in serious loss to the country at large, as well as to the private citizen.

A few have grappled through against all obstacles, who were fortunate enough to command the necessary means, and now have their mines opened and in successful operation. But it has been at the expense of heavy outlays of capital, and nearly two years of industrious application and hard labor ; the results which they have produced has been the means of fixing on a permanent basis, the character of these mines, which it will be difficult to affect injuriously hereafter ; and their integrity as lucrative employments, and safety for capital investments in themselves, is questioned by none who are conversant with their present condition.

Notwithstanding their acknowledged intrinsic value, there is an incubus resting upon them, which prevents, and must still prevent, their more extensive occupancy, and until removed in some manner, will stand as an insuperable obstacle to their future progress. This rests in the doubtful and uncertain tenure, by which these mines are held, being subject, as they are, to the government of the majority of the people in the district in which they are located, and whose interests directly considered, are both unconnected and foreign, though following a profession similar in some respects to that under consideration.

The position of the Placer miner, and those engaged on veins, is different in many respects. In the case of the former, there is but a comparatively small amount of capital requisite to pursue his business advantageously and successfully : in the other, experience has fully demonstrated that he cannot pursue his business successfully without large expenditures. In the case of the former, the extraction of gold is conducted by the simple process of washing ; in the other, it can be extracted from the gaugue often only by complex metallurgical processes, and subjected even then to much uncertainty, and, at times, loss—requiring what the Placer does not, the employment of men who have made it the study of their lives, and the use of means mechanical and scientific, which do not come within the requisition of the former, to conduct his operations to a successful issue.

The operations of the placer miner are generally limited as to time, seldom exceeding a year in the same locality, on his removal his interests in his former residence ceases ; in the case of the miner engaged on veins, he finds that his operations must be continued through a series of years in order to secure a fair remuneration for his labors, and if he removes to other parts of the State, his interests in the locality he left does not cease, as his capital investments still remain and continue a permanent source of revenue to the State and county in which they are located. The implements of the placer miner are few, and easily obtained or disposed of if he wishes to remove but, it is widely different with the other. He is obliged to obtain expensive machinery to obtain profitable results from his labors, and heavy sacrifice is often the attendant, if it is his misfortune to fail in his operations from any causes either natural or artificial.

The effect of placer mining in all parts of the world has been, to produce a wandering and unstable community, no better example is to be found than in our own State ; it is a true illustration of what has occurred in other countries whose features simulate our own ; and to remedy this has been the aim of our State government almost from its earliest foundation ; how far its efforts have been attended with success its present history will clearly elucidate. The attempt to induce a permanent settlement in the mountains can be said to have partially succeeded only, and this has occurred in those instances where the parties thus locating have been enabled to avail themselves of interests that would partake of a degree of permanency for a series of years ; their titles to improvements on the lands such persons occupy, being retained only by the law of sufference, subject to the decrees of the majority residing in their vicinity if found to be auriferous.

On the broad platform of "equal right and equal privilege," which has been the governing principle of this State in its most extended sense from its earliest occupancy, the dim outline of a desire to establish permanency in the settlement of the mountain districts has been manifested, and at the present time it has become a distinguishing feature in a large portion of the mining population, in mining employments it is equally apparent as in agriculture ; among the most stringent advocates of a "*masterly inactivity*" in regard to the government of the mines, two years ago, are now to be found men equally earnest in their advocacy of vesting rights that shall partake of the character of permanency, and protective where his operations require investments, to secure competency and reward for his labours. Experience has taught us that necessity, if we would foster those employments which it has been our pride to boast, and where no subversion of those fundamental principles on which our laws are founded can take place.

In every county of the State where quartz mining has been conducted this will be found a striking feature in each and all of their operations, and has been particularly manifested in some of the northern counties, where more stringency in the enforcement of mining laws of former years existed, than probably any other part of the State ; the effects of this course of action was equally manifest abroad, in the Atlantic States and Europe, when the construction of the present mining code was published in those countries. In one of our northern counties a system has been founded on this code which under certain conditions, (consisting of a given amount of improvements only) conveys a title in fee to all intents and purposes ; and another by which parties have the right of holding all that they may be able to purchase. This course of action among miners themselves must be viewed as a plain and clearly defined wish, on their part, to extend over the country a system of government that shall prove alike conducive to the enhancement of these interests and the public welfare, and offer by these means inducements for the investments of capital from abroad ; its effects would prove beneficial inasmuch as every dollar of capital thus invested would become so much available means of revenue and serve to retain a much greater amount of the gold extracted from our hills, within the State.

From the nature of gold-mining proper, it results as a consequence almost, that those who engage in it, must become permanent settlers, as their operations if successful become the work of years instead of a few months, and their investments, when made, are done with that view. Under these circumstances does it not become a matter of correct policy to separate the interests of the placer miner and those engaged on veins, in such a manner that those engaged in each branch may enjoy that liberty which the placer miner now possesses, and which is enjoyed by the other only by the sufferance of the former in the largest majority of cases ; giving to each the right to enact those laws, which they in their good judgment will find most conducive to their seperate interests, and which from their nature and attendant circumstances are very dissimilar and foreign.

The jealousies and feeling arising from the suspicion entertained by each other, which has heretofore and at the present time exists to a considerable extent, in these two branches of industry would, by the above course be done away, and a much greater degree of stability in mining proper would be the result, (which under the present arrangement of affairs can hardly exist) in which its prosperity to a great extent is involved : its influence would not only be made manifest here, but it would give a confidence abroad in these operations which they do not now possess, and to which we must look for those means by which we shall be able to conduct gold-mining successfully and with profit.

The entire separation of these interests would be regarded abroad as the opening of a new era in the mining history of this State, fraught with beneficial results, and involving a vital interest in her future economy, advantageous alike to the revenues of the State and to the people ; it would remove that serious obstacle at present in the path of its progress, viz : "the insecurity that now exists for invested capital, from the motative policy heretofore pursued," and restore that confidence which such a policy has in a great measure been the means of destroying.

The mines of this State are of a character and value, which if placed in a proper position, will invite investment from abroad, to an amount little less than twenty millions of dollars within the next eight years ; this presumption is founded on the fact that more than one sixth of that amount is at the present time in active operation in this country, and its largest proportion has been derived from American sources, during a portion of that period when public confidence had been shaken in regard to their value. Negotiations are now pending which involve nearly one million more of capital investment in this branch of mining, nearly one half of which is in the cities of Boston and New York.

Considering the disadvantages that now surround them, as shown from the facts relating thereto, they can but be regarded as the prolific sources of wealth in this country ; and every inducement consistent with the liberal policy adopted in the government of the placers, is equally applicable and should be extended to them.

The following pages will contain a brief notice of some of the principal mines of the State with a list of those in successful operation and their locations. Also a table of Barometric Altitudes; and Catalogue of Minerals obtained during the tour, to be placed in the State Cabinet.

LA FAYETTE AND HELVETIA MINE.

This company is located at Grass Valley, Nevada County, and the sketch of the workings of their mine is taken from the La Fayette Hill vein only about two miles south-west of the town. The length of the vein at the above hill is eleven hundred feet; it has a curvilinear course, varying from north-east to south-west; its mean, however, when marked on a right line is north, ten degrees east. The dip of the vein is forty-one degrees east, having a power of three feet at the depth of thirty-four feet; at this point the ore was of a poorer quality than at any other point. The depth of the present working is about 55 feet, and here the vien increases in power and value, being equal to three feet eight inches, and yielding in a large amount of ore, forty dollars per ton. The vien, when discovered, was covered with yellow brown alluvium for five feet, and passed through this and decomposed granite of a purple color fifteen feet, when it entered a mass of decomposed and fragmentary greenstone of five feet depth, thence into compact rock of the same character and continued to the depth of fifty-five feet.

Adit level is 1100 feet in length, exclusive of tram road for conveying ore and attle from the mine; it extends through the whole length of their claim. At their present depth all the ore is obtained by blasting, which adds much to the expense of the mine. The cost of obtaining ore from this mine is from seven to eight dollars per ton at present rates of labor. The company have about 900 feet of vein in Gold Hill, which requires no blastinging and is obtained at the mill for five dollars per ton.

The La Fayette Hill vein was much decomposed for the depth of thirty feet, and contained a large quantity of peroxide iron and free gold; after passing into the compact greenstone the vein becomes quite firm, and highly charged with pyrites investing gold; the crystals were white and well-terminated, generally perfect in form. In some parts of the mine, galena is met with and gold imbeded in it; an examination of this latter mineral has not been made for silver, but from its appearance it is quite probable that it contains this metal. The matrix of the ore is a bluish white and translucent, in pieces of one inch in thickness; the blue tint of the vein in the vicinity of the shafts is due in a great measure to finely divided particles of lead.

The capital of this company is about three hundred thousand dollars, and their receipts in four months has been as high as $98,000, but their average is near $10,000 per month; the mine has yielded with great uniformity since the commencement of operations, and bids fair for future success.

This mine has two Batteries and when in full operation is capable of reducing forty tons of ore per day, but one battery is run at a time as the amalgamating apparatus is not of sufficient capacity at present to dispose of that amount of ore judiciously, the amalgamating instruments consist of Cram's Cylinder and Berdan's Amalgamator, in the latter about fifteen per cent of the gross amount is saved after it has passed through the other instruments; this arises from the fact that Berdan's instrument possesses a levigating power from revolving balls in the instrument which gives a new surface to the material passing under them.

GOLD HILL MINE.

This mine is located in the town of Grass Valley on the first hill to the west of the village. The mine was first opened in 1851 and worked to a considerable extent and profit, subsequently it passed to the hands of the Agua Frio Company under the superintendence of their agent Mr. Atwood in whose possession it now remains; after an examination of the mine the old method of working was given up, and a new system of operations entered upon in order to tap the vein at the lowest possible point and at the same time afford easy transit to the reduction works and drainage to the mine. With this view an adit was commenced about fifteen feet above the level of the creek which flows in front of the town, and carried west through the base of the hill for a distance of seven-hundred feet, cutting through allavium and decomposed granite most of the way, at the west end of the adit which cuts the vein nearly at right angles, the shaft marked A in the longitudinal section was intersected at a depth of ninety feet below the surface; from near the ninety feet shaft a level has been driven to the north on the strike of the vein about seventy feet marked, D, also two other levels east of it, E, F, which intersect the north crosscut D of the ground plan; a winze has been sunk below the water level sixteen feet marked H, of the longitudinal section; this disposition in the working of the mine affords many advantages in the extraction of the ore and attle and easy communication with all parts of the mine and surface, and the intersection of the shaft A produces ample ventilation. The vein intersects the greenstone at the bottom of the air shaft, and as in the case of the Lafayette has cut completely through it; increasing in power as it enters this rock, about one thousand tons of ore was in the yard at the time I visited the mine ready to pass through the reduction works. From the end of the long adit a tram road four-hundred feet in length passes to the mill on which by *mule power*, the ore is conveyed from the farthest part of the mine. The ground plan exhibits the crosscuts and levels and their connection with the mill.

The strike of the vein is north and south diping east at an an angle of 24 degrees, with a vein whose power at ninety feet was nearly three feet; the transverse section is shown the air shaft entering the greenstone and intersecting the vein, with the increase in power of the vein from the surface to the lowest point worked. The ores in the greenstone differ in no particular from those of the Lafayette, with the exception that none of the plumbic sulphuret was observed at this mine though the vein has much the same blue tint. The reduction works of this company were not completed in November and no opportunity was afforded to witness their process at that time; it was expected that their machinery would be capable of reducing over one hundred tons of ore per day, which from its appearance would not be a large estimate, it is probably the most powerful machinery in this country and will compare with any in Europe.

The operations of this mine are looked for with considerable interest at home and abroad, as their capacities for reduction are much more extensive than any hitherto put up in this country.

OSBORN HILL MINE.

This mine is located two miles east of Grass Valley, it has been opened on the course of the vein four-hundred and fifty feet and from sixty-five to seventy feet in depth. Vein strikes north and south dipping east at an angle of forty degrees; the transverse section shows a depth of sixty-five feet; the shaft was carried through twelve feet of alluvium, seven of clay slate, seventeen of a much broken and decomposed greenstone, and fifteen feet of compact rock of the same character; total depth including winze I is nearly seventy feet. The vein at this mine has dislocated all the rocks above it and possesses that half stratified appearance as in the Lafayette, arising from fracture by the intrusive vein. The power of the vein is about three feet at the depth of sixty-five feet. In the longitudinal section, the levels which have been driven are given to scale and their different lengths are found by reference to the sketch. This mine has been one of the most flourishing and profitable of the State and has been conducted with much prudence and economy.

WYOMING MINE.

This mine is situated on the north bank of Deer Creek, about two miles below the town of Nevada; its altitude above the Creek is two hundred and forty feet, and the higher parts of the outcrop on the line of the vein will reach nearly or quite three hundred feet above the same point. An adit was driven about two hundred feet through clay slate, which intersected the vein at this point, at an angle of about twenty-seven degrees. From this, two levels have been driven on the vein, of one hundred and twenty and fifty feet each, and a winze of twenty-five. The vein dips east with an angle of forty five degrees, having a strike north and south, with a power of three feet. Fifty feet below the upper adit, another was commenced and carried to a hundred and twenty-five feet, intending to intersect the vein at one hundred feet below the surface of the shaft F; at seventy-six feet the greenstone was met, and the adit carried fifty feet into it. At the junction of the slates and trap, the former are much changed, evidently from the effects of heat, while at the junction of the slates and vein, above this, they have again suffered from the intrusion of the latter.

On the south side of the hill the vein crops cut through the trap two hundred feet below the summit, with an increased power, leaving no room for doubt of the permanency of its character. In this mine one of the recent veins has cut through from the Bunker Hill Mine, east of this, which produced a valuable nest of ore; the dip of the principal Wyoming

Vein, if it holds its present inclination, must cut the older lodes at the depth of four or five hundred feet, and its situation is such that ample drainage and ventilation can be obtained.

GOLD TUNNEL MINE.

The mine bearing this name is located half a mile west of the town of Nevada, on Deer Creek, and has been worked successfully since its discovery in 1850 or '51. It was originally a placer claim and was found while working the banks of the creek for placer gold. Soon after its discovery an engine was erected upon the ground and the vein opened ; it was commenced by driving an adit level on the vein, which was subsequently abandoned and a new level commenced at the point at which the present reduction works are situated.

The length of the present level is three hundred and seventy-five feet, and has an inclination of ten degrees from the horizontal line ; three winzes have been drove on the lower side of the adit [L. F. H.] which are respectively thirty, twenty and twelve feet, with a level of twenty-five feet between the winzes F. and H. On the opposite side two cements of fifty feet each, and a gallery connecting both, of one hundred and twenty-five feet, with a corresponding one connecting the winzes on the lower side. All the ore included within the dash lines has been stopped out. This vein is situated in granite, and thus far has been loose and incoherent ; this is attributable to the large amount of pyrites contained in the vein, as is shown at any point where the quartz retains any solidity ; the gold is in a free state in the gossan, of which there are large quantities throughout the mine ; the operators on this vein have been eminently successful, and their mine bids fair to continue valuable. The strike of their vein, north ten degrees east, dipping east ten degrees south, at an angle of thirty-eight degrees.

ILLINOIS MINE.

The Illinois Mine is situated directly opposite the Gold Tunnel on the south bank of Deer Creek, and is a continuation of the same vein , it has all the characteristics of the former throughout. The length of their upper gallery is four hundred and fifty feet and that of the lower, two hundred and fifty ; two cross-cuts have been driven which connect the galleries at C. D. each fifty feet in length.

JONES AND DAVIS MINE, HERBERTVILLE, CALAVERAS COUNTY.

The mine of this company is located on the east side of a small tributary running into Amidor Creek, the latter passes through the town of Amidor one mile north of this mine ; the top of the whim-shaft, C, is one hundred and forty-five feet above the level of the creek, and ninety feet below the outcrop of the vein on which the shaft, C, has been sunk ; at shaft 4 the vein is three hundred and fifty feet above the Amidor, and increases in altitude for half a mile, until it arrives at the height of four hundred feet above the town. The company have sunk two shafts of ninety feet on the vein, and drove two galleries, the upper one A being two hundred and eighty feet, the lower, B, one hundred and fifty feet, and are driving in the course of the dotted lines to run a third gallery at the depth of fifty feet below the point B. Figures 1, 2, 3, are stopes from which they are now obtaining their ore, being conveyed along the lower level to the whim-shaft and thence elevated to the surface; from thence it is conveyed on a tram road 600 feet to the reduction works at its terminus.

The design for future operations is to cut an adit a short distance north of the mill, and intersect the vein at a point which will give a depth of three hundred feet from its highest point to a level with the end of their present tram road, and then stope down from this point, which will not only furnish an abundance of ore, if the vein retains its present power, but materially lessen the expense of its extraction. This will be accomplished in a distance of three hundred yards, and probably less. This mine is very systematically arranged for the comfort of the miner, and obtaining all the ores easily, and reflects much credit on its projectors; the sketch of the mine, drawn to scale on the spot, will fully elucidate itself; its convenience of arrangement, considering its local position, will be found equal to all its necessary requirements.

The vein is invested in chlorite and talcose rocks, throughout its whole extent, being nearly three miles in length. On the eastern side of the vein a graphic slate occurs, having a thickness of one or two feet; outside of this a bed of chlorite, from five to ten feet, much discolored by graphite, at times perfectly black and staining the hand easily. On the west side, a greenish chlorite occurs, next the vein, highly pyritiferous and often containing considerable gold; the power of the vein at ninety feet depth is six feet, and has steadily increased from the surface down; its strike is northwest by west, with a corresponding dip east and south, of fifty-five degrees. The color of the vein is bluish-white, with black seams of graphite, giving a ribband-like appearance in the mass; it is highly pyritiferous, and when properly roasted, crumbles easily; some parts of the vein contain an arsenical pyrites, which has an injurious effect in the reducing process, by preventing perfect amalgamation; this is caused by roasting the ores in contact with charcoal which should not be practised in these varieties of ores.

SPRING HILL MINE.

This mine is located on Amadore Creek, at the east end of the town and one mile north of the preceding mine. The company commenced operations on this sett in 1851, and have continued uninterrupted since that time; it is located on the same vein as the former, and crops out to the height of 530 feet on the highest point of the hill between Jones, Davis & Co.

Two inclined shafts have been sunk on the vein to about 75 feet below the bed of the creek, at which point the sett has a power of six feet; in its general character it differs in no wise from the mine one mile south, except in the disposition of investing rocks. At Spring Hill the graphic slates which form the gangue are found on the west side of the vein, in place of the east as at Davis' mine. This was evidently caused by an unequal displacement at the period of intrusion of the dike, resulting from the transverse fracture forming the cross course on which Johnson's mine is situated; the resistance being less in that direction at the time of fracture in the incumbent rocks. This cross-fracture had the effect also to throw the intrusive mass from a right line at the time it broke through, for the entire length of the dike, giving it at first view the appearancne rather of two sets in place of one which they in reality are. There are many similar features attending the veins of this country, which has created no little confusion in regard to their true position; and of themselves though they may appear insignificant, yet with the miner they involve questions of high importance, and exert an influence either prejudicial or favorable upon his operations, as their position may be clearly or distinctly known.

The study of our system of metallic veins and its correct development, involves some of the most important interests of the State; a correct knowledge of their position is much desired, but as the limits of this report will not admit that examination which they require, further allusion to the subject will be omitted.

All the vein between shafts and to the point E, has been stopped out with the exception of a small body of vein to support the walls of the mine and attle F F. The mine from its proximity to the creek has considerable water but is kept free by one of Farnham's double-action pumps placed at the shaft B, while the shaft A is used for bringing the ore to the surface.

AMADORE COMPANY MINE.

This is situated on the opposite side of the Creek from the Spring Hill mine, and on the same sett. Their operations have been conducted below the bed of the creek, to the depth of nearly one hundred feet. Shaft D is the whim shaft, 97 feet, and is to the depth of 100 feet, at the bottom of which a 37 foot horse has been struck, all the ore from the lower level A C has been stoped out, the points I supporting the ottle. Reference to the sketch will present its position at the date of visiting it.

The strike of the vein in both the latter, is north by west, diping east 65 degrees.

RANCHOREE MINE.

Is located one mile north of the preceding, and on the ridge dividing the Amadore and Ranchoree Creeks; their reduction works are about half a mile west of the town of Ranchoree.

The upper portion of their vein is situated 420 feet above the creek; on the vein are three shafts of about 70 feet, and two levels of 110 and 75 feet respectively; they are now driving on the level I, to obtain drainage and easy transit for their ores to the mill; the plan of operations will be seen on the sketch marked by the dash lines. The vein at this lower level gives a good ore, and has the same investing rocks as at the upper levels. The vein strikes north 25 degrees west, dipping east, with a power of four feet. The investing rocks are talcose slates.

KEYSTONE MINE.

This mine is situated on the arroya leading into the Amadore, one mile below Jones & Davis' mine; it appears to be a parallel vein, half a mile west of the line uniting the latter and the Spring Hill mine; the ores partake of all the general characters of the other two mines, and it is situated 25 feet above the level of the creek. The sett of Jones, Davis & Co. and the Spring Hill are in the high hill east of the workings figured in the sketch for the Keystone Mine.

This vein strikes north 10 degrees west, diping 40 degrees east, with a power of five feet; the investing rocks are the graphic slate and chlorites, as found in all the others in this neighborhood.

EUREKA MINE, SUTTER, CALAVERAS COUNTY.

This mine is located a short distance south of the town of Sutter. The company have one shaft, A, which is used for the whim by which the ore is at present taken from the mine: a cross cut, seen at D, in the ground plan, was carried east 140 feet, intersecting the level, D, and main shaft, from this the gallery, B, was carried south 135 feet, and subsequently the lower level, C, was driven each way a distance of 230 feet.

The mine is in active operation, and they are now driving an adit on the east side of the hill, which will intersect their vein at an angle of 65 degrees to its line of strike, this will be 400 feet in length, and will afford easy and rapid communication with the reduction works. At the end of the adit a tram-road is constructed 2800 feet, which connects with the mill; the gallery, B, 2, will be connected with the adit in the dotted line, F, of the ground plan.

The vein of this company is in chlorite, and has a strike north and south, dipping east 55 degrees, with a power of five feet; the vein has a riband like appearance in masses, from small seams of graphic slate running through it. The vein contains some arsenical ores, which are highly auriferous.

LIST OF GOLD MINES

At present in operation in California, with location, power employed, &c.

COUNTY.	TOWNS, ETC.	NAME OF MINE.	LOCALITY.	POWER.
Nevada.	Nevada and vicinity.	Gold Tunnel.	Deer Creek.	Steam.
"	" "	Golden Gate.	Little Deer Creek.	
"	" "	Nevada.	Deer Creek.	Water,
"	" "	Wyoming.	"	"
"	" "	Wisconsin.	East of town.	"
"	" "	Illinois.	Deer Creek.	"
"	" "	El Dorado.		"
"	Grass Valley.	Gold Hill.	West of town.	Steam.
"	"	Crossett and Collins.	Osborn Hill.	"
"	"	Empire.	Ophir Hill.	"
"	"	French.	Union Hill.	"
"	"	Lafayette & Helvetia	Lafayette Hill.	"
Butte.	Jamison Creek.	Washington.	Jamison.	"
"	"	Eureka.	"	Water.
Sierra.	Downieville.	Ariel.	South Fork.	"
Yuba.	Brown's Valley.	Huntley's.		Steam.
Shasta.		Kelby's.		
"	Mt. Washington.	Mt. Washington.		
Siskiyou.	Scott's Valley.	Stents.	Scott River.	Steam.
"	"	Shackelford's.	Scott Valley.	
"	"	Moffat's.	"	Water.
"		Martin's.	Humbug Creek.	"
Klamath.	Sealey's Flat.	McDermott's.		
El Dorado.	Union Town.	Union.	Marthenas Creek.	Steam.
"	Quartzville.	Thomas's.	Consumnes River.	Water.
Calaveras.	Ranchoree.	Ranchoree.	Creek.	"
"	Amidor.	Amidor.	Town and Creek.	Steam.
"	Spring Hill.	"	" "	"
"	Amidor.	Keystone.	Tributary Creek.	"
"	Herbertville.	Jones & Davis's.	"	"
"	"	Lea & Johnson.		"
"	Mokelumne Ridge.	Woodhouse.		"
"	"	Phœnix.	"	"
"	"	"	"	"
"	Sutter.	Eureka.	Sutter Creek.	Water.
"	"	Amidor, No. 2.	"	Steam.
"	Jackson.	Oneida.		"
Tuolumne.	Maxwell Creek.	Harris's.	Creek.	"
"	Coulterville.	Maxwell Creek Co.	"	"
"	Merced River.	Marble Springs.	North Fork.	"
Mariposa.	Mt. Ophir.	Noveax Monde.	Mt. Ophir.	"
	Quartzburg.	Washington & Georg.	Quartzburg.	"

From this it will be seen that there are thirty-nine mines in successful operation in this State at the present date, twenty-eight of which I have personally visited this season, and my excuse for not visiting the balance, was the lateness of the season and distances, with the time necessarily required to compile this report, being now delayed much beyond the time when it should have appeared.

ALTITUDES

Taken by Aneroid Barometer No. 10,811, with the Counties and Localities in which they were taken.

COUNTY.	LOCALITY.	POSITION.	ALTITUDE ABOVE THE SEA.
Santa Clara,	San Jose,	Mansion House,	150 feet.
" "	Almaden,	Hotel,	480 ··
" "	Mine,		1345 ··
" "	Houck's Ranch,	Santa Clara Valley,	190 ··
" "	Gilroy's,	" " "	155 ··
" "	Mission Peak,		2025 ··
Monterey,	Mission San Juan,		210 ··
"	Ranch Tres Pinos,	Cañada San Benito,	220 ··
"	Pass Santa Anna,	Top of hill,	615 ··
"	Cañada San Juan,	Four miles south of the above,	300 ··
"	Cañada Las Muertos,	Entrance,	280 ··
"	Sierra Gibilan,	Summit,	2780 ··
"	Chupedero,	"	2368 ··
"	Chelone,	"	2010 ··
"	Soledad Mission,	Hill on road from San Juan to Watsonville,	312 ··
"			340 ··
San Luis Obispo.	High Ridge,	South Nacismiento,	
Alameda,	Mission San José,	Portico,	2460 ··
"	Sunols Hill,	Entrance to valley,	285 ··
"	" Valley,		505 ··
"	Seven Mile House,	Sunol Valley,	285 ··
"	Livermore's Ranch,	Hill in Pass nine miles from Ranch,	240 ··
"	Store House,	Cañada half mile north of hill,	420 ··
"			865 ··
"		Bottom of hill, one mile,	584 ··
San Joaquin,	Elk Horn,	Mouth of Livermore Pass,	680 ··
" "	Suddenfield's Ranch,	San Joaquin Valley,	220 ··
Nevada,	Nevada City,	Adams' Office,	80 ··
"	*Grass Valley,	" "	1810 ··
Placer,	Auburn,		1950 ··
"		Half-way House to Sacramento,	1080 ..
El Dorado,			370 ..
"	Aurum City,		1200 ..
Sacramento,	Mud Springs,		1430 ..
"	North Fork House,		170 ..
Yuba,	Sacramento City,	Levee,	39 ··
"	Marysville,		76 ··
"	Johnson's Ranch,	Bear River,	1120 ··

* A difference of fifty feet by observations of Mr. Atwood with mercurial Barometer, taken three quarters of a mile south; difference probably in elevation of both places.

Altitudes were taken in the Counties of Butte, Sierra and upper part of Yuba with another instrument, but as it was found not to correspond with the points of departure on my return, the observations were presumed to be incorrect and therefore are not given in this table. Some of the localities in this table have been levelled and their height accurately known, and as the barometric measurements have been found to correspond, they are probably close approximations.

COLLECTION FOR THE STATE CABINET.

The Minerals found in the attached list will represent the rocks of those sections examined and spoken of in the report.

1. Sandstone conglomerate with serpentine, Water Works, San Francisco.
2. Chromic iron, containing Nickel, Panoches, Gabilan Mountains.
3. Chromic iron, containing Nickel, San Benito, Canada of.
4. Chromic iron, containing Nickel, Alameda County.
5. Serpentine, containing free Iodine, Water Works, San Francisco.
6. Serpentine seams of Asbestus, Water Works, San Francisco.
7. Sulphuret Copper in Quartz, Alisal, Monterey.
8. Blue and green Carbonate Copper, Alisal, Monterey.
9. Carbonate and Sulphuret Copper, Alisal, Monterey.
10. Carbonate and Sulphuret Copper, Santa Barbara.
11. Jaspery rocks, Presidio, San Francisco.
12. Gangue of the veins, Alisal Mine.
13. Gossan, containing Gold, Gabilan Mountains.
15. Gold in Quartz with peroxide iron, Washington Mine, Shasta Co.
16. Do. do, do. do do. do. do. do. do.
17. Do. do. do. co. do. do. do. do. do.
18. Gossan, containing Gold, Gold Tunnel Mine, Nevada.
19. Gold in Quartz, Gold Tunnel Mine, Nevada.
20. Gold in Pyrites, Gold Tunnel Mine, Nevada.
21. Gold in Quartz with Galena, Lafayette and Helvetia Mine, Nevada.
22. Gold in Pyrites, Lafayette and Helvetia Mine, Nevada.
23. Gold in Arsenical Pyrites, Lafayette and Helvetia Mine, Nevada.
24. Gold in Gangue of Vein, Lafayette and Helvetia Mine, Nevada.
25. Auriferous Pyrites, Gold Hill Lode, Helvetia mine.
26. Gold and Peroxide Iron, Lafayette and Helvetin mine.
27. Serpentine from the Lode, Lafayette Hill.
28. Pyritiferous and Variegated, Lafayette Hill.
29. Gold in Quartz, Empire Co., Ophir Hill.
30. Gold in Pyrites, Empire Co., Ophir Hill.
31. Ores of the Greenstone, Empire Co., Ophir Hill.
32. Ores Pyritiferous, Empire Co, Ophir Hill.
34. Discoloration of Quartz by *Gold*, Empire Co., Ophir Hill.
35. Gold in Quartz, Gold Hill mine.
36. Auriferous Pyrites in Quartz, Gold Hill mine.
37. Auriferous Cellular Quartz, Gold Hill mine.
38. Surface Ores and Peroxide Iron, Gold Hill mine.
39. Auriferous Quartz in Crystals, Osborn Hill mine.
40. Ore from the Granite, Osborn Hill mine.
41. Ore from decomposed Greenstone, Osborn Hill mine.
42. Ore from the Greenstone Gangue, Osborn Hill mine.
43. Gossan containing Gold, Wyoming mine.
44. Auriferous Quartz, Wyoming mine.

45. Pyrites containing Gold, Ben Franklin mine·
46. Ore from the Greenstone, Ben Franklin mine.
47. Conglomerate and Gold, Little York.
48. Trachyte, Grass Valley.
49. Auriferous Pyrites in Quartz, Mt. George mine.
50. Auriferous Pyrites and Sulphur, Mt. George mine.
51. Auriferous Pyrites, Mt. George mine.
52. Steatite (Soapstone) Jenny Lind Hill (*Rockg Tunnel*).
53. Serpentine, Jenny Lind Hill, (*Rocky Tunnel.*)
54. Asbestus, Jenny Lind Hill, (*Rocky Tunnel*).
55. Cellular Quartz and Gold, Lea & Johnson mine, Calaveras Co.
56. Ore from the Greenstone, Lea & Johnson mine, Calaveras Co.
57. Surface ore of cross course, Lea & Johnson mine, Calaveras Co.
58. Cellular Quartz surface ore, Ranchoree mine, Calaveras Co.
59. Auriferous Pyrites, Ranchoree mine, Calaveras Co.
60. Quartz Talc and Gold, Ranchoree mine, Calaveras Co.
61. Auriferous Quartz, Jones & Davis' Mine, Calaveras County.
62. Pyritiferous Quartz, Jones & Davis' Mine, Calaveras County.
63. Gangue investing Lode Auriferous, Jones & Davis' Mine, Calaveras County.
64. Surface Ores, Jones & Davis' Mine, Calaverous County.
65. Gold in Quartz, Eureka Mine, Calaveras County.
66. Arsenical Pyrites and Gold, Eureka Mine, Calaveras County.
67. East side of Lode, do do do do
68. Middle of Lode, do do do do
69. Average Ores, do do do do
70. Graphic Slate, Jones & Davis Mine.
71. Veinstone with Graphic Slate, Spring Hill Mine, Calaveras Co.
72. Do Roasted, do do do
73. Auriferous Pyrites, do do do
74. Gold in Quartz, do do do
76. Cellular Quartz, Keystone Mine, Amidor.
77. Auriferous Pyrites, do do do
78. do do and Gold, Ariel Mine, Siorra County.
79. Pyrites in Talc, do do do
80. Proxide Iron, do do do
81. Calcarious Travertin, South Fork, Yuba.
82. Galena and Gold in Quartz, Tuolumne Water Co.
83. do do do do do
84. Peroxide Iron and Gold do do
85. Auriferous Talc, do do
86. Talcose Slate and Gold, Calaveras River.
87. Gossan and Gold, New York Mine, Stanislaus River.
88. Carbonate Line, Almaden Mine, Santa Clara.
89. Serpentine, do do do
90. Carbonate Lime in Cinnabar, Almaden Mine, Santa Clara.
91. Cinnabar, do do do do
92. do do do do do
93. Sulphuret Copper, Santa Barbara.
94. Carbonate Copper, Carson Hill.
95. Carbonate Copper, Grass Valley.

96. Sulphuret Antimony, Mt. Oso, Coast Mountains.
97. Carbonate Copper in boulders, Oregon creek. Sierra Co.
98. Gold in do do do do do
99. Lignite and Sulphuret Iron do do do do
100. Hornblende, Monte Diablo.
101. do Cañada San Benito.
102. Silicified Wood, Oregon creek, Sierra Co.
103. Fossil Leaves, Minesota do do
104. do do and Wood, Minesota, Sierra Co.
105. Shells of raised sea-beach, containing Ostrea, Purpura, Mytilus, Benicia.
106. Lignites, Grass Valley.
107. Silicified Oak, Grass Valley.
108. Quartz and Gold, No. 1 level, Pine Tree Sett.
109. do do No. 2 do do do do
110. do do No. 1 Cross cut do do
111. do do No. 2 do do do do
112. do do from the limestone, Dyer Sett.
113. Copper Lode, near Ridly's Ferry.
114. do do Hoyt's Lode.
115. Copper and Gold, Spring Sett.
116. Gossan and Gold, Josephine Sett.
117. Copper and Gold in Quartz, do do
118. Cellular Quartz and Gold, do do
119. do do do do do
120. do do do do do
121. do do Pyrites with Gold, do do
122. Graphite and Gold in Quartz, do do
123. Blue Carbonate Copper and Quartz, Pine Tree Sett.
124. Galena Iron and Gold in Quartz, Mt. Ophir Sett.
125. Hydrated Protoxide Iron and Gold, do do
126. Walls of Lode Auriferous, Mt. Ophir Sett.
127. Veinstone Pyritiferous do do
128. Galena and Copper, do do
129. Pyrites in Greenstone.
130. Medium Ores of Mt. Ophir.
131. Carbonate Copper, Luis Obispo.
132. Agates, do
133. Magnetic Iron, Santa Barbara.
134. Do do in Serpentine, San Francisco.
136. Do do do do
137. Peroxide Iron, Santa Cruz Mountains.
138. Bituminous Shales, with Telina, Coast Monterey.
139. Do Impressions of telina and Venus, with borings of the Pholas, Coast Monterey.
139. Bituminous Sandstone with Pholas and Teredo, Serpulae, Coast Monterey.
140. Yellow Sandstone with impressions of Venus, Southeast Monterey.
141. Do do and Telina, do do
142. Do do do do do
143. Do do do Carmello Creek.

144. Yellow Sandstone and Telina, Cormello Creek.
145. Do do do do do
146. Do do do do do
147. Mactra and Cardium Sandstone, Monterey.
148. Argentiferous Galena, Alisal.
149. do do do
150. Carbonate Copper and Gold in Quartz, Alisal.
151. Mica Schist and Sulphate Iron, Santa Cruz.
152. Granite, do
153. Serpentine and Bitumen, La Brae, Santa Clara Co.
154. Mica Schist with Garnets, Carmello.
155. Carbonate Lime, Santa Cruz.
156. Carbonate Lime in Crystals, Santa Cruz.
157. Marine Fossils, consisting of Pyrula, Telina, Dentalia, Cytherea, Butte Co.
158. Matica, Ostrea, Mactra, Butte Co.
159. Marine Fossils, consisting of Buccinum, Natica, Cytherea, Santa Cruz Mountains.
160. Venus, Venericardia, Santa Cruz Mountains.
161. Marine Fossils, Astarte, San Benito.
162. do do Venericardia, do do
163. do do Mytilus Cytherea, do do
177. Infusorial Clays, containing thirty-eight species, Monterey.
174. Granite, Punta Reys, Marin Co.
175. Limestone and Antimony, do do do do
176. Galena Gold and Quartz, Marble Spring Mine, Tuolumne Co.

Through the kindess of Mr. W. P. Blake, Geologist of the U. S. R. R. Survey, the following specimens have been procured, and which represent some portions of the geology of the routes traveled over by that expedition during the past season:

164. Fossil Wood perforated by Teredo, Colorado Deseret.
165. Silicified Wood, do do.
166. Andalusite, drift of Chouchillas River.
167. Carbonate of Lime, Tejon Pass.
168. Selenite, Posa Creek.
169. Amorphous Quartz, Four Creeks.
170. Coral, Colorado Desert.
171. Basalt, San Joaquin.
172. Marine Fossils; these contain two species of Fusus Bucinum, Telina, Pecten and Turbo, San Diego Mission.
176. Shark's Teeth, Posa Creek.

All of which is respectfully submitted.

JOHN B. TRASK.

Document No. 14.

IN SENATE.] [SESSION 1855.

REPORT

ON THE

GEOLOGY

OF THE

COAST MOUNTAINS;

EMBRACING THEIR

Agricultural Resources and Mineral Productions.

ALSO, PORTIONS OF THE

MIDDLE AND NORTHERN MINING DISTRICTS.

BY DR. JOHN B. TRASK.

[B. B. REDDING, STATE PRINTER.

To His Excellency, JOHN BIGLER,

Governor of the State of California:

DEAR SIR:

Pursuant to an Act passed in May last by the Senate and Assembly of this State, authorizing a farther examination of the unexplored portions of the State, I have the honor to submit the following Report and accompanying diagrams.

Yours, &c.

JOHN B. TRASK.

EXECUTIVE DEPARTMENT,
SACRAMENTO, MARCH 8th, 1855.

To the Senate and Assembly of the State of California:

I have the honor herewith to transmit to the Senate, a Report made by the State Geologist, Dr. John B. Trask, in compliance with an Act passed May 15th, 1854, entitled "An Act to authorize and enable Dr. John B. Trask to complete his geological examination of parts of the State of California.

The copy herewith transmitted, being the only one furnished me, it becomes my duty, respectfully, to request the Senate to inform the Assembly that the same has been received and is in possession of the Senate.

JOHN BIGLER.

PREFACE.

The tour of 1854 was commenced on the 13th day of June, and the first month was spent in the counties of Yuba, the lower portion of Nevada, Placer and Sacramento, for the purpose of completing the examination of those sections which were left unfinished the previous season.

In the month of July, the southern portion of the tour was entered upon, and carried through portions of the counties of Monterey, Luis Obispo, Santa Barbara, and Los Angeles, to the northern borders of the counties of San Bernardino and San Diego. This occupied the time up to the 12th October, a period of three months. My operations were then transferred to the agricultural districts west of the Sacramento River, through the counties of Yolo, Sutter, Butte, Shasta, Trinity, and the eastern part of Klamath. The time occupied in these sections was two months. At this time I returned to the mining counties for the purpose of collecting such statistics as the short period of time allowed.

The whole time occupied in the mines proper, was three weeks; the first part of the season being spent in the agricultural districts of those counties, almost exclusively.

The tour occupied a period of six months and twenty-two days of active labor in the field.

REPORT.

This report will embrace the investigation of the Coast Mountains, commencing near the point of termination of the tour conducted during the summer of 1853, and ending at the northern boundaries of the Counties of San Bernadino and San Diego during the summer and early part of the autumn of 1854. The tour of 1853 in the Coast Mountains terminated a few miles south of the river Nacismiento, in the County of Monterey.

PHYSICAL GEOGRAPHY OF THE COAST MOUNTAINS.

In the report on the "Geology of parts of the Coast Mountains," presented and published by the fifth session of the Legislature, it will be remembered that this chain of mountains laid down as forming the coast line of this State, extended from the 42nd parallel to the southern boundary of the same. This presumption was founded on the erroneous positions of the southern terminus of this chain, as laid down on the older, and also the more recent maps of the State, conjoined with the misapprehension of many individuals who reside on different points of the coast line, and who have blended the base of another and a distinct mountain chain with those belonging to the coast chain proper; these, it will be seen, have no other connection with the latter, other than to traverse its line of trend at nearly right angles to its course.

From the Nacismiento River the coast line of mountains continue on a line, which is nearly direct with the trend of that portion of the chain which extends from Point Pinos to the river above named, and which forms one of the southern boundaries of the County of Monterey; the line being south nearly fifty degrees east to their northern termini or junction with the San Bernadino chain. The latter mountains have their western termination in the vicinity of Points Aguilla and Conception; beyond this to the south, the mountains which front the ocean are derived from this chain or its spurs, which are often projected nearly to the water-line of the sea.

After crossing the Nacismiento River, the coast chain becomes exceedingly rugged and irregular, losing in a great measure that parallelism of ridges which they have heretofore maintained in the more northern districts, from this cause often they become almost absolutely impassable, at other points than those used for public highways; in many cañons south and east of their junction, water is

2

scarcely to be found, and which, as a consequence, renders their study a difficult and laborious task.

Between the middle and eastern ridges of this part of the chain and at a distance of about thirty miles south of the intersection of the Monte Diablo range there are some valley districts occupied as ranches for grazing purposes, but the major part of the entire district present but few inducements that invite it to a permanent and extensive population.

The general characteristics of the mountains west of the central portion of the chain, are repulsive in their character, and ill adapted to any other than those purposes to which this part of the chain is applied, viz: that of affording pasturage for wild cattle and the rearing of sheep.

On the eastern side of the central ridges, the intervening country lying between them partakes much more of the character which is found to prevail in many of the more northern parts of the line ; somewhat extended valley sections, occurring at long intervals, and again breaking up into rough and jagged peaks, with here and there small plats, with detached portions of wild herds that roam these hills almost unknown and unowned.

The ascent to the eastern ridges is abrupt, and the eastern declivities are much of the same character, until the plains of the Tulare lying at their base is approached, when the foot-hills present the same general characteristics as those on the western slope of the Monte Diablo range towards the southern part of the Salinas. There is not that gradual graduation from mountain to plain, which is incident to the descent from the Sierra Nevada. This will be found a prevailing character throughout this portion, and also many other parts of the coast mountains.

The western slope of the mountains towards the sea, from Point Lobos in the County of Monterey, through the entire length of the County of Luis Obispo, is extremely rugged and precipitous, forming a heavy and bold shore line as far south as Point Sal, when the coast begins to assume a much smoother and agreeable aspect. This, however, is but the outline appearance of the plats as they descend from the base of the hills in a gradual slope; for on reaching the water-line, the faces of these plateaus form perpendicular escarpments of nearly one hundred feet in height.

From the facts at present in our possession relative to those parts of these mountains lying south of the city of San Francisco, we are now able to form an opinion that will approximate correctness as regards their geographical position and relations, and it would seem but proper that they should hold that place upon our maps which they respectively hold in nature.

With this view before us, the following proposition will be submitted for the classifying the mountain ranges of this part of the State:

For all that portion of the coast mountains south of the city of San Francisco, and following the line of the coast to the southern part of the County of San Luis Obispo, the same to be denominated *Coast Mountains* and ceasing at their junction with the *San Bernardino Mountains* which enter upon the coast line near this point. The local name of *Santa Cruz Range* to be retained and to comprise the entire group of mountains which extend from the Pajaro River on the south, and terminating at the Presidio Point near San Francisco.

That range of mountains commencing on the south shores of the Bay San Pablo, Straits Carquines and Bay of Suison, and forming the west boundaries of the Valleys of San Joaquin and Tulare—the eastern boundary of the Salinas and Santa Clara Valleys, with the east coast of the Bay of San Francisco, to be denominated the Monte Diablo Range. (This latter range having its southern terminus due west of the central portion of the large body of water known as the Great Tulare Lake.)

That portion of the Monte Diablo Range, extending from the head of the

Cañada San 'Benito in the County of Monterey, to the Pajaros River on the aorth, and forming the middle eastern boundary of the Salinas Valley, and western boundary of the Valley of San Juan, to be denominated the *Gabilan Spur*.

The above arrangement differs but little from that proposed in my report of last year, (Doc. 9, Assembly, pages 12, 13, 18, 19, 21, 23,) and becomes necessary in order to form anything approaching a comprehensive idea of this almost unknown portion of the State. The principal and almost only difference in this arrangement, is in fixing a point at which the Coast Mountains appear to have their termination, a point hitherto unsettled, and one that has caused more confusion, perhaps, in relation to the geography of the State than any subject hitherto engaging the attention of travelers and citizens. The true position of these mountains and their relations with other chains must, at no distant day, command a much greater amount of attention from the people of this State, and the Atlantic States also, than has as yet been bestowed upon them, for it will be found that, in selecting a route for the national railroad, the crossing of this, or an adjacent chain will be necessary, and the principle involved in the great question upon this point will simply be, the best means to be adopted that will avoid the transit of two chains in place of one.

A correct understanding of the situation of these ridges, will explain many of the phenomena constantly occurring in these inland districts, and it affords us the only means of investigating those causes of sterility that are found to accompany and prove a constant attendant of extensive areas enclosed within, as extending to the east of the high ridges composing the chain.

Their study then, becomes a matter not of scientific interest alone, but engages our attention in a practical, and enonomic point of view ; it is fraught with pecuniary public interest, and unless fully understood must result in pecuniary loss to all parties directly interested.

The altitude of these mountains is such that they have the effect to absorb much of the aqueous matter carried from the ocean through the various gaps that occur in the coast-line proper, and when the higher hills fail to accomplish this, the increase of temperature, consequent from the relative position which the mountains hold to the plain lands that may be situated among the immediate ridges, or beyond them to the east, is such that it has the effect to dissipate whatever aqueous matter that might have remained.

This state of the meteorological condition of the atmosphere is admirably illustrated on the northern end of the Salinas and the southern end of the valley Santa Clara. These two districts have the appearance of being subject to a constant drought, so far as external and surface features are concerned ; but a closer examination of all the attendant circumstances that are to be met with in this section of country will convince the observer that an erroneous opinion upon this subject may easily be formed, when mere external character alone is observed during the daytime.

During the after part of the day in the summer season, there is usually a dense fog setting in through the opening made by the Bay of Monterey, which sweeps across the Gabilan Spur over on to the south part of the Santa Clara and the valley of San Juan ; and although this fog is often sufficiently dense to obscure the view for any considerable distance, while it rests upon the northern portion of the Salinas Plains, and west of the Gabilan, still it is not apparent often in the atmosphere four miles east of that ridge. The atmosphere is perfectly transparent, nor would the traveler suppose for one moment that any material change in the condition of the air had taken place, or that it was in any way different from that through which he may have been traveling during the entire day.

It is only at evening that the change is perceptible, for as the temperature decreases after nightfall, a heavy mist from the condensation of the moisture held in solution by high temperature takes place, which is often equivalent to a light rain.

On the middle portions of the Salinas, much the same features are observed, and it is no uncommon circumstance to be in a cloud of mist at one point, and at another on the same plain not three miles the atmosphere as clear as nature can produce it; it is instructive as well as interesting to stand in a commanding position and witness the solution of the cloud of vapour as it passes a given and well defined line.

The same features are prevalent on the valley sections lying east of the Mount Diablo Range, and the effects of condensed moisture are very apparent even in the western foothills of these districts. In this fact lies one of the secrets of the productive capacities of the soils of many of these interior sections, and were it not for this peculiarity of our atmosphere a large area of our inland country would remain a perfect Sahara, suited neither for man or beast.

On some parts of the valley sections there have been observations conducted through a short period of the last year, for the purpose of eliciting some information relative to the hygrometric condition of the atmosphere many miles from the sea. These observations if continued for one or two years hence, will furnish us valuable and interesting information relative to the amount of atmospheric moisture of the interior of the State, from which we shall be able to deduce some conclusions of the productive capabilities of many parts of the valleys that are now neglected, under the prevailing idea that water sufficient for the propagation of grains does not exist in these sections; from what information upon this subject, is in a tangible form, I am led to the conclusion that the atmosphere of the central portions of the Plains of San Joaquin and Sacramento, is nearly or quite saturated during seven months of the year. The prevalence of southerly winds on these plains is always marked by an increase in the height of the dew-point, and they are found by tables, kept during the year 1854, to constitute nearly sixty-nine per cent. of the winds of the summer season.

Beyond the junction of the coast mountains, the San Bernardino Chain makes its inception, and forms the coast-line for a considerable distance to the south. It is at this point where one of the great errors relating to the physical geography of this part of the State has been committed, viz: *that of blending the western terminus of this chain with the coast-line of mountains proper.* From Point Aguilla the coast begins to assume a much more easterly direction, than at any other point north of this locality (except perhaps in the immediate vicinity of Cape Mendocino,) and on passing Point Conception it pursues nearly a due east trend until arriving at Point Dessolata to the south of the Mission San Juan Capistrano, when it again assumes its easterly course after rounding that point.

At a short distance north of Point Aguilla the base of the San Bernardino chain fronts the coast, at times miles distant, at others approaching the water-line; after passing the south-eastern point of the Santa Barbara channel the chain is seen stretching away in the distance nearly due east towards the waters of the Colorado, and across the Jornada del Muerto dividing this desert into two unequal parts.

On approaching San Pedro in the county of Los Angeles we find that the nearest part of this chain is not less than forty miles distant from the coast, and to the northeast of this place the distance is much greater. At the distance of seventy miles in the same direction may be seen the high peaks of San Bernardino, and beyond it again, that of San Jacinto; farther to the west are mountains near the Cahon Pass, while to the left of this line of view and at nearly the same distance are the rugged peaks of the Sierra San Jose and San Gabriel.

Farther to the north and at the distance of fifty miles are the mountains of San Fernando, the whole of which are but the more prominent peaks of this transverse chain. On the northern base of these mountains flows the River Mohave, through the central and northern parts of the great desert.

Within the district above named, and on the south base of these mountains lies the great plain of Los Angeles, which from the northern to its extreme southern lines cannot be less than one hundred and eighty miles in length, with an average breadth of forty miles, comprising within its limits an area of arable lands equal to three-fourths of the valley of the Sacramento, or about one half that of the Sacramento and San Joaquin combined.

The local positions of the mountains bordering the western and southern portion of the State must it will be seen, modify to a great extent the productive capabilities of the adjoining districts, and no better illustration of this fact is necessary than an examination of the flat lands lying contiguous to their base; in the case before us the lands at the southern base of the San Bernardino chain, though coarse and harsh in texture, are at the same time highly fertile, while that found upon the northern base, though derived from the same sources, is wholly incapable of vegetable production, or at least to but a very limited degree. From this then it will be seen, that the climatal conditions necessary for a healthful and abundant vegetation are influenced more by position and altitude rather than from any defects in the soil itself.

Hence it is, that we find the Santa Clara and Salinas valleys are more uniformly productive, than the portions of the San Joaquin lying immediately to the east of the former, while at the same time the latter is more productive than the section to the south known as *Desert*, but which under favorable circumstances has proved inferior to none of the best lands in any part of this State; this if a plain contradiction to the general idea prevailing, and promulgated from high sources, that this portion of the State is valueless, and if individuals see proper to publish conclusions made up from hasty examinations, and unfavorable predilections, they must not expect others to follow in their trail, and pervert truth to save individual responsibility.

The only requisition necessary to make this *desert* a productive field, suited to the growth of our southern staples, is the introduction of water in sufficient quantities for irrigation. This done, no district of this State will present greater capacities.

The position and course of the San Bernardino chain, with its extent and altitude forms a striking feature in the geography of the State, and the climatal features incident to the effects produced by position and altitude, are equally distinctive; the products arising from these peculiarities, are equally marked in all their forms, while its zoology partakes of the general mutation which supervenes to as great an extent as is manifest in the peculiarities of the climate; not less characterized are the native inhabitants, their pursuits and interests; there seems but little to unite them with other parts of the State, as each and every natural product, methods of living, and political feelings, are as distinct as the almost impassable mountain barrier that separates them from the northern portions of the State.

GEOLOGY OF THE COAST MOUNTAINS.

The geology of that portion of the Coast Mountains south of the River Nacismiento, differs, but little from that observed a short distance south of that line.

The talcose rocks and their derivations extend south of the river for the distnce of about thirty miles, forming a narrow belt, and flanked on the southwest by the trap rocks, and on the northeast, by coarse granites and sienites, at times composed almost exclusively of massive hornblende, and at others considerable quantities of the latter is found imbedded among the other primitive rocks. The primitive group of this section of the country, exhibits itself in a belt of about one and a half miles in breadth, and is most evidently contemporaneous with the rocks forming the Santa Cruz mountains, and that part of the coast-line, extending from Point Pinos south to the northern line of the county of San Luis Obispo.

Among the magnesian rocks of this district there were seen many small specimens of the chromic iron, but none in such massive quantities as that noticed in the Gabilan Spur, in the vicinity of the Sierra Panoches, near the southern junction of this spur, with the Monte Diablo range. The talcose varieties of the rocks of these mountains, as well also as the sienites, and granites, have been intruded and dislocated by the quartz, but no veins of any considerable magnitude were met with, and there was but little indication of any auriferous deposits within them.

On the head of a small creek which is probably a tributary of one of the southern branches of the Nacismiento, a heavy bed of chlorite slate makes its appearance, having a strike east and west and dipping to the south with a high angle. This bed is cut through by a dike of trap rock having a dark grey color, and immediately adjoining the latter is a small vein of quartz some nine inches diameter, holding the same course and having a westerly dip. This vein contains galena, and sulphuret of molybdenum, holding the same relations of mineral disposition, that are found to exist in the vicinity of the Pittsburg Mine in the county of Nevada.

I was unable to discover any valuable metallic associations in any of the rocks belonging to this group, and am forced as a consequence to say, that in this instance, the metallic associations hitherto found to be unexceptionable in all other parts of the State, viz: of gold in quartzose and talcose rocks, when found adjoining each other, does not hold good in this instance, it is one of the very few exceptions apparently to that general rule.

On the west flank of the eastern ridges, and at the distance of about twenty-five miles from the rancho Santa Maria, there are beds of a crystalline or primary limestone, similar in all its general characteristics with that found in the vicinity of Santa Cruz; a large proportion of this calcareous rock, possesses a high crystalline character, and is unsuited for other purposes than the manufacture of lime. On a small valley to the west of this bed and at the distance of about half a mile west, a heavy deposit of calcareous travertin is found, but like the toro beds in the county of Monterey, the springs that rise to the deposit, seem no longer to exist; this bed covered an area of nearly one-fourth of a mile, and having a depth of nearly seven feet.

The geological position of these limestones is among the primitive rocks like its equivalents among the more northern parts of the same mountain chain, and is the same in age as that group extending through three hundred miles of the Sierra Nevada.

From the valley above alluded to, this rock extends south in detached groups or beds for a distance of about thirty miles, and will be found on the west flank of this line of ridges to a point nearly due east of the head waters of the Rio Santa Clara in the county of Santa Barbara. A similar group of these rocks is also met with near Lake Elizabeth, near the main waggon road from Santa Barbara to the Cañada de los Ubas and the Tejon Reserve.

In the cañon of the rancho San Francisco the limestone is frequently met with on the sides of the hills to the left of the road, but at this locality it cannot be considered *in situ*.

The rocks have been carefully examined for organic remains, but in no instance have I as yet been able to detect the slighest vestige of organic life, and from those who have succeeded me in the examination of these rocks, I learn that they have met with no better success.

It is not uncommon to find impressions of marine plants at least, in rocks of this character, but even these are absent in the group under consideration.

A distinguishing feature in these limestones, is the small proportion in mass which they bear to the other primitive rocks with which they are associated and invested, and when found in contact, (as was the case in two instances) with the more recent igneous intrusions, their structure was found materially changed.—They were more often found imbedded in the granitic rocks than in any other position; but little of the entire line of beds possessed a fine crystalline texture, and this even was usually much discolored by iron.

The limestone rocks of these mountains are well represented on the west flank of the Sierra Nevada, their equivalents may be found in various mining localities, as at the Marble Springs, Sonora, Ringgold, Murderer's Bar, Carson River Falls, also as far north as the county of Plumas, it passes through all the intermediate counties lying between Mariposa on the south and Plumas on the north. In some of the above localities it has been found to answer the purpose of a good building material, this however is merely local, but its principal use in this State is the manufacture of lime.

The granitic series probably underlies the entire central and a large portion of the eastern line of ridges, although it does not make its appearance upon the surface to that extent which this supposition would seem to imply. I am satisfied of this fact however, from the examination of the debris found in and about the small streams, which are found traversing some of the deep cañons of these mountains; in all the sedimentary beds, of sand and drift thus found, the granitic constituents of the same formed by far the greater proportion, and it may be said constituted their entire mass. How far this formation may extend westward, or towards the coast, and north of the San Bernardino is yet quite uncertain, as I am not aware of any outcrop of the granite north of this chain and south of San Simeon.

TERTIARY ROCKS OF THE COAST MOUNTAINS.

The tertiary rocks of this part of the coast mountains, are interesting in a scientific point of view, in directing our attention to those periods of the earlier history of this portion of the western continent, when it was submerged beneath the waters of the ocean. The prevalence of the tertiary rocks in these mountains fully corroborates all that has heretofore been said respecting almost the entire range of country stretching from the base of the eastern Sierras to the present eastern confines of the sea. On the summits and sides of the hills, we find the fossiliferous rocks of this part of the country, maintaining the same relative positions which they occupy in other and distant parts of the State; the equivalents of the Monte Diablo groups are found as well marked as at any part of that particular range, while at the same time we find in this connection other beds of widely different forms, and belonging to different periods of the same era, and which are found again hundreds of miles distant in other directions.

Sufficient is now known respecting the distribution of the vertebrate and invertebrate animals inhabiting the country during these remote ages, that we are able to frame, at least, an approximate opinion of the relative periods at which the different classes of animals existed, whose remains have been found within the limits of this State.

With those relics of the vertebrate animals now in our possession, from the counties of San Luis Obispo, Santa Barbara and Los Angeles, and what has been brought to light in the Counties of Tuolumne, Placer and Siskiyou, it appears evident that not less than eight species of these gigantic animals formerly existed upon these shores. The relative situation of these remains in different parts of the State precludes the idea that they could have existed during the same identical period, therefore, it will probably be necessary to construct a different arrangement than that at present acknowledged, for the date at which allied genera and species in other parts of the world existed, compared to those of California.

We are warranted in this assumption from the appearance and character of the marine fossils adjacent to the district from which many of these bones have been exhumed, and as in the case of those remains from the northern districts of the State, their association with relics of the works of art would certainly appear to bring them down to a much later period than that usually assigned; but of this subject we shall treat again at a future day, when farther, but perhaps not more decisive evidence is in our possession.

In the mountainous districts of the Counties of San Luis Obispo and Santa Barbara, the predominating fossiliferous rocks are miocenes holding an age contemporaneous with the Monte Diablo groups. Among the higher hills of these Counties, the Miocene rocks are in many instances largely developed; this will be found to be the case in an eminent degree in the La Questa San Marcas, a pass in the mountains, and on one of the trails from the town of Santa Barbara into the Valley of San Inez.

The cañon of this hill cuts through heavy beds of sandstone, which is loaded with fossils of marine origin, among which Pectinea, Cardia and Ostrea are in greatest abundance, while it is prolific in univalves and spiral shells, with other additional bivalves. Immediately east of the Mission of Santa Barbara among the lower hills, there is an extensive bed of Ostrea, the cementing medium being made up of lime with an admixture of a small quantity of sand.

In passing through the Valley of San Inez and entering the coast mountains in the County of Luis Obispo, the same fossiliferous rocks occur for forty miles, and in a large valley lying in the centre of these mountains a portion of the rib of a large whale was found by Col. Norris, of the U. S Land Survey, at an altitude of nearly twenty-five hundred feet above the level of the sea, and about thirty-six miles into the interior. It is not uncommon to find the remains of these large cetaceans among the mountains forming the coast, and some fragments of similar bones have also been brought from the borders of the Tulare Valley. From careful examinations of those bones which have been brought into situations where they have been made the subject of careful investigation, it is believed that the larger proportion of all that have yet been found, are referable to present existing genera and species, though from fragments alone, it would be difficult to individualize at the present time.

The fossiliferous sandstones of the mountains possess many of the lithological characteristics which are found among the rocks of the same age in the more northern parts of the State, and belonging to the same chain, and when differing from this rule, the cause will be found entirely local, and of limited extent. Any diversity in species that may be found imbedded in these rocks, will be more attributable to local climatal influences rather than to any difference in relative age which the rocks of the southern mountains may hold to those of the northern districts.

In the County of San Luis Obispo, at the distance of about fifteen miles from the coast, and from thence into the interior, both east and south, are to be found beds containing an uncommonly large Gryphæ at times weighing twenty pounds; it is far superior in size to those found in the vicinity of Livermore's ranch, in the county of Alameda, and like them, they at times have been found to contain the impress of the animal that formerly inhabited the shell; it is not improbable that the age at which both species existed was contemporaneous, the difference in species, size and form, being attributable solely to local climatal effects. Such is the fact at the present time with the Mollusca inhabiting our coast, within the parallels of latitude inclusive, and we have no reason that such was not the case in relation to the fossiliferous groups.

The large bivalves form an interesting feature in the paleontology of our State, and undoubtedly are of different species from many already known in other parts of the world; but their peculiarities must be deferred until a future period.

The area over which the tertiary rocks are distributed, leaves but little room for doubt of the former submergence of the entire district; and the different periods of this era points us to so many successive elevations, which were probably gradual in their character. If it should be questioned that this was not the fact, during the earlier age of these deposits, we would simply refer the observer to the terraced outlines of the fossiliferous groups from the present shore of the ocean to the summit of the first and western ridges of the chain. These elevatory effects have undoubtedly been continued through the subsequent periods of this epoch, and will be considered more in detail when the coast line of the southern part of the State is under consideration.

PRIMITIVE ROCKS OF THE COAST MOUNTAINS.

The primitive rocks of the Coast Mountains consist of the granitic series, in which are included the the Sienites, Micaschist, Granite, Gneiss, Porphyries, and the older Greenstone, including also the serpentine rocks. On these rest the greater part of the older sedimentary rocks, and some few of the Pliocene period. Their general distribution has been noticed in the preceding pages of this report, and it remains now only to mention more particularly the points at which they may best be observed, with any peculiarities that may attend them.

The granite forms the summit of a high ridge to the east of the San Inez Valley; from about half the southern centre of the valley, and on the flanks of the mountain, the serpentine rocks creep out and extend in a southwest direction for about two miles, crossing the ridge at this point and forming its summit for about half a mile. The entire line of this summit is bare and jagged, and the white appearance of the granite at a distance gives it the aspect of a large bed of quartz; a closer approach, however, developes its true character. I have seen but one other bed of the granite rocks of this State which presents the same peculiar features, and those are situated about half way between the town of Jackson and that of Volcano in the County of Amidor. In the middle portions of the comb of this ridge is a large bed of Micaschist, containing imperfect specimens of garnets which closely resembles those found on the Carmello Creek, in the County of Monterey.

On the sides of these ridges and fronting the southwest, the sedimentary rocks are found in detached masses, with imbedded fossils which are usually very imperfect, and therefore, of little value; their distinguishing features fixing their alliance to the Monte Diablo group. They maintain a high angle of inclination in most instances, and have suffered much disturbance from the subsequent intrusion of later igneous rocks through and among the primitive series on which they rest; many evidences of the intrusions are manifest throughout this entire range, but as a general fact, they appear much more local in their character than in many parts of the more northern equivalents of this part of the chain, or more particularly such as may be found in the Santa Cruz and Monte Diablo ranges.

The Serpentine rocks of the country included in the southern branches of the Nacismiento River support in several localities heavy beds of the Miocene sandstones, the fossils of which agree in all particulars with those noted as occurring in the same group of rocks throughout this part of the State. On the northern extremity of the talcose series, a vein of quartz has cut through the inferior rocks, and also through the sedimentary group, resting upon them; among the sandstones it has sent out several lateral veins, and the points of contact exhibit very marked changes in structure, equally distinguishable with any of those cases noticed in former reports, where the contact of lavas were observed on an extensive scale.

Nor are the changes of structure confined to the intrusion of the latter veins alone, for in following out the igneous intrusions, it was found that considerable dikes of the trapean rocks were manifest, the effects of which were apparent both by change of position and structnre, the latter to an eminent degree. Another illustration of the effects of those late trapean intrusions is most clearly marked in the case of the Los Angeles sandstone about one mile north of the town, where the latter beds containing impressions of marine plants and other fossils have been most completely metamorphosed, so much so was this the case that the rocks would fracture transversely to the lines of stratification with as much ease as in any other direction. The fracture was usually conchoidal with sharp, well defined edges, and the fragments had a distinct sonorous sound.

Leaving San Inez and passing in a southeast direction to the San Fernando Mountains, we find a continuation of the primitive groups which are apparently connected with and continuous into the coast mountains to the north; they are met with in the Cañada Los Ubas, and are continuous from thence into the coast mountains to the west, and the southern terminus of the Sierra Nevada.

The rocks in the vicinity of the Tejon are granitic, consisting of Sienite, Hornblende Granite, a goodly amount of the more felspathic rocks, containing imbedded crystals of hornblende and schorl, with Mica and hornblende schists. They evidently belong to one and the same group, having an age contemporaneous with that series found some two hundred miles farther to the north. South of the terminus of the Sierra Nevada, and on the western edge at the desert, are to be found small masses of scoria with small fragments of Obsidian, the latter not abundant.

The above general characteristics are sufficient to fix the relative ages of these distant groups, of allied rocks, and when we remember that nearly throughout the entire range of the mountains they traverse, that another and widely distinct formation is found reposing upon them, the features of which either at its extremes or centre are congenerous in character, or but slightly variant. The great uniformity thus manifested in the primitive rocks below, and the sedimentary group above leads us most irresistibly to the conclusion that cotemporaneous origin in each is most distinctly marked.

It must not be inferred from the above that more recent disturbances in these districts have not taken place, for this fact has been before noticed in former reports while speaking of other parts of this range, and the same is also observable in the district under consideration. The principal differences in fossiliferons character among the superior sedimentary deposits of this particular period will be found attributable more to climatal influences, rather than to any apparent differences in relative age; for latitude exerts a much less influence on species than temperature.

The differences in species found at the extremes of this group of sedimentary rocks, are not more marked than are the present living Mollusca now inhabiting the waters of the coast at corresponding points to the west of any portion of the range. At Point Conception we may find some few of the species that are abundant on other parts of the coast north of this locality, but as a general rule it will be found that the large majority of all the species thus met with will differ very widely from those, even one hundred miles farther to the west, and even at less distances. The same rule will apply to the fossil organic remains of this section of the State, and with much more strictness, as we find the evi-idences of an inland sea, whose natural boundaries were such that a higher temperature must have existed than ever that which is so characteristic on the south flank of the San Bernardino Mountains at the present time.

The topography of the country investing its shores was mountainous, and the hills of sufficient altitude to protect it from the harsh winds of the north; an augmentation of temperature was the natural result producing different organisms from those at the base of their western declivities; it is thus that we find in the fossil forms of those districts the species that now exist only in the lower latitudes, and which are marked by the Murex, Typhis, Arca and Cucullea. On these premises are we able to reconcile some of the apparent discrepancies which have arisen, and place the deposits in their proper geological position as regards the periods at which any portion of this group had their origin, and it explains one of those causes of diversity in species among beds evidently contemporaneous.

We have very conclusive evidence before us in this State, that the climatal conditions prevailing during the period in which the Miocene beds were forming was much greater than that prevailing at present, and confined to particular districts, though extending over considerable areas; this arose evidently from the causes above noted. That the shores of the Miocene sea were primitive is proved from the fact that these rocks are imposed directly on the latter, thus demonstrating that its relative age with that of the northern and eastern chain is widely different and far more recent.

Since the period of their deposition other and important changes have taken place, and upon the coast line we find the superior beds of the Tertiary epoch elevated in regular succession above the element in which they originated. How far into the southern interior of the State these groups may extend is yet in an uncertain state, the reports to the present session of Congress from explorations of these districts will probably determine this point.

VOLCANIC ROCKS OF THE COAST MOUNTAINS.

We come now to the consideration of another and different group of rocks, found in connection with the primitive rocks of this district. Their appearance among the latter demands some consideration, as it is to this group that we must look for many of the mutations observable in this part of the State, as causes producing them were undoubtedly instrumental in producing those manifest changes so frequently observed among the sedimentary rocks of these mountains. The volcanic rocks of this part of the coast mountains consist for the most part of intrusions of a scoriaceous and vesicular lava, at other times it becomes much more compact in form, and again exhibiting itself in the form of a light volcanic froth, its colors are various, passing through all the different shades from a yellowish white to a dark iron-brown and black with a semi-metallic lustre. From what opportunities occurred for their investigation I think there can be but little doubt that their intrusion took place, for the most part, during the miocene period, as they appear to have disturbed this group much more sensibly than any other in these particular sections. We are warranted in this conclusion to a considerable extent, by an examination of the equivalents of the southern rocks, found nearly three hundred and fifty miles north, as in the case of the tertiaries situated among the Buttes in the county of Sutter. Here the recent volcanic series is found intruded through the sandstones of these mountains which bear the same fossils as those noted in the preceding section, while at the distance of twenty miles to the north-east the fossiliferous rocks of later date are found entirely undisturbed by any of those particular intrusions.

The scoriaceous lavas of this date are well represented by a dike of similar character passing through the upper portion of El Dorado county, and which is found very often in detached masses on the hills betweeu Georgetown and the Middle Fork of the American River. Specimen No———. In the vicinity of the Tejon Pass and on the desert to the south it forms isolated hills known as "Lost Hills," but in passing into the mountains this characteristic becomes immediately lost; we here find that they enter and cut through nearly all of the primitive rocks, as well as the sedimentary, and where large dikes are formed, changes of structure are easily observable, the original structure being entirely destroyed.

It was not uncommon to find jasperoid rocks in the vicinity of these dikes, where they had intruded through either sandstone or slates. In these cases every trace of former organic existence was dissipated, and were recovered only by traveling often considerable distances.

Among other disturbing agents and differing in general appearance from the lavas, are to be found frequent intrusions of a recent trapean rock (green stone) which is common in many parts of these mountains, but more abundant in the transverse chain to the south; these rocks are found to penetrate the latter to their southern base, and approach nearly to the coast line in some places; they cannot be considered of cotemporaneous origin with the former by any means, as we find them disturbing a distinct and more recent group of sedimentary, as well as the older rocks. There is every reason to believe that they were intruded as late as the miocene period, as they are in contact with rocks as late as those found on the Carmello and near Monterey, a part of which Mr. W. P. Blake considers as quarternary, and they certainly are not earlier than the Post Pliocene.

It is probable that these rocks have been principally instrumental in disturbing nearly all the late tertiaries, as we find the greatest amount of dislocation among these rocks, when found in contact with this intrusive suite.

GEOLOGY OF THE SAN BERNARDINO MOUNTAINS.

The trend of this mountain chain has been stated as being nearly due east and west; this will be found to hold good for the greater part of its entire length; and it now becomes necessary to trace as distinctly as possible the peculiarities of the geological structure of its mountains, in order to draw legitimate deductions respecting the character of adjacent arable districts lying at their base.—The inception of this chain on the west was stated to occur a few miles north of Point Conception, and to follow the above trend nearly or perhaps quite to the Colorado River.

The geographical position of this chain must exert a powerful influence in modifying the productive capabilities of the adjoining lands as well as also the production of diversified species in the neighboring seas, which we find to be the case, the latter having been fully demonstrated within the past year.

These mountains are made up for the most part of the primitive rocks, and consist chiefly of the granitic series; they form by far the most of all the higher ridges and more elevated peaks belonging to the chain.

The primitive series is flanked on the south by coarse-grained sandstones in the county of Santa Barbara, a large proportion of which is fossilliferous, the species not corresponding with those found in the adjoining mountain chains, except perhaps to a very limited degree. A high ridge of this chain lies to the north and east of the town of Santa Barbara, and sends a heavy spur down to the water-line of the coast a few miles from the town ; this spur approaches so closely to the beach that the traveler is compelled to take its sands for his road a distance of twelve or fifteen miles, at the end of which he rounds the base of the spur, after which he finds a more agreeable road until he arrives in Los Angeles. West of Santa Barbara the ridge is more distant from the coast line, but carries the same lithological characteristics to the pass of the Gaviota, and thence on to the Punta Sal, a short distance beyond which the base of the ridge again approaches the water-line, and forms a rugged, bold shore. The Pass del Gaviota is a deep, rocky cañon composed for the most part of large boulders of coarse sandstone, portions of which contain imbedded fossils of marine origin, (the pass furnishes a rough avenue to enter the Santa Inez valley from the coast and is sometimes used to avoid the ascent and descent of the La questa San Inez in traveling to or from San Luis Obispo.) These rocks continue to the hills, forming the south-west border of the valley, and are found also upon its northern and eastern limits. On the right of the road leading to San Luis Obispo and about four miles from the valley of Santa Inez a large bed of Ostrea are found, and immediately to the west among the lower hills, beds of sandstone containing but very few fossils. On ascending the high hill at this place we find the equivalent of the fossil Ostrea perched high upon the summit of this ridge ; the difference between the respective levels of the two beds being near nine hundred feet, and the distance but little short of one mile and a half.

This is but one of many instances that might be mentioned, of similar occurrences among the fossiliferous groups of this State, in which we find parts apparently of the same bed occupying widely different levels and both *in situ*, and it will be necessary for us to account for these apparent discrepancies on some other hypothesis, more consistent with the existing facts, than that of mere uplifting from volcanic action alone, although this agency has undoubtedly performed an important part, in many instances, in elevating parts of these beds in certain localities. It is very evident that the differences in elevation among the tertiaries of the same period, and as we have just seen, parts of the same bed, must be referred to other causes than the one generally assigned in this country, and when we come to consider the species found in different beds, their present habitat will afford us a basis on which to found a theory, at least, that will in some measure account for the discrepancies observed.

The geology of the San Bernardino chain, so far as it has been examined, affords us some instructive examples relative to the disposition and distribution of the fossils found upon its flanks. On both sides of this chain we find the miocene deposits, evidently of the same period, occupying different levels, and the same beds presenting different lines of dip ; in one case a great degree of horizontality prevailing while in another the beds will be highly inclined.

The fossiliferous beds rest mostly upon the primitive rocks. When an exception to this rule occurs it is found to be entirely local, and extending over inconsiderable areas, this may be considered true of the western portion of these mountains, but how far to the east it may extend I am unable at present to determine. The more horizontal beds of these rocks were usually found nearest to the summit of the ridges, those upon the flanks and near the base possessing the highest degree of inclination, and the latter occurring on the southern base to a much greater extent than upon the north. This is easily accounted for in examining the country near the coast-line in this vicinity. At the distance of about forty miles from Santa Barbara on the road thence to Los Angeles, these mountains have suffered to a small extent comparatively speaking, in those disturbances which have been alluded to as occurring in the coast mountains ; this is manifested a few miles east of the rancho Poseto in the county of Los Angeles. At the distance of fifteen miles further in the same direction, and to the northward of the Conejo ranch eight miles, a scoriaceous lava bursts through the base of the mountains, and is found in the second range of hills north of the latter locality ; this continues at intervals until you enter the locality of the lower mountains north of the Pesos River, and was found to continue eastwardly as far as the Semma and Papa, beyond which point it was not observable.

This lava has burst through the primitive rocks and apparently overflowed some few of the sandstones, but the principal effect on the sedimentary rocks has been that of tilting them from their former position. This volcanic action has continued, apparently almost uninterrupted from the eocene or miocene periods down to the present time, though evidently not to so great a degree at present as formerly. This is evidenced by the continued action of a number of small volcanic vents at different distances from the coast, and extending from the county of Luis Obispo to the northern portions of Los Angeles, the most northern of these vents occurs on the south side of San Simeon Bay at a distance of a little more than three miles from the ocean. As you advance south from this point the next in importance is found in the hills fronting the coast, on the rancho of Guadalupe in the northern part of the county of Santa Barbara ; another le s active is found on the ranch of Dr. Robbins about five miles from the town of Santa Barbara. Again at the Rincon twelve miles from the town another of these vents is found. These localities emit light, heat and smoke at different intervals during the year, and some of them are dangerous to approach ; they are undoubtedly closely connected with the phenomena of earthquakes that often affect this district of country, and which apparently have a tendency to expend their principal force in an easterly and southerly dircection. The records of earthquakes that have reached us from this section of country furnish us evidence in support of this supposition.

By referring to the number of shocks which have occurred since 26th of November, 1851, up to July 14th, 1854, in this part of the State, we shall find that they amounted in the aggregate to 31, and of this number 23 have not been felt north of Luis Obispo, their principal force being exerted south into the ocean for a distance of fifty or sixty miles from the land,(as in the case of the marine volcano 25 miles southeast of the Island of San Clemente, observed by Capt. Cropper and officers of the steamer Cortes on the 1st of March, 1853, and now known upon American and English charts as "Cortes Rocks,") and east beyond the Colorado River ; (as in the disturbances which occurred on the desert, at Camp Yuma, and south and west of the Colorado River, on the 26th of November, 1851, the latter "Mud Geyser" being still active as recent accounts from this section of country declare.) The latter shocks were felt in various portions of Los Angeles county, and were particularly severe at the Mission San Gabriel.

The effects of these subterranean agents over so large an extent of the southern part of the State furnish us with the means of judging of what the effect must be on all the superincumbent strata, over which they exercise an immediate influence. The natural effect must be either to raise or depress the country in rather a uniform manner than otherwise, (as great intensity of action is not manifest,) and we have no better means of forming an opinion than by an examination of the sedimentary groups along the coast-line. A careful examination of these rocks will lead us to conclusions that are not only interesting in a scientific view, but also of a practical and economic character, as their true positions must exert a beneficial or injurious effect upon operations that will be presented in the improvement of the soil in this part of the country.

The dip of these rocks is peculiar in some respects, following as they do a direction different from that which might have been anticipated, from any features which the relative positions of the mountains and plains present on their exteriors. We should expect to find a linear dip from the mountains to the sea, where the inclination of the surface is so regular from the former to the latter ; but in place of this we find that the dip of the stratified rocks is the reverse of this, inclining to the east, while those of the mountain ranges directly opposite are found inclining to the west. Were these peculiarities limited to a small area they might be accounted far from local causes acting in such immediate districts, but as we find them extending along the coast-line for a distance of nearly 250 miles, we cannot but regard them as the results of extensive local action, elevating the coast-line.

There is but one other method of accounting for the position of the rocks, (extending as they do from the southern shores of San Simeon to the northern lines of the counties of San Diego and San Bernardino,) which is, that the Islands forming the west coast of the Santa Barbara channel were originally united and formed part of the main land, holding those relations to the plains at the east, that the coast mountains do to the valleys of the Sacramento, Salinas and Santa Clara. There may be some reason for a supposition of this kind, as many of these islands contain quiet elevated lands, and the island of Catalina is in reality an almost unbroken mountain ridge, (with the exception of what is called the Isthmus,) for 30 miles in length, as elevated as many parts of the coast mountains.

Should this position be assumed, we must suppose that an area of plain lands equaling three-fourths of the length of the Sacramento and San Joaquin valleys by about 200 miles in breadth, (for these islands extend through four degrees of longitude and nearly six and one half degrees of latitude) must have been submerged during one or a succession of those turbulent periods that have formerly been in existence on the western portion of this continent, or that a rupture having occurred, the inroads of the seas have gradually denuded these lands, and thus effaced them.

It would be unnecessary to travel thus far into the abyss of time, to reconcile a feature that may present itself, like that under consideration, where we have an agent at hand, in active operation, and adequate to produce all the features which these rocks manifest ; more simple and satisfactory will it be to account for their present dip by the agents above alluded to, than to seek for causes beyond our comprehension and our powers of satisfactory demonstration.

In an economical view these rocks will claim our attention. It has been observed that the rocks on the coast-line for the most part have an easterly dip while those of the mountains to the east dip in an opposite direction. The effect of this is to produce a basin-shaped structure, under the surface of the plains and as this section of the State is strictly agricultural and but little improved, it becomes an inquiry of no little importance to ascertain the probabilities that exist for obtaining water through artesian borings.

The structure of the rocks which form the basis of the plains of Los Angeles are such that we may reasonably suppose that subterranean waters are flowing among the slates and compact sandstones beneath the surface. The character of these rocks should first be understood and also their positions relative to each other.

STRATIFIED ROCKS OF THE SAN BERNARDINO CHAIN, AND PLAINS OF LOS ANGELES.

The stratified rocks of this chain consist of clay, clay-slate, sandstones, conglomerate and bituminous shales ; these comprise those rocks only which have been observed by outcrop along the coast-line and on the flanks of the hills to the east. Commencing at Point Aguilla we find the coast-line presenting high bluffs of a light brown sandstone, interlaminated with thin seams of clay and slates, possessing the same color as the arenaceous rocks in which they are imbedded. As you recede from the sea, the land is found to become depressed to a considerable degree until within a short distance of the base of the mountains, when is is again observed to be more rapidly ascending. This fact will hold good with regard to all the level lands fronting the coast from the above point south and east of San Pedro in the county of Los Angeles..

In traveling over this part of the coast another general and striking feature will arrest the attention, and if the pedestrian has traveled in any of the great valleys of this State, he will be struck with the remarkable coincidence which is manifest along the entire range of that terraced structure found so general throughout the whole extent of those valley sections. The superficial soil of the coast terraces is composed of rich mould of a grayish brown color, this is mixed with a fine sand, and a small quantity of mica with a little clay. The sub-soil is composed of a brown loam mingled with a blue clay and and white sand, the blue clay alone forming a thick bed beneath the whole, and resting upon the rocky structure forming the basis of these plains ; this may be considered the general structure of those lands laying at the base of this chain, but will probably be found locally modified in portions lying adjacent to the hilly regions.

The first suite of indurated rocks beneath this consists of a bed of loose sandstone seven feet in thickness. Below this again is found a bed of light yellow and brown infusorial clays interlaminated with thin seams of sandstone ; four feet below this again are found sandstones of a brown color with thin seams of slate containing much calcareous matter thirteen feet in thickness. A heavy bed of bituminous shale succeeds the latter of about eighty feet in thickness, from which issues in many places large quantities of fluid bitumen, and below this again is found a bed of dark sandy clay above which I have frequently seen waters issue in small quantities and under all the strata above named. The aggregate of their thickness inclusive of the alluvial coverings amounts to 124 feet, and the above description applies more particularly to the country stretching from the coast-line towards the east or the interior. The following tabular arrangement giving the line of dip will serve a better purpose of illustration of the position of these strata :

Front of cliffs at San Pedro.

Alluvium 20 *feet.*
Sandstone infusorial clays, 4 *feet.*
Sandstone and calcareous slate, 13 *feet.*
Bituminous shales, 60 *to* 80 *feet.*
Dark sand and clay.

Sea.

At the bottom of the cliffs and near the sea level the drainage from the strata above is observable, and where water is not seen to issue there are unmistakeable evidences of its presence in the growth of plants requiring much moisture for their propagation even within a few feet of the sea.

From the above section it will be seen that the bituminous slates, from a heavy underlying bed to all the strata above, and though apparently firm and compact in texture they admit the percolation of water, probably between the lines of stratification. The freedom with which water issues from beneath these rocks is best observed about one and a half miles east of the town of San Pedro, on the beach ; here the waters come up through the sands of the beach in the same manner as is observed in small bubbling springs situated in soft wet lands.—From the appearance of these plains it is evident that the dip of the coast strata assumes nearly a level position and reversed inclination at the distance of seven or eight miles east of San Pedro and towards Los Angeles, and that the edges of the reversed dips, are covered by the superincumbent drifts from the primitive mountains west and north of the city and plains.

Among the sandstones, clay and slates of this district, are to be found large quantities of marine mollusca in the fossil state, they are usually found in alternating beds, at times upon the summits of the cliffs among the fine alluvium and soil, as in the high table ridge west of the town of Santa Barbara, or resting in soft and indurated calcareous sandstone in the same vicinity. Again they are found in the firm sub-soil or upon the left shores of the estero from one to three miles northeast of San Pedro, in beds ranging from a few inches to several feet in thickness. The bituminous slates with a few exceptions contain no fossils of marine origin; there are occasionally impressions of fucoids to be met with, on the surfaces of the lamina composing the group, and although other organic forms are almost entirely absent this fact is sufficient to prove that they have had their origin beneath the waters of the ocean.

The great extent of territory which these shales cover is rather a novel as well as an interesting feature in the geology of this State. They manifest themselves first in quantities which entitle them to consideration as a distinct formation, in the upper parts of the counties of Santa Clara and Santa Cruz, extending into the county of Monterey ; the district is small however when compared with that which we find further south, and appears continuous for a long distance. The southern group is found to commence in the county of Luis Obispo and traverses the whole of the west portion of that county and extends through the entire length of the counties of Santa Barbara and Los Angeles, evidently underlying the greater part of their territory from the mountains to the sea. To what extent these slates may pass beneath the surface of the ocean is of course unknown, but there are good reasons for the supposition that the distance is considerable, from the fact, that during storms when a heavy swell is occasioned there are large quantities of these rocks brought up and distributed upon the shore, in fragmentary masses. Attached to these fragments often are mollusca and marine plants belonging to deep water and differing widely from the shoaler littoral deposits which are also found in great numbers. Another evidence that this formation extends for some distance beyond the coast-line seaward is the fact of the emission of liquid bitumen and its appearance on the surface of the ocean miles distant from the main land. It might be argued that the currents of the ocean would have the effect to transport this material to considerable distances from this shore, and this is undoubtedly true to a great extent ; but in forming this conclusion we should remember that the greatest amount of force is manifested during the setting of the flood tides, and that all floating materials are soon landed on our shores from great distances at sea. I have been informed by persons engaged upon the coast that this bitumen so often seen upon the waters south of Point Conception has often been noticed west of Catalina, and that they have sailed through large quantities of it beyond the Island, while the waters in the channel have been for days free from its presence. Such facts would lead us to infer that these shales extend probably as far to the west, forming the bed of the ocean, as they are known to extend to the east under the surface of the extensive plains of Los Angeles, the distance in the one case being about equal to that in the other.

The remaining sedimentary rocks of these mountains consist of sandstones and slates, the former composing by far the greater bulk thereof. The sandstones contain the larger proportion of the fossils found in these districts, and lie in all cases superior in position, to the bituminous slates. In the vicinity of Santa Barbara they form a large portion of the covering on the flanks of the mountains extending to the summit of the southern ridge, their aspect is repulsive and barren, vegetation being almost entirely absent, except in the deep, precipitous ravines between the hills ; the foot-hills below are made up of large boulders having evident marks of abrasion by water, and coarse gravely drift derived from the same sources. On these lower hills the oak and indigenous growths flourish, although the soils are harsh and coarse, as they naturally must be from the sources from which they have been derived. This is but another evidence of those powerful fertilizing agents that are so lavishly distributed through our soils compelling the otherwise sterile hills to produce abundance for flock and herd.

One of the causes of this fertility is found in an examination of the fossiliferous rocks, it is evident from their appearance that the animals lived and died on the spots where their remains are now buried, they do not present the appearance of a littoral deposit, there is not that variety in species which we should look for under those circumstances, or those broken, rolled and fragmentary remnants usually found in the latter. Whenever a bed of fossils is met with in this section of the country among the indurated sandstones, either the shells of the bivalves are entire or casts of their interior exist ; when the latter occurs is is not unfrequent to find upon the mould of the shell a true imprint of the animal that inhabited it. I have seen the palial impression of a Venus with its sinus and muscular cicatrices nearly as perfect as though a cast had been taken from a recent animal.

The rocks found in these mountains and at their base contain marine animals, inhabitants of both deep and shallow water ; with those also that live upon the verge of highest waters ; this fact would indicate that gradual elevation has been exerted over a considerable area in this part of the State, as forces are still in activity that are commensurate with the production of the features manifested, but it should be remembered that the area thus affected is not applicable to the entire suite of fossiliferous rocks incident to these and the ranges of the coast mountains.

We come now to consider another group of sedimentary rocks, skirting the base and foot-hills of these mountains and confined to the county of Los Angeles and northern part of San Bernardino. These were traced from the mountains lying between Arroya Peros and Rio Santa Clara on the west to a point east of Los Angeles as far as the Arnaci and San Jose ranches lying to the east and south of the Monte.

To convey a clear idea of the position of these rocks, we will commence to the north of the city of Los Angeles, and at the base of the higher hills, or where the sandstones and slates are found in direct contact with the primitive and other igneous rocks.

As before observed the principal rocks of this chain are granitic. The first rocks of sedimentary origin met with and in contact with the granite is a bed of arenaceous slates. These so far as I was able to form an opinion appeared to be about thirty-five feet in thickness and dipping south fifty-five degrees.—Beyond this, coarse sandstones were met with having the same dip interlaminated with their beds of fine brownish clays. These rocks apparently have been but little changed by subsequent volcanic intrusions and contained many fossils, all of which were marine consisting mostly of the cardium and allied species. Advancing south we now approach the first foot-hills of the valley and such as are found within one mile of the town ; here a change of character specifically different from any of the aqueous rocks to the east, is to be observed. This latter suite constitutes the only material change of consequence, among the tertiaries of the San Bernardino chain.

By way of distinction these rocks will be denominated the infusorial group, to separate them from the earlier and later rocks of this era, and as there will be occasion to speak of them as occupying the position of distinct groups, belonging to one or more of the periods. These rocks are made up of beds of sandstone 100 feet, having a buffy yellow color and which pass almost imperceptibly into a sandy clay-slate, and thence into a fine, whitish, soft and light chalk-like deposit 16 feet, perfectly stratified and often receiving the name of *chalk clay* ; this is again covered by a light fossil slate 28 feet, containing fragments of small and as yet undetermined species of animals ; the dip of these rocks is very uniform, maintaining nearly a vertical position or but slightly departing from it. On these rests the drift 30 feet, which in hills fronting the plains forms an imperfect coarse conglomerate, made up of the sienites, granites, trap, indurated and metamorphic sandstones. All this suite have been disturbed by recent intrusions of trap rocks and as in the case of the buffy sandstone half a mile north of the city, the transition near the points of contact is such that the rock will fracture transversely to the lines of stratification as readily as in any other direction, the fracture is always conchoidal, breaking with sharp well-defined edges, and the stones when broken having a sharp sound much resembling the dolorites. The high inclinations of these beds are due undoubtedly to the later intrusions of the igneous rocks, and they must have received their dip anterior to the deposit of the coarse drift, as the latter appears to rest unconformably upon their upturned edges. This is the fact with respect to this entire group generally, whether found in the county under consideration, or in any other part of the State, in which it has been observed.

The artesian boring in the city of Los Angeles has developed to a certain extent the character of the plain beneath the surface to a depth of 400 feet ; the position of the strata through which they have descended is as follows (as near as could be learned) : a heavy blue clay for 30 feet, followed by a bed of coarse gravel, (drift) 18 feet ; clay, sand and gravel blue, 16 feet. These contain small marine shells followed by a thick deposit of tough, blue clay, 150 feet, (containing fossils,) the character of the earth below this point has not as yet been ascertained, nor have they yet struck the superior strata of the sedimentary rocks a few yards to the north of the well.

EXTENT OF THE INFUSORIAL GROUP.

This group of rocks was found as far east as the foot-hills of Sierra San Jose, and continue along the southern base of this part of the chain to the south of the hills on the banks of the Arroyo Peros ; they were also observed among the hills near the Conejo and La Poseto ranches. On the east bank of the Santa Clara River a small deposit was found at an elevation higher by nearly forty feet, than at any point east of this place ; after crossing the Santa Clara River it is not again seen until near the Mission San Buenaventura ; here it again assumes its usual position as regard altitude and continues thus to the Mission of Santa Barbara. After leaving this locality it is met with as a thick bed capping a low ridge in the vicinity of the ranch Coral, and also between the latter place and Paso del Gaviote. In crossing Point Conception the coast assumes a more northerly trend, and the infusorial deposits follow the same line and make their appearance at La Espada in the county of San Luis Obispo, continuing along the line of the same direction nearly to the Bay of San Simeon. Beyond this point I possess no information of its existence or position, until reaching the Bay of Carmel, when it is found nearly continuous to the heavy deposits three miles from the city of Monterey.

In the County of Santa Cruz these rocks are again met with to the right of the road crossing the Sousal, and also on the north bank of the Pajaro River near the junction of the Pescadero. They are invested by sandstones and slates in nearly every instance in which they are found, and their uniformity in altitude is one remarkable feature attending the entire group. An observance of each and all of their main characteristics may be noticed by one locality, viz: near the town of Monterey, and what is observable here in this particular, will be found a true index to all the rest of the group above alluded to, in any portion of the State. It will be seen from what has been said respecting these rocks that they are general in distribution within the limits of certain districts, holding as they do an average height above the sea of about 330 feet, varying at no place so far as known, over 22 feet from this line; the linear extent of the group exceeds 461 miles. Their constancy with respect to the tertiary, *miocene*, (or perhaps later periods) would induce me to apply a name to this group that shall at once identify it as a marked feature of that portion of the tertiary era to which it may ultimately prove to belong. Its uniformity of character in every particular, connected with its extent and associations, fix it as a guiding mark that will serve to separate the group to which it belongs from those that preceded or followed it; I therefore propose the simple term of the *Infusorial period*, belonging to the tertiaries of California.

As before observed, the regularity of position and altitude of these deposits leads us irresistibly to conclusions respecting the elevation or depression of this portion of the Pacific coast. The evidences which they furnish are to the effect that since the emergence, there has been but little of those violent disturbances which agitated the country prior to that time, and that the recession of the sea from those points has been gradual; an idea which is borne out most fully by corroborating evidences in other and more distant parts of the State.

PLAINS OF LOS ANGELES.

In the preceding pages we have given a brief summary of the general characteristics relating to the geology of a portion of the coast and San Bernardino mountains. We shall now proceed to examine the probable positions which the sedimentary rocks of the latter chain occupy beneath the surface of these plains. From what has been said of the positions of the rocks among the foot-hills skirting the northern edge of the valleys, it will be seen that it is with the latter or infusorial group that we have to work in forming conclusions respecting the structure of these plains below the surface. The great extent of these plains requires more than a passing notice, and their value can only be appreciated by a careful examination of all their characteristics both below as well as on the surface. We cannot judge of the value of a district of country by a superficial glance at its exterior features, and nothing but a searching and discriminating view of its hidden resources can give us an adequate idea of either its present worth or its prospective facilities. This remark will apply with great force equally to the Plains of Los Angeles, the Valley of the Sacramento and the lands bordering it, as well as to the broad district embraced in the valleys of the San Joaquin and Salinas Rivers, especially when we come to consider their agricultural fitness, or their application to any pastural purposes. It is needless here to dilate upon the importance of a knowledge of the geological structure and mineral affinities which often influence the virtues of soils rendering them more or less adapted to certain purposes of an agricultural character. Great error might doubtless arise in many instances were we to attempt a judgment of some of the districts alluded to, without such knowledge; for instance, a stranger passing along portions of the Plains of Los Angeles in our long dry summer season would find the beds of streams dry, the herbage and vegetable growths seared, the earth parched and cracked open as it lies baked in the burning heat of the sun, the timber sparce and of a gnarled and almost useless description; upon these external appearances he would conclude with great error that he had found a region unfit for the habitation of man, when in truth, such is the sub-structure of these plains that their soils are unsurpassed in fertility by any others in the United States, as the returning seasons of rain would prove to the same traveler, when he should find himself almost buried in the luxuriant growth of the grasses, wild grain and herbs of these districts. And it ought to be observed that vast portions of these lands may be irrigated, so that even in the summer they can be brought within the profitable control of the husbandman.

These portions of the country which are not found to yield the precious metal, or any other useful mineral products to any great extent, can be interesting in an economical point of view only with reference to their means of agricultural occupation. It will be with the purpose of precluding erroneous conclusions from being drawn out of any remarks we may make in this connection, that we propose at this time to consider the geological structure of these sections in the bearing it may have upon the prospective interests alluded to, interests which we think are destined sooner or later to test all the capabilities of these valleys for agricultural and horticultural production.

The first question in importance to be settled on this subject is the one of irrigation; what are the means to be used in order to bring within the reach of the farmer a supply of water sufficient for the thirst of the land and for the necessary wants of stock during the long dry seasons of our climate? Two methods have been proposed to which we will address ourselves at this time. The one is that of *tanks* which may be found amply sufficient for present purposes in supplying the lands now occupied with water enough for the farmer and horticulturist. The other method is by canalling, for the purpose of drawing water from the rivers out upon the plains in sufficient quantities to supply their entire surface with the essential element of cultivation of the soil.

The tanking system has been used for many years in India and the oriental nations, and has proved successful beyond the expectations of its originators. The positions of the hills forming the northern boundary of the plains of Los Angeles are admirably situated for the accumulation of water by this means, and the expense of constructing the dams necessary for its retention would be comparatively small, when considered in connection with the advantages to arise from their erection. There are many natural reservoirs skirting the line of these plains, which, if obstructed by small dams, would furnish water sufficient for all ordinary purposes of cultivation. Immediately to the north of the city there is an opportunity afforded for accumulating a body of water nearly one mile in length, with a breadth of one fourth of a mile, and a depth of from 20 to 30 feet, by the construction of a single dam across the entrance of the ravine. This lagoon would be filled and kept supplied for at least six months of the year from the rains which annually fall, and from which several remitting springs in this vicinity are now supplied. This is given as an instance, but only one of many of a similar character which may be found to prove that from the constructions of these hills, nature seems to have designed a plan which would force itself upon the mind of man for meeting the exigencies of our long dry seasons, and in this way inviting him to the enjoyment and possession of her rich fields. It is a practicable and feasible plan which would at once strike the eye of a hydraulist, and which has no place in the theories of visionary speculation.

The other method alluded to, and which we esteem one which promises to be advantageous, if applied in this region, is the construction of a canal of about three miles in length, which will divert a portion of the water of the Los Angeles River from its natural channel, and connecting it with the semi-natural reservoir spoken of, so as to keep it constantly supplied with an abundance of water. An objection might at first view be interposed by the public of this locality to this latter project, on the ground that it would interfere with the supply of water for irrigation which is already used in considerable quantities for the lands already in cultivation, yet a little reflection will make it convincing that the lands now irrigated by the use of this stream would not necessarily suffer from any scarcity of water, as its present wastage is sufficient to supply irrigation to at least double the quantity of ground to that which now occupies the area of irrigated cultivation in that vicinity. This plan would present another advantage in the fact that the water thus diverted would be retained at a much higher level than that occupied by the point at which it is at present taken from the stream for its distribution along the lower bottom lands bordering the river. This would expand the area of distribution, while the drainage passing through the higher terraces to the north and west, would again find its level on the *sanjons* now used for conducting it through the lower bottoms. This river discharges a greater quantity of water than that flowing in Bear River during the dry season, which is entirely lost in the loose sands a few miles west of the City. Here sinks beyond the control of the farmer a sufficient supply of water to irrigate successfully a large surface of the richest soil, if it were saved by the plan already proposed, which might redeem these lands from their parched and arid condition, which in the summer months now prevents the growth even of their indigenous herbage and grass, and entirely unfits them for agriculture. We have sought in vain for any valid objection to this proposed use of the water of the stream alluded to for agricultural purposes on the plains beyond the City, as it would be impossible for the waters to escape to any great extent either by evaporation or sinking; which, as it is at present, is the means of robbing the lower bottoms themselves of a sufficiency of water for needful purposes, and leaving the higher terraces entirelv parched. The sub-soil of these higher lands, as already observed, is composed of a very tenacious blue clay from 30 to 40 feet in thickness, and as impervious to the percolation of water as a solid mass of granite. The water on reaching the clay will immediately pass into the bottoms through the same avenues which now convey it, and it will have performed its double office of irrigating both the higher and lower portions of the impending surface. A proper and judicious distribution of this stream will, I am convinced, supply abundantly more than three times the area now under cultivation in the immediate vicinity of this City, while the attendant expense would be comparatively inconsiderable.

ARTESIAN BORING.

We come now to another means of obtaining water in addition to those mentioned, and as the subject is one of vital importance to the growth and settlement of large portions of our State, so far as regards its heavier agricultural productions, I shall endeavor to elucidate as far as possible, the principles involved in the question, and also the probabilities of success in undertaking the enterprise. This of necessity brings us to a detailed examination of the structure of the plain from one extremity to the other, and which will be followed in as concise a manner as possible.

The City of Los Angeles is situated twenty miles from San Pedro to the north, and has an altitude of 253 feet above tide level, giving an ascending grade of a little more than twelve feet per mile. The level surface of this plain alone will afford no correct idea of its substrata, either in their positions or direction and degree of inclinations, but may serve in some measure as a guide to direct us in making an appropriate estimate of the probable depths to which they descend, and consequently, the probable depth that will be required to sink these wells in order to tap a perennial stream or fountain; the ultimate depth of boring the artesian wells will depend in part on the thickness and dip of the sedimentary rocks beneath, should it become necessary to pass through them. The stratified rocks composed of sandstones, slates of different kinds, and clays, will first of all demand our consideration, as the position they maintain below the surface, will necessarily affect any process which may be adopted for obtaining water, and this remark will hold good whether the source of supply shall rest either above them, among them, or below them all upon the primitive rocks upon which they stand.

In the preceding pages, when speaking of San Pedro, it was observed, that the rocks which form that point, and also Point Fermen were stratified sedimentary rocks, composed of sandstones, slates, and infusorial deposits between two beds of sandstone, and the whole of these, are on the top of bituminous shales, the bed of which rests conformably upon a bed of very dark arenaceous clay, above which or rather between which and the bituminous shale just mentioned, fresh water is constantly flowing and issuing out. At a much higher level and at a distance of twenty miles to the north we find the same group existing, and each bed holding its precise relative position, which it is found occupying at the coast, with this exception, that the bituminous shales is no where seen to crop out in any of the hills lying at the base of the mountains. The absence of this out-crop, however, is no evidence that the bituminous shales does not exist there, but on the contrary we have strong proof of their continuation and underlying position here as on the coast, from the fact that the principal springs of bitumen are found among the lower hills in the immediate vicinity of the outcrops of their associated rocks as found near the sea. As the organic forms in each bed of the rocks are precisely identical, we have good reason to believe that the rocks on the coast line are continuously from that line to the mountains inclusive, and as a consequence form the basis of all the superficial deposits of the intervening plains. The thickness of these deposits, as determined by their outcrop amounts to nearly 200 feet, and it is hardly to be supposed that they much exceed that depth.

The dip of these beds on the south base of the mountains being much higher than those at San Pedro, it is probable that they would not be reached by boring so soon as in any other part of the valley. The dip of the stratified rocks near the edge of the plains, and at the point selected for sinking an artesian well, ranges from 48 to 53 degrees, and it will be probably impossible to reach them below the surface at that point at any distance less than 375 feet, presuming that their dip is the same, or nearly so at the distance of 1000 feet from the outcrop. It is more than probable that the inclination of the strata decreases as the distance from hills increases, and that at some point a little more than midway between the City and San Pedro these rocks have a horizontal position. This must certainly be the case or we shall be forced to the supposition that the equivalent group on the coast to the south lie unconformably, and that the two overlap each other. This would be contrary to all reasoning upon similar cases, as there are no evidences that there has been any volcanic disturbances which could have produced a false position of such a character.

The opposite inclination of the two extremes of the group favor the above presumption, and if this be true, then the superficial deposits upon the beds must be much thinner than at that point where the rocks assume a horizontal line. From the inclination of the surface of the plain from both margins, towards its centre, we should be induced to suppose that near the points of horizontal position of the basis of the plains, not only would be found a corresponding depression upon the surface, but also other attendant circumstances which might have lead us to infer that if water was percolating even among the superficial strata of clays and other earthy semi indurated masses, resting upon the rocks above referred to. Such should be the case if water exists among any of these strata, and this is the fact, thus furnishing the best evidence which we can obtain on this and similar points. We find the water leaking out of the lamina of the deep clayey sub-soil in quantities sufficient to form small lagunas and perennial springs for several miles, and at a point not less than 200 feet below the level of the City of Los Angeles and twelve miles to the south from the town. It is to be greatly doubted that anything approaching a constant supply will be found in any of the superficial material resting upon the rocks, notwithstanding wells of this character may be sufficient for the supply of local demands, and although they may rise above the surface at first, still it will ultimately be found that mechanical means will have to be employed in obtaining water in sufficient quantities for the supply of agricultural purposes.

It will most probably be necessary to pierce the stratified rocks before a sufficient amount of water will be obtained for the ample irrigation of farming lands, and to accomplish this will require heavy expenses to be laid out, for labor at its present prices in this country; yet I think there is but little risk as to obtaining an abundant supply, if these rocks are perforated. There is one condition, however, that should be mentioned, which is that in the event of striking a bed of loose sand or gravel beneath the heavy clay bed, there is almost a certainty of obtaining an abundant supply of water, without descending below that point. I have seen but one or two instances which would lead us to suppose that such a presence is to be found beneath the clay, and above the rocks, and they were not of sufficient extent to found an opinion upon, and it may be reasonably doubted that such a bed of sand and gravel would be met with; the evidences, I think, are against it.

The thickness of the superficial deposits and stratified rocks, beneath the surface, so far as my opportunities of examination extended, are as follows: (The thickness of the rocks is from my own measurement, and the thickness of their superficial covering is from the results of the boring of an Artesian well near the town of Los Angeles.) Commencing with the alluvium and descending:

Alluvium,	6	feet.
Blue clay,	30	"
Bed of drift gravel,	22	"
Arenaceous clay,	16	"
Tenaceous blue clay,	160	"
Coarse sandstone,	35	"
Infusorial sandstone	100	"
" Clay,	16	"
Fossil Clay slate,	30	"
Total,	415	feet.

This is the smallest depth at which water will probably be found, except in the contingency above named, and it is more than probable that a greater depth will be necessary, but of this we have no direct evidence. A careful examination of each stratum belonging to the entire group of rocks, so far as the same are uncovered on both sides of the plains, did not enable me to discover any point through which water would probably percolate and issue, except at the points named, to wit: immediately below the bituminous shales, and we cannot reasonably expect to find it short of that point in boring on any part of these plains. I speak thus positively, for the purpose of preventing, if possible, any useless expenditure of money, in undertakings of this character, when they have not for their object the penetrating of the whole, or a part, at least, of the rocks which underlie the basin; as from the evidences before us, there are no grounds for the supposition that a permanent supply would be obtained short of that depth.

It may be expected that some additional reason should be given, besides what has already been advanced, why water might be expected to flow unremittingly from the depths designated. In order to meet such expectation, I will state that an examination of the accompanying diagram exhibits the fact that the Los Angeles River flows for miles at an altitude much greater than that occupied by any of the sedimentary rocks which have passed under our consideration, and that for several miles its course is along the line of strike and parallel with the dip of the series belonging to this group, and crosses those lines only when it approximates the edges of the plains, and where the drift and alluvium covers the whole.

Again, the sources of the river furnish a much greater supply than is found to reach the valley sections, the proportion arriving at the latter point comprising about one-third of the quantity supplied at the sources. We cannot account for so great a loss in volume on any other ground than that of absorption, and we are not left to presumption in this case, but have the best of evidence that such is the fact, for in observing the stream as it issues from the primitive rocks, even but a few miles from the City we find that its volume is much heavier than at any point below, after reaching the sedimentary rocks. This is found to be the case with several of the streams in the northern part of the State, and is particularly observable in the Yuba, West Feather and Cosumnes Rivers, during medium stages of water. From Foster's Bar to the junction of the Middle Yuba, there is a greater volume of water than at any point below the junction, while in the vicinity of Marysville the volume is nearly fifty per cent less than it is thirty-five miles above, notwithstanding that the main river receives all of its principal tributaries from the Middle Yuba down to its confluence with Feather River. The same condition of things is observable on the Cosumnes below Cook's Bar and the Sink, and on the West Feather River from just above Rich Gulch, and the same features are also distinctly marked on the Main Feather as far down as the White Rock. The cause of this irregularity in the volumes of our principal mountain streams seems to us quite apparent. These streams which we have named, as well as others, rapidly approach the stratified rocks as they descend towards the valleys. These rocks are nearly all open and of a loose texture; the streams, like the Los Angeles River, often flowing for miles along the line of strike belonging to the groups, and crossing the same only when they approach the alluvial deposits, either among the lower hills or at the edge of the plains. These facts being established, we then have another reason for the presumption that water will be obtained by the means suggested, and the evidence is strong in support of the presumption. The disappearance of heavy springs among the stratified rocks near the surface, indicates that the waters which pass beneath them are probably discharged into the sea, as these rocks carry a southerly dip far enough for this purpose. One other fact is worthy of notice, and furnishes stronger evidence of the feasibility and probably successful termination of operations by boring than perhaps any which has yet been adduced. It is this: on the high hill to the west of San Pedro, about four miles distant from the shore, and at the altitude of nearly one thousand feet, the out-crop of the sandstones belonging to A. in the diagram are observed, being interlaminated with their seams of slate. The dip of these rocks on the hill is nearly vertical, the inclination being to the north, corresponding in direction with those on the shore. From among these rocks and at this height there is a perpetual spring gushing out, which furnishes water for a large number of cattle which graze upon this mountain, while no particle of water is to be found during the dry season for a long distance around; there are no sources from which this water can be derived in any part of this hill, and none such corresponding in altitude within thirty-five miles of the spring mentioned. Upon the flanks of the mountains on the other side of the valley at about the last mentioned distance, the identical rocks from which these waters emerge, are found at sufficient altitude to furnish such a spring; the same rocks are also found twelve to sixteen miles north and east of Los Angeles, where the river flows parallel with their course, and upon them for nearly three miles. At the distance of four or five miles further west along the coast, at a locality known as the "*Cave*," there is also, I am informed, a constant stream flowing out among the stratified rocks, which was formerly resorted to as a watering place by vessels, and by the seal and otter hunters.

These facts are sufficient to induce the belief that Artesian borings will succeed on these plains provided they are carried to sufficient depth, and also that failure is as certain if due discrimination be not used in conducting these operations. When we consider the amount of expense which will be required in order to attain this object, and the hazard of failure to individual enterprise, we think it would not be unwise for a County like Los Angeles herself to set an example as a County, by securing the idea in the minds of the people, and exhibiting to them the proof that the work can be made successful by proper management, especially when we know how deeply the failure or success of such means for obtaining water will affect the future growth and welfare of the plain country. After a successful operation of this kind by the County, individual enterprise would readily embark in similar works wherever they could be made valuable.

The accompanying diagram will elucidate more clearly the position of the rocks included within the range of country under consideration. The section is projected on a direct line from San Pedro to the City of Los Angeles, and is intended to give a suppositious position to the rocks beneath the surface, as deduced from an examination of their out-crops for several miles along the borders of the plains on both sides.

The capital letters, A. B. C. D. are levels at which the Los Angeles River flows, at different points north of the City.

A. being 14 miles,
B. " 11 "
C. " 5 "
D. " 2 "
E. Station staff at San Pedro.
F. Old Fort near the City.
G. The City.
H. A spring on the hill back of San Pedro.
I. San Pedro.
J. Banningville.
K. Outliers of gravel drift on the hills back of the City.

The numerical figures represent the rocks and their coverings and outcrops.

Nos. 1. 1. 1. Infusorial sandstone 322 feet above tide.
" 2. 2. Infusorial clay.
" 3. 3. Clay slate.
" 4. Calcareous Shales.
" 5. Bituminous Shales.
" 6. Bed of gravel drift between beds of clay.
" 7. Blue clay above.
" 8. Blue clay and sand below gravel.
" 9. Heavy bed of blue clay containing marine fossils.
" 10. 10. Probable position of stratified rocks beneath the surface.

In the diagram at the point marked I., we find a constant but small supply of water; this supply issues from between the beds 7. and 8. and follows the course of the deposit of sandy gravel drift marked 6. in which water is usually found. On the summit of the lower hills marked K. K. is found this drift in sites, forming outlines of a larger bed which formerly existed, and which has been removed by denudation, and deposited farther down upon the plains as in the case before us.

At no very distant day the Los Angeles River has flowed to the north of the City, and was undoubtedly the principal agent, concerned in the removal of the drift beds. Very unmistakable evidences are observable of changes of this character having taken place several successive times in years past, and recently. It has changed its course a distance of three or four miles. It is now producing the same effects upon the high terrace to the southeast of the City, as it has already done farther to the northwest.

SOILS AND PRODUCTIONS OF LOS ANGELES

The soil and productive capacities of these plains will now be considered; for in these alone consist the present and prospective value of these lands. Referring back to the rocks composing the mountain chain, which forms the northern borders of these valleys, we can readily infer what would be the constituents and general features presented in the coverings of the plains. The diagram exhibits two distant terraces, the lower one occupying a little more than one-third of the transverse extent of the plain, the upper terrace holding a much greater inclination from the borders towards the centre, and the whole having an average grade of about 13 feet per mile from datum to the level of the City. On examining the hills either at San Pedro or between the City and the mountains, we shall find most distinct outlines of other terraces rising above the levels of these plains, to the number of two or three, beyond which this characteristic is not clearly defined.

These terraces play an important part in modifying the characters of the soils upon the plains adjacent, and as a consequence affect the productive capacities of the lands as far as their direct influence extends. A peculiar and striking feature found in the soils of these plains is, that even to the base of the mountains or their foot-hills the components of the earth are found as finely comminuted as at any point near the centre, or upon the lower alluvial bottom in the vicinity of the settlement known as Banningville.

Along the northern base of the low mountains of San Pedro the same features occur, and as far toward either extremity of the plains as an opportunity offered for an examination, this peculiarity presented itself. From the great preponderance of the primitive rocks (and those mostly granite,) in the mountains, and from which the soils of these plains have been derived, we should *a priori* have been led to suppose that a coarse, harsh and almost worthless range of country lying at their base would have been found, but quite the reverse of this is true, and a soil both soft and mellow covering these plains is found in its stead. It is very doubtful if a soil more fertile, and capable of greater production, is to be found anywhere along our Pacific coast south of the Isthmus of Darien, independent of the influences of climate. The depth to which this soil extends below the surface ranges from 18 inches to six feet—the average depth is about 3 feet; the color is usually of a dark grayish brown when dry, and on close examination it is found to contain a great quantity of decomposed vegetable matter, consisting of the dead roots and stalks of its indigenous productions. In many places it would remind a person of some of the rich moulds formed in small quantities in the ravines of hills producing luxuriant vegetation. On the lower bottoms this soil is mixed with a fine micaceous sand which renders those districts highly fertile. It is upon these lands that the major part of the extensive grape crops of this County are produced; and a mere inspection of the ground alone, when free from moisture and unconnected with the crops it is capable of producing would be very apt to be considered unproductive and worthless. On these lower bottoms and beneath the soil there is found a bed of stiff blue clay; (7. Diagram) when the waters are turned off from this earth, and the sun is permitted to dry the surface, a white efflorescence is often observable over considerable areas. This efflorescence consists of the salts of potash and soda, the nitrate of potash forming an important article in the crystalization. In other parts of these bottoms the principal salts thus found upon the surface are composed mostly of the carbonates of potash and soda, and much smaller proportions of nitre. It is a singular fact that on many of those lands covered by these salts in such quantities as to give the earth a white appearance, plants and vegetables requiring much nitrogen for their healthy propagation are found to flourish far better than upon many other apparently more favorable portions of these valleys.

The active fertilizing agents contained in the lands of these plains have been derived from two sources; first the alkaline salts from the decomposition of the primitive rocks, (the granite furnishing the soda and potash, from the segregation and subsequent destruction of the felspar contained in them;) secondly, the lime and nitrous constituents have been derived from the marine fossiliferous rocks resting upon the former; with the destruction of mammalia which were abundant in the earlier periods of the Miocene tertiary. The greatest proportion of the latter salts, however, were probably derived from the marine Mollusca which undoubtedly lived and died in the materials in which we now find remaining imbedded, and as these remains constitute large beds of rocks at the present time, we should find them fully adequate to produce the fertilizing salts above mentioned.

The great amount of vegetable matter intimately commingled with these salts and earths upon the surface of these plains, it will be seen would render this district of country capable of an abundant production, and whether applied to agriculture or horticulture, or to its present grazing uses, it will still be found capable of supplying even in its unimproved natural condition a sufficient sustenance for ten times its present numbers of flocks and herds. A very small amount of artificial aid in the improvement of these plains would add greatly to the richness and expansion of the pasture grounds, and would prevent the present necessity for the wide roaming now so prevalent among the stock which is placed to graze in this broad unfenced surface of country. One example of the rare capacity of these soils is exhibited, both in the higher and lower plains of this and the adjoining counties, in the luxuriance of the growth of the native productions. Among the indigenous growths, is a plant known as the "*Burr Clover*," which spreads over the valleys and up the sides of the hills; this plant produces a great quantity of seeds in its small "burrs," which, as the stalk dies, is distributed upon the ground, at times covering it to the depth of a half inch. (Allusion was made to this plant in my report of last year when speaking of the productions of the Salinas Valley.) The cattle and horses find in this seed a nutritious food upon which they subsist during the dry season, and of which they seem to be remarkably fond, whilst their fine condition after living upon this alone, attests the cereal richness of its qualities. The traveler unacquainted with the ground over which he is passing would be both puzzled and surprised at the fine appearance which the herds present, especially when he is informed that the apparent desert upon which he sees them is all they have upon which to feed; for in passing over a district of country on which not a blade of grass or any other edible plant is visible for miles, and the surface of the ground has more the appearance of a burned prairie than any other, being of a dark ashy gray color, no stranger to the nature of our soils and seasons would for a moment suppose the land could be ever applied to any valuable use or cultivation. The color of the surface is that of the seed mentioned, which, as before stated, covers the ground in great quanties. This fact alone would be a sufficient evidence of the fertility of these plains did no other exist to which we might refer, and it is to be much doubted if any other part of the world possesses a degree of fertility to that extent that the seeds of its indigenous productions alone scattered broadcast upon the plains are capable of supplying with nutriment over 100,000 head of neat cattle and 20,000 head of horses, with sufficient to keep them in the best marketable condition for months without resort to other subsistence. The stock of these plains at the present time, is not over twenty-five per centum of that which they probably maintained some six or ten years since, and for which there was always an abundant supply. Those only who are familiar with this part of the State can fully appreciate its productive capacities, and they can be realized only by visiting and subjecting its natural resources to the strictest scrutiny; this done, and I have no fears but the above remarks will be fully endorsed by all who make the investigation.

The culture of grain upon these plains warrants the most sanguine anticipations, and so far as the experiment has been made, the yield has been largely above the average crops of the more northern districts, and should success attend the experiment of the introduction of water for irrigation, full thirty per cent of these plains may be applied to the rearing of cereal crops, and leave a large margin still for pasturage.

The advantages of water near or on the surface in this section of country is manifested in the experimental crops of last year on the "*Monte*" a few miles east of the City. The corn crop of this locality, comprising about 1800 acres, was immense in its yield as in the size of its stalks; a large proportion of it was planted late in the season, but notwithstanding this, the ear was full-formed and well filled in the month of October, and the crop still in the silk. It was no uncommon circumstance to find six full ears on one stalk, and the number of four was much more frequent than any figure below it. I think that it may be safely estimated that the *Monte* lands will yield an average crop of sixty bushels to the acre.

These facts are noticed more particularly as corroborative of what has been advanced respecting the fertility of this line of plains, and with evidences such as have been adduced on so grand a scale as a mere experiment, there seems but little room left to doubt the high qualities for production which these lands will exhibit, should they be tilled with judicious management.

We come now to the consideration of the exotic productions of this part of the State. The position of the mountain chains which separate this part of the State from the districts north of it, their trend and altitude are productive of far different climatal conditions from those noticable in any other portion of the country. After passing Point Conception upon the coast, or crossing the last ridge of the San Bernardino chain, in traveling from the north, the traveler is ushered into a widely different climate from any with which he has before become acquainted. The atmosphere is entirely divested of that harsh coldness which is found on the seaboard and to some distance in the interior, and at the same time is unaccompanied with that scorching heat incident to the plains and valleys situated among or lying to the east of the ridges comprising the coast mountains or their spurs and ranges. From these circumstances it will be seen that a different class of products would naturally be found, and that exotics of a more southern nativity would flourish while their destruction would be almost certain beyond this chain. First among the exotic growths of Los Angeles, is the sweet orange; this tree is found to flourish well without any artificial protection from the atmosphere, and attains the height of forty feet, and in some cases even more than this; its fruit is fully equal to any imported article which has yet arrived in this country. The tree produces bountifully, and is in fruit throughout the whole year. The fruit is generally large and plump, with the pulp well filled, there is not the slightest evidence of anything uncongenial connected with its appearance, it may be said truly to have become habituated to our climate, or to have found in it the kindred qualities of its own tropical native home. I have seen the young tree of two years from the seed producing full, well matured fruit. During the palmy days of the old Missions, they were in the habit of cultivating somewhat extensive groves of these trees, but since their decline, the trees and their culture have been neglected, and the groves in many instances cut down. It is a pleasing fact to know that the attention of American citizens resident in this portion of the State are turning their attention to the propagation of this delicious fruit, and it will be but a very few years before our markets will be supplied from domestic sources entirely. In the Cities of Santa Barbara and Los Angeles and the adjacent Missions I have seen the orange tree forty years old, and in some few instances much older.

The citron is also another fruit belonging to the same natural family, and was formerly cultivated to a considerable extent, and flourishes well at the present time. I have seen this fruit in the gardens of private residences growing to the size of six inches in length by three inches in diameter, its weight could not have been less than two pounds.

The date tree, fig, pine, apricot, guava, pomegranate and kindred fruits find a congenial climate, and a soil adapted to their successful cultivation, and are to be met with at several points in this section of the country. No attempt, so far as I have been able to learn, has as yet been made to produce the pine-apple, although the climate and all other concomitant conditions of locality essential to its culture abound. Some experiments have been in the culture of tobacco, which have proved highly successful and satisfactory—the Cuban variety is found to flourish as well here as upon its native soil; the great consumption of this article in California will render its cultivation an object of some considerable importance, and as so little care and labor is necessary in rearing it here, it is more than probable that but a few years will elapse before it will find a place in our commercial tables, as an article of home production, and perhaps of export.

The climatal conditions of these plains, and the adaptability of their soils are such that we may reasonably expect, ere a few years shall pass, that cotton, coffee, tea, sugar and rice, the four latter articles particularly, will find a place in our catalogues of home productions, and the only impediment that now stands in the way of their immediate production, is the high price of labor which is consequent upon the sparseness of population. The unoccupied or rather unimproved lands extending from Point Aguilla to San Diego on the land of the coast, and into the interior for distances varying from twelve to fifty or sixty miles, and the extensive valley ranges beyond the first and eastern line of ridges of the San Bernardino mountains offer strong inducements to the immigrant and settler who may be seeking a permanent and agreeable home, and who wishes to cultivate the soil as a means of livelihood and source of profit. To such this district of the State furnishes an ample field for his operations, and equally profitable with any other portion of our wide domain.

MINERAL PRODUCTS OF LOS ANGELES, &c.

A brief review of the agricultural capacities of the soils of this part of the State has been given, and I would say in this connection, that in these particulars lie the strength and principal value of the lands throughout the district generally; the mineral resources of this range of country so far as examined, being comparatively of little value.

The transverse chain of the Pacific coast (San Bernardino chain) appear thus far to act as a barrier, and to have cut off almost completely the rich mineral deposits found in the mountains of the more northern sections. There are a few localities, it is true, where auriferous deposits of limited extent are met with, but no general features which would in the slightest degree indicate that they extend over any considerable areas. So far as I have been able to learn, both from personal inspection and information derived from others of localities which I have not visited, I entertain the opinion that no extensive deposits of gold will be found south of these mountains, and few, probably, that would warrant mining explanation. There are some evidences existing that silver may be met with in the southeastern spurs of this chain, but to what extent is yet undetermined. The limestone rocks of the Armagosa, and the granite and quartz of this section, contain both gold and silver, but they are situated to the north of this chain, yet the *gypsum beds* found near their southern base and on the southern part of the Colerado Desert are found to contain gold in small quantities, not sufficient, however, to pay for working. The predominating metaliferous rocks of these mountains, so far as known, consist mostly of copper containing lead and silver; the heavier quantities of these ores lying upon the Rio Santa Clara, in the County of Santa Barbara. Bismuth and iron are also met with in these mountains, the former to a limited extent, the latter more generally disseminated and forming small veins among the primitive rocks. Both of the latter minerals are found in the immediate vicinity of the Mission of San Buenaventura, and the former (Bismuth) in the mountains near the coast in the vicinity of the rancho Guadalupe. The principal mineral products of these counties, of any commercial importance, are the beds of sulphur; they commence in the County of San Luis Obispo, and through alternate distances of two to six miles, extend to the County of Santa Barbara, and northern part of Los Angeles. The larger proportion of these beds lie near the coast, and form the investing surface material of those volcanic vents found upon this part of the coast, and which have been alluded to in the preceding pages of this report. These sulphur deposits will, at a future day, be worked with profit when the demand for this article shall exceed that of the present time, and still I think the present demand is sufficient to warrant the investment of capital in this quarter, where the mineral is found in sufficient quantities to render the working of its mines a lucrative operation.

The appearance of magnetic sands among the drift found in the beds of the arroyas led me to the supposition that gold might exist in their connection, which, upon examination, was found to be the case, although in very trifling quantities. The same thing was found to exist upon the beach three miles southeast of Santa Barbara. This metal was probably derived from the heavy gravel drift which is found in the immediate vicinity.

Bitumen is another of the more abundant mineral products of this portion of the State, and is found in very large quantities. This article is available and well adapted to the manufacture of gas for the purposes of illumination, and will probably be used to considerable extent in this country, the only practical objection to such a use of it, being the fact that no valuable residuum is left in the retort after the extrication of the gaseous constituents; as this mineral yields a much greater volume (being nearly double,) of illuminating gas, than any other in use, it is very questionable whether it would not be equally profitable from this circumstance. In the use of coal, we have the coke remaining which may be applied as an article of fuel, but the value of the latter in the market would probably be counterbalanced, by the increased volume of illuminating matter contained in the simple bitumen. The expense of transportation of coal from distant regions must very materially enhance the price of the commodities resulting from it, but in the use of the asphaltum upon our coast, this heavy item would, as a necessary consequence become materially diminished. The only real objection to the introduction of the latter article for the above purposes is that there may not be sufficient quantities of the mineral obtainable for so extensive uses as would be required ; this is a valid objection, and should be well considered before entering upon a speculation of that kind ; from what is already known of these beds, they certainly have the appearance of being adequate to the supply of any ordinary demand for those purposes, as they are frequently to be met with covering many acres of ground. This fact however in regard to quantity can only be determined positively by clearing one or two of the larger springs, and thus ascertaining the actual amount of the mineral discharged per day or per week, and should it be found anything near adequate to the demand for gas manufacture, its collection and transportation at fair rates of prices, will form a much greater source of revenue to this district than the entire cattle trade of these counties at the present time. A little attention to this subject will convince us that a heavy and lucrative business may be conducted in this department of trade, if the necessary measures are adopted to bring this element into practical notice, for as stated in the preceding pages these springs extend from the county of Santa Clara to San Diego, and most of them near the coast.

To illustrate more fully the advantages to be derived, and the extent of business that now lies untouched in this particular, it will only be necessary to allude to the quantity of coal required for the purposes of illumination at present in this State. The requirements for the city of San Francisco is about 5000 tons per annum, at an average price of 22 dollars per ton, equal to 110,000 dollars, the demand for Sacramento is equal to about 2000 tons, which at the same price equals 44,000 dollars, the total amounting to 154,000 dollars. Allowing the coal to produce, (which the best quality will,) about 1100 pounds of coke from the ton of coals, the value of the coke as sold here, at about 62 cents (high price,) per bushel, will yield a return upon the original cost ; of a little more than twelve dollars per ton, or a sum total of nearly $87,000. This estimate is based on the product of the Scotch coal, the specific gravity of which is but 1.27. The Asphaltum of this State has a specific gravity of about 1.62, the difference in the excess arrising probably from the earthly matters contained therein.

There cannot be less than 4000 tons Asphaltum lying upon the surface of the ground in the counties of Los Angeles and Santa Barbara alone, within a few miles of the coast at the present moment. Its value delivered in San Francisco would not be less than sixteen dollars per ton, equal in value to 64,000 dollars, and this amount alone would offer sufficient inducement to embark in the enterprise independent of any other consideration. The amount lying upon the surface in other adjacent counties is probably equal to the amount in those specified, so that 8000 tons would be a safe estimate to place upon the quantity already available.

The analysis of this mineral exhibits the following available constituents for the manufacture of gas ; in one hundred parts there is found a a limpid oil equal to thirty per cent, and the same amount of charcoal with a large per cent of ammonia, the balance consisting of earthly matters and water. Here then we have 60 per cent of the gross weight applicable to immediate use, the charcoal holding the same relations to the bitumen, that exist in the coke to the coal. That the supply of this article is abundant, there can be but little question and fully equal to 5000 tons per annum, (the requirements of the State will not fall short of this figure for years to come,) equal in value, at 16 dollars per ton, to 80,009 dollars, and should it possess no more than an equal amount of illuminating matter, it will be seen that it will be far more economical than the present use of coal. The only, or rather the principal question asked by those interested in gas manufacture, is this, is there a sufficient quantity to meet the demand for 3000 tons per annum, in other words, if there is a sufficient quantity, is there every evidence of quality also to make it a reliable resource?

The proper opening of these springs would undoubtedly furnish an ample quantity of the mineral, and if the business should be judiciously managed, it would prove lucrative and permanent. It is to be hoped that this brief allusion to this subject, may elicit attention from those who are intimately acquainted with the localities in which it is found, to its proposed value, as well as to the quantities which may be supplied.

Limestone is found in considerable quantities among the higher hills of this part of the State. Without any exception I believe it is primitive, and the greater part of it possesses a high crystalline structure. It is well calculated for the manufacture of lime, and proportionately less fit for any other application to building purposes.—The granites which form the principal basis of these mountains, is usually of a hornblendic character, often running into true Sienite. It is ill adapted to purposes of building. both from its constituents, and its general consistency, and it is generally in situations remote from navigable waters, a fact which forbids at present its transportation for such purposes, even were it found to be of a better quality.

I have thus given a general outline of the geological characteristics of this part of the country, and the more prominet economic adaptations of its resources, which may be derived from them, by the enterprise of our citizens, when the industry of the people, as well as their capital shall be invested in their development. It would be incompatible with the limits of an abstract report like this, to enter into the minutiæ of the more scientific details which might naturally be drawn from so abundant a field of investigation. I have thought it advisable in this as in former reports therefore to omit them, with a view to furnishing such as may be deemed useful, together with accompanying illustrations, in a final report of a more complete form in detail, upon the geology of California.

In the appendix of this report will be found a catalogue of the fossils, minerals and specimens representing this portion of the country, less full however in detail than that which will hereafter be presented, when they can be systematically arranged so as to convey a clear idea of their relative ages and positions.

With these remarks on this part of our subject we will now leave it for the purpose of turning our attention to the more northerly and equally interesting portion of the State.

COUNTRY NORTH OF THE AMERICAN RIVER.

The district of country lying north of the American River was entered upon in the early part of October. The examinations were carried through the upper portions of the county of Yolo, through the west part of Placer, through Sutter, and crossing the Feather River, was pursued through the counties of Colusi, Shasta, portions of Trinity, the eastern part of Klamath nearly to Siskiyou. Returning to the southward again, the eastern side of the River Sacramento was followed, through the counties of Butte and Yuba.

I shall confine myself first to the observations made in the more exclusively agricultural portions of this part of the State, and subsequently to the mining counties beyond and upon the upper sections of the Sacramento River and Valley.

What has been said of the physical geography of the mountains forming the borders of the great valley is equally applicable to a large part of that section under consideration, and wherever any material differences occur they will be noticed in the course of our remarks upon this region. The lower bottoms of the Sacramento Valley, over which the principal traveled road now runs, have an ascending scale of about five feet per mile from the city of Sacramento to the junction of the Pitt River, the distance between these points being about the same as that between Sacramento and the town of Shasta, and nearly on the same level. The principal agricultural lands of this part of the valley lie upon these bottoms, which in the county of Colusi are often of several miles in width on both sides of the river. As we advance towards the coast mountains in this county, and also in the south-west part of Shasta, we immediately enter upon an elevated plateau, which apparently extends to the base of the mountains to the west. This plateau, or more properly speaking, middle terrace of the valley has an ascending grade towards the mountains much more rapid than the lower bottoms, its altitude above the latter varies from 60 to 70 feet, and the ascent to its top is usually quite abrupt. As this terrace advances towards the west, another table is seen to ascend from its surface, exceeding this middle terrace in height, beyond which the heavier rolling hills, constituting the base of the coast mountains commence, and which in a short distance terminate in rugged and elevated ridges.

Throughout the county of Colusi, and also for a short distance and to the south part of the county of Shasta, this middle terrace contains a large area of arable land, differing materially from its equivalent in the more southern portions of the same valley producing there but a limited vegetation and being composed of coarse, harsh gravelly soil. These peculiar characteristics of the middle section of the plain are carried southward from the vicinity of Red Bluffs for a distance of ninety miles, when they gradually come to partake of the sterile features above noticed, and which are carried into the western part of the county of Yolo, on the same line of elevation above tide level.

On this middle plateau is situated some of the best land for farming purposes to be found in this part of the State. The soil has been derived from the mountains of trapean rocks which constitute the eastern ridges of the coast chain, and is composed of a soft loam mixed with little sand, and the detritus of a few of the slate rocks which are found in comparatively small quantities along the base of these ridges. The almost total absence of the granitic rocks, which are usually productive of harsh, dry and uncongenial soils, unless modified by particular local circumstances, and the admixture of the extensive limestones which stretch from across the Pitt River and appear in the mountains to the west renders the lands of these counties peculiarly adapted to the culture of the grain and root crops, and desirable to the farming population of the country. The constituents of these lands renders them valuable, for the culture of fruits. They contain all the elements necessary for their healthy and successful propagation, with the advantages of an extensive market, which is immediately surrounding almost the entire section. The advantages presented by nature are not entirely overlooked by the inhabitants in this part of the State. This is apparent from the fact that flouring mills have already been erected, of capacities much greater for grinding than those which have been seen in other counties.

The county is as yet but sparsely settled, but an examination of the character of its lands, and of the inducements it will present to the strict agriculturalist, will lead to the most favorable conclusions respecting the future appreciation and settlement of this district. Its capacities for the production of the cereals and also extensive corn crops, were evidenced during the last year, in which we find that the reputation which this district had acquired for the rearing of these products, was fully sustained.

The lower bottoms of this part of the valley present a somewhat anomalous feature in their native productions compared to their equivalents farther to the south. It consists in the forest growths which extend for miles from the banks of the river. On the bottoms below Tehama, the oak, maple and other trees which skirt the banks of the stream usually extend but a very short distance back into the flanks of the valley, never I believe reaching in any instance the foot of the middle terraces. At the distance of about twenty miles south of Tehama we first enter the valley forest (for so it may be called.) which continues to increase both in density and extent as we approach the upper end of the valley, and soon after passing Red Bluffs it is seen to extend from the base of the coast mountains to the Sierra Nevada. The greater part of the trees are situated upon the middle plateau, and extend themselves into the upper tables and thence into the foot-hills of the mountains where they soon become commingled with the pine and other trees of mountain habits. The trees growing upon these lands offer a good criterion to judge of the character and condition of its soils on which they are found. They exhibit to us the fact that the soil possesses those elements which are necessary for the propagation of the cultivated trees, and which can be made doubly useful in supplying woods, either for building, for fuel or other purposes, and the production of fruits, at present a great desideratum in the State of California.

This part of the State has every appearance of possessing superior advantages for the culture of the northern fruits, the apple, peach and pear, either or all of which would find here a soil and climate congenial to their healthy and luxuriant growth.

Before dismissing the agricultural districts of the upper Sacramento, I would call the attention of the residents of this part of the State, to the means of irrigation which may be advantageously used in this district. All the streams which issue from the mountains, lose a great part of their water before they unite with the main river, and in some cases, it has been found that the waters of these streams were entirely absent from their beds for miles above their junction. When this is found to be the case, and even but a small district of valley lands intervenes between these points where the waters thus disappear from their surface channels, there will usually be found between the main river and the sink, some point at which the waters issue from beneath the surface, which is manifested in these cases by small lagoons, swampy ground, and wet places, none of which are usually of any great extent. This fact has led me to suppose, that a clay bed might probably exist beneath the superficial soils, which is nearly impervious to water. This upon examination has been found to be the case. The limited superficial discharge of these waters, is accounted for in a sandy admixture which is found in the clay, and which of course would admit a much freer percolation of water, than the compact clay alone would allow; the natural inference from which is, that by far the greatest proportion of the waters which flow through the tributary streams of the northern Sacramento, pass beneath the surface of the valley and emerge from the same many miles distant from the places of their disappearance. As the structure of this basin will be examined more in detail in another part ot this report, further remarks in relation to this part of our subject will be dispensed with at this time.

MINERAL DISTRICT OF THE UPPER SACRAMENTO VALLEY.

We come now to the consideration of the mineral resources of the Upper Sacramento Valley. The upper portions of this valley lie for the most part on the east banks of the Sacramento River, with the exception of a small section above the junction of Clear Creek, on the west side of the main stream. The southern boundary of what may be considered properly as the Upper Sacramento Valley (and which is mineral land for nearly its entire extent,) I have proposed to comprise within the range of mountains, crossing the Pitt river and forming a part of its southwestern banks, on the north, and the junction of Cow Creek on the south. This district will have a line of distance from north to south of about thirty-five miles, and a breadth of fourteen miles lying immediately north of the emigrant road leading from Noble's Pass, aad entering the Sacramento Valley.

In passing across this section it was found that a large portion of the area included was a placer district, similar in most respects to the equivalent ranges on Butte Creek, and extending southerly through Long's Bar on the Lower Feather River, which is also observable in the vicinity of Camp Far West, on Bear River, and thence on to Rhode's Diggings, in the County of Sacramento.

Within this area there is at the present time a large mining population, and three considerable mining towns have been built up by the enterprise of that portion of our people who arrive annually by emigration across the territories and enter the northern parts of California through Noble's Pass, also coming through the American Valley. In the middle portion of this district there are situated some of the most extensive auriferous quartz leads, of any to be found in any part of the State, and from which the gold found distributed through the soil is derived. This entire district may be said to constitute a single large placer embracing an area fully equal to two hundred square miles, and probably the largest uninterrupted placer to be found in this country. The situation of this plain, enclosed as it is by high mountains on three sides, renders a climate mild and agreeable, with the exception of a short time during the dry season, when like all valleys in this country, the temperature becomes somewhat elevated.

This placer range extends in a northerly direction beyond the Pitt River, on which stream the mining town of Pittsburgh is situated; it is said also to extend up McLoud's Fork, the principal northern tributary of Pitt River; of this, however, I am unable to speak from personal knowledge. I think there is no question but such is the fact, for my informants were men on whom reliance could be placed in matters of this character. In this district as in many others in the State similarly situated, scarcity of water is the most serious impediment in the way of the miner in seeking for the profits of his occupation as well as to the general growth and progress of the country. And wherever an ample supply of this agent is furnished for mining purposes, the Upper Sacramento will give abundant employment to a large and busy population. I think there is no hazard in expressing the opinion, that this placer alone exceeds in area the aggregate of all the other known placers of Shasta County, in which it is situated, and is capable of giving employment for many years to four or five thousand men.

I consider the mining sections of this county equal in value to those of many parts of El Dorado, Placer and Nevada as they existed in the years of 1851–2–3. They are much in the condition in which the flats and ravines in those counties were during those years, and which, since the introduction of water by canals, have yielded vast sums of gold, and such high remuneration for labor.

These mines are as yet almost untouched, and they require only that stimulus which has been applied in other counties to the south, to bring them into immediate use and occupancy. The rapid ascent of the Sacramento River after it enters the cañon immediately above the Upper Ferry is such that any amount of water would be easily obtained by diverting a portion of the stream, and carrying it by canals or ditches to the west of the river to be distributed among the high flats to the west from the town of Shasta, which flats abound in auriferous deposits similar to those of Middletown, Briggsville and other localities. A distance of six or seven miles from the mouth of the canon would give sufficient altitude to carry the waters nearly as high as the summit of the hill on which is situated what is known as the Upper Springs, and within the town of Shasta.

A distance of three or four miles above the first settlement on the plain east of the river, the waters of the Sacramento may be diverted to any extent that might be requisite, and in quantities sufficient, if required, to nearly inundate the upper plain on that side of the stream, and a natural channel may be found of sufficient elevation a portion of the way, to convey the waters over the undulating hills on the southern and middle portions of the prairie beyond.

The inducements for the investment of capital in mining operations which offer themselves in this immediate vicinity are unsurpassed in any county of the State south of this point, and it is a remarkable feature in the history of this district that they have not attracted that attention which their intrinsic merits suggest.

GEOLOGY OF THE NORTHERN COAST MOUNTAINS.

The term Northern Coast Mountains is used in this case for the purpose of separating a portion of this district, which differs materially in mineral aspect from any other part of this chain south of the County of Colusi. The counties of Humboldt, Klamath, Trinity, Shasta, and the southwest part of Siskiyou, if not the whole of the latter county, are situated in this part of the chain, and which collectively form a portion of the mineral districts of this State. My line of travel did not extend sufficiently far north to determine with certainty what portion of the mountain district, in the northern part of the State should strictly constitute the coast chain. But from what evidences there are in our possession at the present moment, respecting their peculiar disposition, the presumption is strong that even Mount Shasta belongs to this chain, in place of its forming a part of the Sierra Nevada as heretofore believed. This will prove to be the case, provided the Cascade range which extends through Southern Oregon is found to be a continuation of our coast chain as is now supposed.

In this case we shall have the Sierra Nevada terminating at Lassen's Peak, or rather at a point not farther north than this moumtain, and the structure of the county extending northward from this towards the southern line of Oregon fully warrants such a conclusion. North of Lassen's Butte there is not a mountain to be seen on the line of trend of the ridge country, which consists apparently of low, flat table lands, similar in structure and appearance to the table hills north of the main Feather River or those which extend through the southern, western and northern parts of the Counties of El Dorado, Placer and Amador, as we approach the plains from the mountains in these several counties.

The only mountains in this part of the State are those belonging properly to the coast ranges, and of these Mount Shasta forms probably the line of eastern limit; its distance from the sea is a due west line not exceeding seventy miles, being a much shorter distance from the ocean than many parts of the same chain situated farther to the south.

The mountain districts of this part of the State are divided by bold and rapid streams, and as a consequence, are designated by local names which serve to fix their geographical and relative positions, forming the boundaries of counties and the lines of water-shed, which unite with the ocean at widely different and distant localities. Thus we find the waters which flow into the Sacramento separated from those which flow into the Klamath by the range known as the Trinity Mountains, the latter river draining a portion of the waters belonging to the Great Basin, and which rises east of the Cascade range.

The rocks which comprise this part of the coast mountains are made up mostly of the primitive group, and simulate in almost every particular with those found in the mining counties of the Sierra Nevada, and also the southern portions of the coast chain. In the eastern and middle districts of this part of the mountains, the sienites and other members of the granitic series are largely predominant, and commingled irregularly with them, are found the serpentine rocks and their derivatives, consisting of the talcose and chlorite schists, alternating with all the other members of the primitive group.

Resting upon these we find the slates of an argillaceous origin frequently disturbed and maintaining every conceivable degree of inclination, as in the other mining counties of the State, but still holding their parallel with the mountains in which they are situated, which is observable elsewhere, and the same line of strike or linear direction. The constancy and regularity of the strike found in these rocks at such remote distances from those of the southern range of mining counties leads us irresistibly to the conclusion that they belong to one and the same period and co-relative age, having their origin from the same class of rocks as those of the other sections. The subsequent igneous intrusions which have disturbed the one are found to be of the same character as those which disturbed the other, and have apparently acted with the same force and at the same time with those of the Sierra Nevada. The intrusions of quartz dikes and veins appear equally as numerous and well defined as those found in any other part of the State, and even much more extensive than many of those observable in the midland counties. They simulate more closely with those veins found in the counties of Tuolumne, Calaveras and Mariposa.

In the depressions lying between the principal divides of the various rivers, the heavy drift deposits are met with; in some localities they extend to great depth, as in the vicinity of the town of Weaverville, they have been found to the depth of nearly five hundred feet, which was proved by the sinking of the deep shaft near that town. This drift, or the greater part of it at least, has all the evidences of having been deposited during the tertiary epoch, the manifestations of which are found in the great amount of the impressions of dicotyledonous leaves, many of which are apparently of present existing species found growing in the neighboring mountains; the silicified woods and lignites all present thesame general features.

This district is peculiarly interesting from the great amount of drift deposits which are present in many localities, and the character of the organic remains contained in it is well defined, and will probably be the means of modifying our opinions in some measure, relative to the probable age of the drift deposits of the different portions of this State. There are apparent grounds existing, (which, however cannot be fully demonstrated at the present time) that these drift beds are assigned to two distinct periods of the tertiary era, but more time and further examination must be had before this point can be satisfactorily settled. In an economical point of view it matters but little to which of the two periods, either of them may belong, so far, at least, as their mineral products are concerned, for the deposit in whatever portion of the State it may be found (except south of the San Bernardino Mountains) is highly valuable for its auriferous accompaniment which is generally found throughout the whole of it in general distribution.

The drift beds are found extensively dispersed through the northwest part of the State, and are found much elevated on the flanks of the ridges as well as in the depressions between them. In this particular they simulate with the extensive and wide-spread placer ranges which traverse the mining districts from the County of Plumas to that of Calaveras, and thence through Tuolumne and Mariposa. From their general character, so far as they have been opened and examined, (which has been but to a limited extent) they present all the physical and integral features which have hitherto warranted our conclusion respecting gold deposits within our borders, and which have guided to those practical proofs, by opening the mines, which have developed to us the natural hiding places of the immense resources of wealth which abound in our State. There is every reason to believe that those drift beds situated in the northern coast mountains are equally as valuable, and will, when worked, prove as abundantly supplied with gold as those of Sierra, Nevada, Placer and El Dorado Counties. This opinion is based on the fact that the deposits on the flanks of the hills in the coast chain are co-relative in age with those of Minesota, Mameluke Hill and White Rock, in the Counties of Sierra and El Dorado, their fossils being identical, and their elevation above the sea about the same.

The outlines of these beds begin first to show themselves as well defined formations on the east and west banks of Clear Creek above Frenchtown, and also on French Gulch, in the County of Shasta, and are distincly traceable from these localities across all the rivers lying to the north and west of this creek as far west as Salmon and Scott Rivers, and on the hills forming the sides of all the larger basins lying between these points; the great Weaverville basin furnishes one of the best examples of the kind in this part of the State, and is observable on what is known as Musser's Flat to the northeast of the town. It is similar in all respects to the localities in Nevada County, in the vicinity of Moore's, Orleans and Eureka Flats, opposite to Minesota.

LOCAL GEOLOGY.

The local geology of the Northern Coast Mountains presents but little diversity from the other mineral districts of the State, and as a general fact the rocks maintain that uniformity of character which is found to exist in almost every locality within any given area.

The first locality that will claim our attention is that of the middle and northern with the eastern part of Shasta County. Nearly as soon as we leave the valley, and among the first foot-hills the slates are met with standing in nearly a vertical position. This trait, however, extends but a short distance, and we are suddenly introduced from the fossil clay slate into a district in which the latter is most completely metamorphosed. This is found to occur within two miles of the point at which these rocks maintain their true laminated character of the slates. In the immediate vicinity of Shasta City, the changed condition of these rocks is noticable and directly east of the town, the intrusion of the igneous is presented on an extensive scale. On the hill opposite to the City the intrusive rocks have broken through each series that preceded them, and we find the slates in the immediate vicinity of the trapean dikes, most completely changed into true jaspery rocks. To the east and north of the hill we meet with the first beds of the serpentine rocks which have been disturbed by the same agents which have disturbed the slates; this bed of the primitive group extends in a northerly direction about six miles, and is flanked on the west by the sienites and granites, and on the east by the older trap rocks. Among these serpentine rocks are frequently to be seen small veins and also large dikes of auriferous quartz running parallel, which will be seen from their course to correspond in trend with those of the more southern part of the State, and this general characteristic belonging to these latter rocks (the quartz) was found to prevail as far north as my observations extended.

Nearly all the quartz dikes of this part of the State are situated in the serpentine rocks, and it is rather an exception than otherwise, to find them associated with other series of veins of any considerable magnitude. There are but very few exceptions to this rule, and when these dikes are found to occur in other rocks, the investing walls are usually granite. The predominance of these veins among the class of rocks alluded to, fixes to a certain extent their probable age, and like the dikes of the counties of Nevada and Amidor, come under the classification of former reports in which they have been arranged as primitive, in order to separate them from a class similar in constitution, which appear to have been intruded subsequent to the deposition of the slates.

Up to the present time, there have not been observed any extensive quartz ranges which have the appearance of having protruded through the slate formation of this part of the State. I have heard of two localities of this character, one of which I have subsequently visited, but found on examination that the *Slate* belonged to the stratified rocks of the primitive series, and were almost exclusively talcose schist. In those localities where opportunities occurred for the examination of the trapean rocks which were found adjacent to these dikes, they presented the same appearance and evidences of having broken through that class of rocks.

This is manifest in nearly every vein to be met with for the distance of five or six miles from Shasta City, and is particularly well defined in the vicinity of what is known as the Quartz Mountain, eight miles north-east of the town and on the head of the Sacramento Valley. From this brief outline of their general features and associations, it is difficult to form any other conclusions than those at which we have above arrived, respecting their strictly primitive character; and as such, when found to be auriferous, they are discovered to be equally valuable with those in other parts of the State. In traveling north-west of the town, and well on to Tower's Bridge we find a diminution in the outcrop of these rocks, but after crossing Clear Creek and assuming a more northerly course they again make their appearance in well defined lodes running parallel with each other for long distances. The best position for examining their relations with the adjacent rocks is three miles from Frenchtown at the Mt. Washington Mine. At this locality the parallelism of the dikes is observable along the flanks, and over the hill on which this mine is situated. A level has been driven about 200 feet on the main lode of the mine, which has exposed the walls of the vein for that distance and at a vertical depth of about 150 feet below the outcrop. It is here found that the lode traverses the primitive rocks exclusively, and like the other mines in the State the power of the lode is increased as it descends. In the vicinity of the reduction works of this establishment are large masses of an amygdaloidal trap, which is found in situ a short distance west of the buildings. This rock is cut through in every conceivable direction by small threads of quartz, which I have found to contain gold, showing most conclusively that the mineral was injected at a subsequent period to the formation of this trapean mass.

In traveling up the canon from the bridge above alluded to, the quartz dikes are found to crop on the sides of many of the hills as we pass along; as the ascent of the Trinity ridge is made from McLaughlin's ranch, which is situated in the canon spoken of, no veins are again met with, until the base of this ridge is approached, towards the Trinity River, when they are again found crossing about two miles to the east of Lewis's Bridge on this stream ; but we shall for the present defer their consideration till we come to examine them again in the county of Trinity, where they belong.

CARBONIFEROUS LIMESTONE.

In the eastern part of the county of Shasta, there is a group of calcareous rocks, stretching obliquely across the head of the Sacramento Valley, whilst the mountains in which they are situated, or more properly, the mountains of which they compose the chief part, hold a due north and south trend. Their color and altitude when seen from a distance of twenty or thirty miles in either direction, form striking features in the landscape scenery of this part of the country, peering upward in their more northern portions to the height of about 3000 feet. Their light blue tint projects them in strong relief, against the dark rocks and darker herbage of the mountains beyond, in such a manner as to display their rugged and bold outline in the clearest and most distinct picturings.

These *limestone mountains*, thus termed because there are no rocks of any other description to be found upon them, extend across the Pitt River in a northerly direction for a distance of about thirty or forty miles, forming a portion of the canon of McCloud's Fork, and are situated on the western banks of that stream, between which and the Sacramento flows the rapid stream termed by Mr. Dana, Destruction River, a name which it still retains.

The dip of these limestones is to the east at an angle of about 20 degrees; the strata, which are very distinct, vary from a few inches to eight feet in thickness, and the thicker beds appear extremely solid, scarcely exhibiting even a small seam. Those which lie near the base of the mountains are much darker in color than those above them, and form a most beautifully variegated marble, inferior to none of those varieties used in ornamental architecture, or for making furniture. The lower, the middle and a considerable portions of the upper beds are highly fossiliferous, consisting of marine species entirely. The fossils are composed of several species of encrinite, orthis and small spirifers, in the middle and upper beds, and of corals among the lower ones. This I believe is the first fossiliferous limestone, as yet found in any portion of this State, it has heretofore been entirely wanting.

The discovery of this group of rocks brings us in close connection with a new geological era within the State, and enables us to present the outline of a strong hope that we may yet be able to discover that article of comfort and economy so much needed on these western shores. These rocks belong to the carboniferous system and appear to be the representatives of that system developed during the survey of the north-west Territories by Mr. Owen. They appear almost identical with the superior portions of that group known as the "Carboniferous rocks of Iowa and Des Moines" and in which the coal measures are found.

I do not wish to be misunderstood in this matter, nor to say one word which might induce individuals to invest capital or time, in what would be considered fruitless attempts in search of coal. The only evidence existing, that this article may be found in quantities that would be adequate to the demands of this State, will depend upon the character and extent of this group of rocks under consideration.—My time did not permit that extensive examination of the group, which I wished, but it was conducted far enough to determine the fact of their carboniferous character beyond question. As before stated, these are the first rocks which have been found in our State, of that series to which the coal measures belong, and they furnish us reason to hope that we may yet be able to say that California can supply herself with coals from her own mines, and thus avoid in all time to come the enormous expense of the importation of this most valuable commodity from vast distances over seas.

During a hastily conducted line of travel in 1850, through the district east of the Pitt River mountains, I observed a few scattered masses of a secondary conglomerate. This gave me the first impression of the probable existence of the coal measures in those districts of country, and there was a brief notice of the subject in the short report to the Session of 1853. On the 15th page of that report, on the Geology of the Sierra Nevada, the following remarks were made:

"These conglomerates have but little interest connected with them further than geological position is concerned, except the modifying influence they may exert through their debris on the formation of the valley sections; but there is a belt of these rocks in other parts of the country which will be entitled to much more particular consideration. In addition to the buhr stone of this district, this section of the State contains some few traces of the secondary rocks, a suite almost entirely wanting with this exception in other parts of the State so far as explored. The existence of any portion of this suite should command our attention, and any measure which would be likely to develop this formation, or any part it within the limits of this State should meet with public approbation. The importance attached to this group is the fact that to this suite we must look for a home supply of the mineral coals, if even found within the State."

And on the 16th page of the same report we read as follows:

"As these rocks have exhibited themselves in the northern districts, and in those sections most immediately connected with the coast-line of mountains, it is to be hoped that judicious explorations in that range may develop its existence (the existence of coal,) either at the points alluded to, or in other and more distant parts of that chain.

From the structure of the country generally it is doubtful whether any other portion of the State presents the slighest ground for hope that this necessary material of economy will be found in other parts than those indicated, and every effort compatible with prudence should be made that will tend to elicit information on this highly important subject. The frequent discovery of small patches of mineral coal in those mountains, would seem to lend aid to the suggestion that its development in this chain may be looked for with more confidence than at any other point."

The foregoing remarks upon this subject penned in a hasty manner more than two years since, (and the observations which gave rise to them being conducted in a district of country where at that earlier period of our history the explorer found his attention well occupied rather in the preservation of his life against the dangers of the wilderness and its denizens, than in searching for geological formations,) have during the past year been strongly confirmed. We have reason now to believe in the correctness of our suggestions then thrown out, from the discovery of fossils belonging to that period, and required as a basis for such conclusions. These fossils have been found at distances of miles from those points where the first indications of the secondary series were thus hurriedly observed. It should be remembered that it is no easy task to define positively the true position of a formation or group like a conglomerate from its mere lithological characters alone; and it receives its additional value, when it is found to hold a direct relation with groups of a homogeneous character, presenting fossils of a known age, and known position.

Such is the case with the fossils of the limestone rocks before us, their relative position being well known, as well as the period to which they belong, that they place the subject of the existence of a coal field in this part of the State, or Southern Oregon, in a more tangible form than any which has been before presented. We are able therefore to arrive at something like a satisfactory conclusion, not only as to its existence, but approximately as to its probable locality. The fossils before alluded to, are always found *below the coal beds*, and in no instance *above them*. Their depth below the coals is generally within *three hundred feet*. These facts will lead us to look for some other locality more elevated, and on the line of trend to the north in which these rocks may be found with their appropriate superincumbent strata, in which we may naturally expect will be found the proposed beds of mineral coal. The dip of the rocks to the east at an angle of about 20 degrees, and the elevation of the lands lying in that direction with their outline, would warrant extensive explorations in those quarters with strong grounds for the belief that success would attend the search; while to the north the beds should be sought for among the higher hills and low mountains east of Shasta Butte, or perhaps as far north as the Siskiyou Range, beyond the Klamath River.

I feel but little hesitancy in saying that a great degree of certainty exists, of the mineral coals being found in the counties of Shasta and Siskiyou, but in the former more particularly. I cannot with respect to the latter named county, speak with the same amount of confidence, as my examination did not extend sufficiently far north to determine with any degree of certainty the probable extent and position which these rocks maintain through the middle and northern parts of that county. My remarks in relation thereto are based on the fact of an extensive bed of limestone, similar in character to that under consideration, existing on a tributary of the Klamath River, a short distance to the west of what is known as Bridge Creek, a specimen of which was in my possession three years since, but was destroyed in the great fire at Sacramento. This specimen, I believe, contained no fossils, so far as my recollections serves me at the present time.

Should no coals be found adjacent to any part of this group, there are other circumstances connected with it, which render it of considerable economic value. The depth and solidity of the strata composing the great mass of the hills, and the firm character of the stone, will render it desirable for building purposes, to which it is well adapted, both in quality and quantity. It would make a more durable material by far, for those purposes, than a great portion of the stones at present used, either on public or private works about this country. Indeed there is none to be found so good, except, perhaps, the better qualities of granite, such as is found in the eastern parts of the county of Sacramento. The facilities of transportation, too, are very good, as this rock is found within six or eight miles of the navigable waters of the Sacramento River, at its higher stages, and which, with light draught boats, could be made available for four months of the year, and probably for a longer season.

The lower beds of these rocks are composed of corals, and the stems of encrinites, distributed through a very dark base, and traversed with veins of white spar. It receives a high polish and is obtainable in slabs of almost any dimensions and thickness. It will be found a most superb article for ornamental housework and for furniture. There are sufficient quantities and variety of qualities of this stone to answer the entire demand of this State for many years to come, and capable of affording an extensive and lucrative business to persons engaged in this department of industry. The value of ordinary marble in this State, is about $2 50 per cubic foot, and the demand constantly increasing. For the finer varieties, the prices are much higher, and rule as high as $3 25 and $4 00 per cubic foot. I have obtained the opinion of practical stone artificers on the fine dark varieties of these rocks, and they unqualifiedly pronounce it but little inferior in quality to the Italian stone known as the "*Black and gold*" marble. The stone of the Sacramento does not possess the rich yellow veins, which distinguish the above-mentioned article, but in all other characteristics it closely resembles it.

The situation of these rocks is such that water power may be used almost directly upon the ground from which they are extracted, from the current of a small stream, the tributary of a creek which flows directly to the east of one of the main ledges, and carries water throughout the year. With these advantages, and the character of the rocks combined, it is to be hoped that attention may be turned to this department of trade, and thus add another to the list of our available resources.

TRINITY COUNTY.

The southern and south-eastern line of this county is separated from that of Shasta by the high ridge known familiarly as the Trinity Mountains. These attain an elevation of about 4000 feet, at the points at which the trail crosses this ridge. There are but few points along the line of travel that exceed this height; it may therefore be considered very nearly the general mean altitude of this range, or rather spur of the coast mountains. The rocks composing this ridge, are granite and sienite, deeply underlaid by the greenstone trap which descends to the beds of the streams, and forms the principal *bed rock* of the placers of this section. On the flanks and near the base of the ridge, there are frequently to be met with, isolated masses of the metamorphic rocks, the chief of which are slates. These rocks often present a porphyritic structure, especially when found in contact with the trapean rocks, or with quartz.

I do not remember one instance in which the sedimentary rocks were found in an altered condition, when in contact either with the granite, the sienite, or any other member of that cotemporaneous group alone. I therefore infer that they were deposited upon the latter subsequently to their consolidation, and any changes which they may have undergone since their deposition and uplift, are occasioned by the intrusions of more recent igneous rocks, which have alike disturbed the slates, and the primary rocks on which they rest. In using the word primary in this case, it is applicable to the granitic series, including the serpentines, and is intended to separate the series of this part of the State, from rocks of identical constitution in other localities, which are beyond question, not older than some of the lower members of the tertiary era. These latter rocks were merely alluded to in my first report to the Legislature, and will be found thus noticed on the 12th and 13th pages of that report.

The deposits of placer gold found in these districts lie superior in position to the metamorphic series, and also superior to most of the slates. It is usually found imbedded in the gravel drift, which is composed for the most part, of rolled masses of the primitive group, almost unmixed with any other of the adjacent rocks. The entire district west of this range exhibits the marks of old water lines, from which the waters have since receded, the outlet being probably through the Klamath to the ocean. The waters were apparently fresh, and the drift beds and clays which formed the bottom are charged with large quantities of vegetable remains; but as yet no relics of animals have been found.

The small amount of deposits found among the drift, and belonging to the more recent rocks leads naturally to the inference that the gold deposits of these basins were derived mostly from the primary suites, and such was subsequently found to be the fact on examining the geological relations of the rocks found among the mountains. This characteristic was prevalent as far as the crossing of the Scott River mountains, and westerly for a distance of not less than 40 miles. In this place we shall resume the consideration of the quartz veins and their relations to the other rocks, which will more fully illustrate the character of this portion of the State.

The examination of these rocks was continued from Lewis's Bridge on the Trinity, in a northeasterly direction to the base of what is known as Brown's Mountain, a ridge which forms the eastern border of the Weaverville basin.— On this ridge there are no vestiges of any other than the primitive series, and trapean rocks, comporting in character with those spoken of on the Trinity ridge. On the western declivity and a little more than half way down to the level of the basin, the veins were found to be situated in talcose slates, which extend in a broad band from this point to the bottom of the hill ; as usual, the vegetation within the line of its range become much more sparsely distributed than upon either of its flanks where the trap rocks and granites were found to predominate. Following this line for several miles, these talcose rocks were found to be part of an extensive range which composes the major portion of the four prominent peaks situated north of the town of Weaver, which are designated as the Weaver Mountains, and which may be known by their peculiarly barren aspect, when approaching this town from any point of the compass. This belt extends entirely across the basin, and has been struck, at various points, in sinking shafts and driving tunnels for placer mining.

Taking a westerly direction along the base of the ridge, and following that line for four or five miles, I observed three dikes of quartz cutting the granite, and one near a small branch which empties into Weaver Creek, which entered the greenstone below the granite. In company with some three or four of the citizens of Weaver, a visit was made to the high ridge west of the west branch of the main creek. In the distance of two miles in reaching the summit of this hill, we crossed as many as five distinct parallel lodes, three of which I subsequently found to contain gold. On the following day, an examination of the southern end of this ridge was made, and a heavy dike of this rock was found occupying the summit, and cropping out at various points on the declivity towards the river. I think that this dike is identical with one which is found on the south-east flank of Brown's Ridge, and it unquestionably cuts entirely through that mountain.

In all the veins which passed under my observation during my rambles in this section of the State, not one was found to enter any of the rocks of sedimentary origin, but were confined exclusively to the primitive group. On the Trinity River and between that and the Scott, the same features were prevalent in this particular with one exception, which was found at the distance of about two miles from Palmer's Ferry ; here the Argillite slates on the left of the trail were cut through by a single small vein which was traceable for a distance of nearly one mile, and like several veins in the more southern counties of the State ; this lode had a strike nearly due east and west, nearly at right angles to what are known here as the primitive lodes. This is an interesting fact in this county, and serves to show a regularity in those perturbations to which this part of the continent has been subjected at different periods. Under the article of *Mines* I shall have occasion to allude to this subject, in connection with the comparative value of the metalliferous character of these lodes, so far as they have been examined and are at present understood in this State.

From the allusions made to the primitive veins in my report of last year, some idea of their intrinsic value may be gleaned with reference to the prospects which they present for mining operations.

Finding so great a preponderance of lodes of this character in this district of country, I took occasion to collect and examine a considerable number of these rocks from different veins, and situated miles apart. These collections were from the counties of Shasta, Trinity and the eastern part of Klamath, the aggregate number of which was forty-three, and of this number fourteen were from the Weaver Basin and its surrounding ridges, of which nine specimens, or about three-fifths contained gold; of the remaining twenty-nine specimens twenty-two were found to contain the same metal. As but one of this entire number of veins was found to be located for mining purposes, within my knowledge, I hope that I may not incur the charge of giving a favorable report on private property for pecuniary considerations, for to be frank in this matter, I found a less quantity in the vein which was claimed than in any specimen which proved to be auriferous.

The above facts respecting the auriferous character of the quartz veins of the northern section of this State are detailed for the purpose of calling attention to that important source of wealth, which in other parts of the State has proved of so high a value, and which thus far in the extreme northern portion of the County have been engaged in to so limited an extent. One of the greatest causes, however, which have acted in preventing capital investment in this branch of mining, is the hitherto almost inaccessible condition of this section from bad roads, preventing the transit of heavy machinery which is so necessary to success in the reduction of ores. This difficulty at present seems likely to be overcome, for active measures are now being taken for the construction of good avenues of communication, which will insure the means of the transportation of heavy freights to almost any portion of the northern interior.

IRIDIUM AND OSMIUM.

This County, like many others of the State, produces the above metals, but in much larger grains than any heretofore discovered. This alloy is the metal usually denominated *Platinum* in the mines of this State. It is found in the greatest abundance on the south fork of the Trinity River, occurring in large and small rounded grains, and nuggets weighing from one pennyweight upwards to half an ounce. Thus far the south branch has been most productive in this mineral, although some of the adjacent streams contain notable quantities. The size of the grains from this stream will render it of some commercial importance, as it appears well adapted to those uses to which it is ordinarily applied, (that of forming the points of gold pens) although its price, like that of every other commercial commodity, will be variable according to the supply or demand. During the past year the price of this article has exceeded that of gold; but a considerable quantity being thrown into the market in the early part of last spring, its price diminished very materially; the effect, however, was but of short duration, as the article was found to be of an inferior quality.

It was thought at one period that the large quantities of this metal found at Port Orford, Coose Bay and Cape Blanco might affect the price of the article to an extent that would render its collection in this State of little importance; but the size of the grains from the above localities renders it almost valueless, being but mere thin scales in an extremely fine state of comminution. The large size of the grains found on the banks of the Trinity, imparts to this article one of its principal values, and as it is found in considerable quantities upon that stream, it is to be hoped that attention may be directed to its collection.

IRON.

A short dislance to the north of the town of Weaverville are small veins of magnetic iron ore. It is seldom found in veins exceeding one or two inches in thickness; but from its position and other attendant characters, it is fairly presumable that this will prove an extensive bed of this ore. Our reason for this supposition is based on the fact, that what appears to be its equivalent, was found on the opposite side of the basin, on the south bank of Brown's Creek, and at the distance of four miles from the point at which it was first discovered. The distribution of the metals in this and other Counties that were visited during the past year, will be noticed more in detail when making out the tables illustrative of that portion of our subject.

STRUCTURE OF THE SACRAMENTO VALLEY.

A farther examination of this valley during the past year has placed us in possession of additional information in relation to the peculiarities of its structure, and as this part of the State promises in a few years hence to become the theatre of extensive operations in agriculture, it becomes an interesting and important point to ascertain what may be the probabilities of obtaining a supply of water to conduct those pursuits successfully on so large a scale. The portion of the plains of this valley to which I would call your attention in this particular, is that which lies to the north of the County of Sutter, and the extreme lines of the valley section towards the Pitt River, which stream may be considered as constituting the northern terminus of those plains.

It is found that this plain carries an ascending grade of about four and one-half feet per mile from a point opposite to to the town of Marysville to the entrance of the canon leading from the plains to the town of Shasta, the air-line distance inclusive, being that one hundred and five miles, giving us as the altitude at the entrance to the canon, a rise of five hundred and twenty feet above the line at which the observations were commenced, and five hundred and ninety-six feet above tide level.

In this part of the Sacramento Valley there are ten streams flowing, which carry water throughout the year in the hilly districts forming its boundaries; but the greater portion of the waters flowing at these higher points are lost upon the surface almost as soon as their streams reach the alluvial covering of the plains beyond the lower hills, with the exception of the freshet season. The larger streams, the Sacramento and Feather Rivers, furnish the principal channel for the escape of those waters, which, rising to the east of the slate and conglomerate ridges, discharge themselves into the ocean.

In order to form an approximate idea of the probable amount of waters which pass beneath the alluvial coverings of the plains, it may be stated with safety that it exceeds the quantity flowing in the Feather River, below the confluence of the Yuba. This estimate is founded on the known fact that the tributaries which furnish the waters flowing in the Sacramento, *during the summer months*, are neither as numerous nor as large as the streams which sink before uniting their waters with that stream during the same period, and which are also direct tributaries to the upper portion of that river during the rainy season.

Much of the water which flows in the Sacramento as it approaches the Bay of Suisan is derived from drainage through and between the superficial strata of the plains, or from the small subterranean courses which flow out over the middle clay beds, which form the substratum of the sandy and gravelly clays above. One of the best proofs which is presented, of the existence of these latent currents along the plains from the Upper Sacramento, as far down as Yolo County on the south, is found in the fact that there is derived a constant supply to the large lagoons of the plains, which we can trace to no other source, thus driving us to the conclusion which the known formations of the valley corroborate. Another fact is worthy of attention in connection with this subject, which is that these lagoons have outlets which distribute their waters over the *tule* grounds, where they maintain quite uniform stages during the summer months, which is traceable to no other known and visible system of supply, and compels us again to the belief that the subterranean courses of the lost mountain streams must furnish its elements. If the lagoons were filled merely by the overflow of the plain during the rainy season, they would not maintain their uniform height throughout the dry season as they now do, and they would furthermore necessarily exhibit all the features of mere standing pools of stagnant water, no signs of which is now to be seen about any of these bodies of clear water west of the Sacramento. It has been asserted, though I have no personal knowledge of such a fact, that a light current is at times perceptible to the south, in some of the larger lakes.

The water in many of these lakes is of considerable depth, perfectly clear, and much colder than the waters in the rivers, their dimensions varying from eight to twelve miles in length, and three to five miles in breadth. The existence of these bodies of water and their number, temperature, and their uniform depth and volume teach us plainly that the source of their supply must be traced to some other cause than that of the mere periodical overflow of the surrounding lands. If this be admitted, we must look for that supply to the more elevated borders of the valley on the east and west, or at their northern extremities. A sufficient supply of water is not to be found on any part of the west border of the plains, to produce these lagoons until after we pass the Cottonwood and Clear Creeks to the north, and we cannot, therefore, look to that direction alone; but we find the apparent source of an ample supply in the numerous streams that sink upon the upper and eastern sides of the valley which, as before stated, hide the greater portion of their contents before reaching the main channels through which they conduct their discharge in the rainy season. An additional evidence that the waters of those streams pass beneath the surface, and in a certain degree are superficial, is a fact that heavy forest growths frequent different levels, and in their distribution are found at distances of miles from any currents of water which would be at all adequate to the support of such forests, by imparting to the soil in which they grow the necessary moisture for their nutriment.

The structure of the plains below the surface, has been inferred from an examination of the changes which take place in the soils which are met with in traveling from the higher terraces of the northern end to those of the more southerly levels, which latter are but a few feet above tide water, and in the position of the clay beds which are found lying upon the first outcrop of the slates which are found in the lower foot-hills before entering the more elevated mountain districts. A vertical section of the country spoken of, would give a depth of about four hundred feet as the superficial covering of the valley where it is exposed to view. The various depths of the principal groups of this part of the State will be found in the table in the following pages, and the respective positions from the surface, as demonstrated by the boring of the Stockton well, which has perforated them to the above noted depth of four hundred feet. The thickness of the lower clay bed is, of course, unknown, and there is as yet no method of reasoning upon its probable depth from any data in our possession which would amount to more than mere speculation. There is no evidence respecting it beyond twenty or thirty feet, which is all that has thus far been known.

This deposit has all the appearance of having been originally covered by the waters of the ocean, as small fragments of what appear to be marine shells have been met with at different points, though none of them in a state of sufficient preservation to enable us to determine either the genera or species to which they belong. Should this prove to be the equivalent of the Santa Clara deposit, its average thickness might be put down at about one hundred feet, or if like the Los Angeles bed, then the boring of four hundred and thirty-five feet has not yet penetrated through it. There are reasons for the supposition that this blue clay is not less than that of the valley of Santa Clara, and the likelihood of its being much thicker is admissible. We think two hundred feet might be set down as a reasonable supposition respecting its depth, which, should it prove correct, will present the probabilities of obtaining water from beneath it, at a distance of fifteen miles from Sacramento City, about at the same depth at which we estimated it last year,—the difference between the estimate of last year and the present, being only forty-five feet, and both estimates being made without any reference to each other. In the northern part of the valley, the heavy deposit of clay which has been mentioned as resting on the slates, so far as opportunity offered for examining it, seemed but little disturbed, and from its general appearance, I was subsequently led to the belief that it was the same as that found on the surface of the lower bottoms further south. But I am unable to speak with much certainty upon that point, as no organic remains were observed by which its identity could be satisfactorily proved. The presumption upon this subject, that it is identical, is based on the very tenacious character which it possessed, and its peculiarity of color, two features noticeable only in these lower beds on the southern levels of the plain.

Should this bed ultimately prove to be identical with those forming the surface of the lower bottoms, for which result we have good grounds of supposition, then its thickness as indicated by its outcrop in the upper part of the valley cannot be less than we have herein estimated it, and would fix the bottom of that deposit at the depth of a little more than seven hundred feet. Short of this water will not probably be found in that of the country in any permanent supply.

The depth of seven hundred feet for an artesian well is not excessive, and may be esteemed even small, when we consider to what depths this description of wells have been carried in other parts of the United States and Europe. A failure to obtain water at this depth should not discourage the enterprise, for the structure of this basin, in every part of it, is such as to warrant a certainty of obtaining water beneath its surface if the operation of boring is carried to the extent which the geological conformation of the ground requires. The case of the artesian well in North Carolina which has been completed within the past year, furnishes a good illustration of the depth to which it may, at times, be necessary to descend to obtain a permanent supply of water. This well has been completed at a depth of 2700 feet, and a copious supply obtained. This fact alone should be an incentive to perseverance in the prosecution of such enterprises beyond any depth to which they have yet reached in our State.

A great uniformity appears in the disposition of the earthy deposits forming the superstructure of the San Joaquin and Sacramento valleys, above the rocks at their base. The interesting suite of specimens from the artesian boring at Stockton, sent by Mr. George E. Drew to the Academy of Natural Science at San Francisco, with an accompanying paper giving the depth of each of the beds, and their respective distances below the surface, assists us much, with other collateral evidences in forming an opinion of the relative positions of the beds below and those above the surface, and which are equivalent, the one with the other. The following table will exhibit the relations of these beds, though nearly two hundred miles apart.

With the exception of the upper gravel beds, which occur in the higher terraces of the northern part of the Sacramento Valley, the beds below the surface on the San Joaquin will be found to correspond in their general features very closely with the deposits which are traceable above the surface, from the City of Sacramento to the south banks of the Pitt River.

The figures give the maximum depths at which each of the deposits were met with in both sections of the State, and the diagrams exhibiting the transverse and longitudinal sections of the plains, show the relative positions of the respective beds as far as known at the present time.

TABLE SHOWING THE POSITION OF THE EARTHY DEPOSITS OF THE PLAINS OF THE SAN JOAQUIN AND SACRAMENTO ABOVE AND BELOW THE SURFACE.

Beds of the San Joaquin below the surface.

Light dark red clays and sand,	40
Grey sand and clay,	170
Blue clay, gravel and sand above,	237
Light grey sand,	265
Fine clear gravel,	346
Blue clay,	400
Total,	400

Beds of the Savramento above the surface.

Alluvium, lava, light red clays,	52
Upper gravel beds,	66
Light sandy clay,	160
Sand, gravel, blue clay below,	225
Light greyish sands,	276
Fine gravel, sand and blue clay,	338
Blue clay,	358
Total,	358

The above table exhibits a strong coincidence in the coverings of the v at nearly two extremes of the State, and the observations leading to th results being entirely unconnected with each other, there certainly ex reason for the belief that the earthy coverings above the stratifie maintain a great degree of uniformity over the entire basin.

The depth of the Stockton well is not so great as the boring r the latter being 465 feet below the surface point of starting, 4 has been carried through the blue clay entirely. This clay h sity and hardness as they descend, and contains embed rocks.

For the above information I am indebted to Messrs. Angeles, in a letter describing the progress of the we the State, during the month of October. The San supply of water from a bed of fine gray sand, wh the heavy clay bed, which varies from 75 feet t

On the plains of the Sacramento there are some additional aqueous deposits which have not made their appearance in the line of the Stockton well, but they may have arisen from changes in the respective levels of water courses, such as have been known to have taken place within comparatively short periods, an illustration of which is to be found in two instances with respect to the bed of the Sacramento River. The old bed of that stream, about nine miles south of Shasta City, may be easily traced at a distance of four to eight miles from the present course of the River, at a level of about three feet above medium stages of water, and running nearly at right angles to the line on which the River now runs.

The differences caused by these additional beds, however, are very trifling. Their aggregate would only amount to about 34 feet in a line of distance of 290 miles, and would not, therefore, affect any general result in relation to those wells.

The annexed diagram, exhibiting a longitudinal and transverse section of the plains of the Sacramento and San Joaquin, will exhibit more plainly than language can convey, an idea of the structure of these plains so far as known at the present time.

The diagram No. 1 shows a section carried through the major axis of the valley, comprising an air-line distance of 160 miles, or from the upper terrace at the northern extremity of the valley, south to a point opposite to the City of Sacramento in the County of Yolo. The lower clay bed is indicated at the different points at which it was noticed, which will be seen, by reference to the sketch, in the arroya south of Tehama; and again on the banks of the lake on the western side of the Sacramento River. This is probably the same bed which is found resting upon the slates some twenty-five miles north of the limits represented in the sketch. By reference to the letter of Mr. Drew, respecting the Stockton well, which we have exhibited in a tabular form, a close similarity of the beds of the two districts will be observed, and if the waters which sink beneath the surface in the more elevated districts of these plains, pass beneath this bed, (and from the evidences before us, such seems to be the fact), it will be necessary, as a consequence, to penetrate it in order to obtain any considerable supply of water. I entertain but little doubt that the foregoing remarks afford a correct idea of the true position of matters below the surface of the plains, and we are warranted in these conclusions from an examination of the outcropping materials on the flanks of the valley for miles in extent. The outcrops of the slates, sandstone and clays, on the west sides of the plains, are the equivalents of those which we may expect to find beneath the surface of the valley, and from the positions of the sedimentary rocks on the eastern borders, we are not warranted in any other conclusion than that waters are flowing in subterranean streams on the more impervious materials comprising the basis of these plains.

From the observations which I have been able to make during the past season upon these districts of the State, there have been no new facts elicited which would induce any modification of the opinion entertained and expressed in my former report, respecting the probable depths which it will be necessary to reach in order to obtain water from artesian wells. If there exists any reason for a change of those opinions, it rather tends to the increase of the depth which may be required. I still feel confident that the former conclusions will be found correct, and the figures true as to the point at which perennial springs will be reached. All the evidences I can command only tend to strengthen this confidence. Still it should be recollected that it is beyond the power of man to demonstrate, with *absolute certainty*, the depth of the stratified rocks which form these plains, without actual penetration through them, and the feasibility of an operation of this kind is demonstrable only so far as may be legitimately inferred from the natural position of the substratum as presented in their outcrop upon the borders of such plains. We should have in view, at the same time, the probable effect of those disruptive agencies which have elevated the edges on either hand, and the law which governs those effects, when exerted over long distances. In this country, as in every other which is similarly situated, the smallest amount of inclination will be produced on originally horizontal strata at the greatest distance from the immediate center of disturbance. On this rule was founded the position assumed in my former report, in relation to this subject, which is here referred to, together with a transverse section of the valley, in order the more fully to illustrate this portion of the present report.

The superficial structure of the plain is now known to a depth of 400 feet below the service, and if it be admitted that the rocks beneath the surface at the center are in their proper position, which will be found to be the case, taking the preceding rule as the basis of our calculations, we may thus be enabled to make an approximation of the depth to the surface of the underlying rocks, the superior of which is probably sandstone imposed upon a firm conglomerate beneath them.

It was stated in the report of last year, that a permanent supply of water would not, in all probability, be obtained before the sandstone had been perforated, unless, perchance, an arenaceous deposit should exist below the heavy upper clay beds, and this underlaid by a deposit of plastic clays or argillaceous slates; in that case the depth of water would fall within 800 feet.

I am not aware of any facts which would modify that opinion, and it is far better for us to have the probable maximum before us rather than the minimum of depth required, for, should we base our estimates of cost upon the latter, there are strong probabilities that failure in obtaining water from these sources would be the result even though a comparatively small depth might intervene between the point of suspension and the point at which water might be found.

An examination of the diagram exhibiting the transverse section of the basin will develope the fact that the Stockton well is in all probability but little more than half way down to the position assigned to the upper beds of sandstone, and it is quite certain that if water is not obtained before reaching those rocks, that it will be necessary to penetrate through their beds and obtain the supply on the surface of the conglomerate. The only prospects of a permanent supply of water being obtained at any depth less than twelve hundred feet, are the probabilities which may exist of a deposit of sand being found immediately below the beds which are now being bored, and this resting on an impervious deposit as above mentioned.

The following table of estimated depths under such a contingency as last proposed is given in order to direct attention to all of the favorable constructions which may be adduced upon this interesting subject, and hoping that citizens interested in it may be properly encouraged to persevere to the attainment of successful practical results. The depths in this table are estimated for a supply of water above the sandstone, and at given distances east and west of the City of Sacramento, and will be equally applicable to other localities upon these plains, so far as they maintain nearly the same level above tide water.

TABLE SHOWING THE PROBABLE DEPTH OF A PERMANENT SUPPLY OF WATER ABOVE THE SANDSTONE.

	FEET.
At Sacramento City,	775
Twelve miles east of Sacramento City,	700
Seventeen " "	660
Twenty " "	625
West of Sacramento, (at Washington),	775
Eleven miles west of Sacramento,	700
Fifteen " "	650
Twenty-two " "	550

To this table may be added 380 feet, should it become necessary to descend through the sandstones and upper beds of slates, which we have arranged as belonging to the superior beds which form the basis of the Valley.

It would be impossible to estimate the increased value of the lands lying upon these extensive plains when the fact has once been demonstrated that water can be obtained from these sources; at the same time it must be seen that individual enterprise alone will not be equal to the task of penetrating such depths, in consequence of the heavy expense which must be incurred in the undertaking. Few individuals are possessed of a landed estate of sufficient extent and value to warrant their embarking in such an expensive and costly operation. The State has, perhaps, a much greater interest in this matter than any other landholder, from her large landed possessions on these plains, and we here suggest the wisdom of the policy on her part, which shall take the initiative, if it were only to carry one shaft to the required depth at which water can be obtained. Not only would one success of this kind greatly enhance the value of her own lands, but it would also prove a strong incentive to combinations of individuals for the attainment of similar objects respecting private property. It is evidently the fear of failure which now deters many from undertaking the enterprise, consequently each district is now waiting for some neighboring section to enter the field, the effect of which is to retard the settlement and cultivation of the country, and affect materially the general prosperity. The effect of partial failures in obtaining water at small depths, and with limited means, will be that these operations will be esteemed unavailable, and it therefore becomes a matter of both public and private pecuniary interest to determine at what depth it will be necessary to descend, in order that a permanent supply may be obtained. After the solution of this matter by fair practical experiment, it would be found that all individual and corporate enterprises would be governed by its results.

I have conversed with two intelligent gentlemen who have been large contractors in well boring, in the Atlantic States, and they have given it as their opinion, that an eight inch bore cannot be carried to the depth of twelve hundred feet in California for any sum less than $14,000. This fact alone would be sufficient to deter almost any individual from an attempt to sink a well of this character, unless there should be a probability almost strong enough to approach a reasonable certainty that success would crown the enterprize. The sinking of one well to the requisite depth, would have the effect of imparting confidence in the undertaking, which no other circumstances can ever inspire. If this were done by the State, the extensive area of lands lying upon the valleys, and belonging to her, which under present circumstances must be sold at vey low rates from their desiccated character, would rise in intrinsic and market value sufficiently to more than repay the State for the expense of their reclamation.

The immediate occupancy and improvement of the broad plains of California would follow fast upon the steps of any system of irrigation which would successfully redeem their lands from that arid condition which for half the year gives them more the character of deserts than of habitable countries. Such a process of improvement would thus lead the State to new sources of revenue, not only in the enhanced value of her own lands, but also in the greatly increased value and amount of the improved lands of individual property taxable for governmental purposes.

There is no part of the country more inviting in point of fertility of soil and salubrity of climate than these valleys, and none which would be more tempting to the ambition of the agriculturist, if the additional feature of a plentiful supply of good water could crown the advantages which these lands possess, being in their central position between the markets of the mining towns on the one hand, and the cities of the seaboard on the other.

It is to be hoped that general attention may be turned to this subject, and that it will meet with such deliberation too on the part of the State Government as its importance would suggest. The higher portions of these plains, where nature has supplied them with moisture, are found to be abundantly productive, both for pasturage and the culture of grains, and if this moisture could by any means be secured throughout the summer season in the now arid portions, there would be no obstacle to the settlement through the valleys of an active and prosperous agricultural population.

TERTIARY ROCKS AND OTHER DEPOSITS OF THE SIERRA NEVADA.

We shall now pass to the notice of the rocks belonging to the tertiary periods, which are found in the Sierra Nevada, and which extend from the middle sections of these mountains to the east of the foot-hills and under the eastern borders of the valleys of the Sacramento and San Joaquin. They consist of sandstone, slates, conglomerates, and heavy beds of gravel drift, alternating with sands and clays—of the latter group, many are found in an indurated state, at times possessing a stony hardness, and at others the same bed is frequently found loose and incoherent.

On examining the rocks of this district of the State in the month of June last, it was found that the tertiaries were resting upon the granites direct, and that the granite had been uncovered by placer mining to a much more westerly extent than had previously been assigned to their positions. These operations placed us in possession of the facts, that they formed the base of the table lands near Willow Springs, and within 22 miles of the City of Sacramento. The aqueous deposits which are found resting upon the granites, exhibit themselves as out-liers, forming the main body of the first range of plateaus above the plain, and are of the utmost importance in determining the relative ages of contiguous rocks to the east.

West of Willow Springs, in the county of Sacramento, the slates and sandstones crop out near the edge of the plains; they soon become covered with the alluvial drift, and are not met with again in travelling to the east until arriving at the first range of hills beyond the above mentioned locality. *Between the springs and these hills, the only surface rock is the granite, forming the "bed rock" of this section for several miles*, and lying at an average depth of about twenty-five feet below the surface. At the distance of eight miles (air line) east of the Springs, these rocks disappear, and are replaced by beds of indurated gravel drift, having large quantities of a coarse granitic sand commingled; this latter article being heavily charged with iron, which forms the cementing medium of these beds. This drift-bed has been pierced to the depth of ninety-four feet with shafts sunk for mining purposes.

At the depth of forty-three feet from the surface, a bed of marine shells was found in fine gravel and sand, cemented by iron, giving the mass a considerable degree of firmness. Below the first fossil bed there were alternating beds of sand and gravel, in which were imbedded the teeth of sharks and other portions of the skeletons of fishes; commingled with these were the remains of mollusca in large quantities, and of various species. From the specimens obtained, it appears very certain that these beds were deposited upon the granitic rocks direct, as the fossil specimens in the State collection will abundantly prove, for in these the fossil may be seen adhering firmly to that rock.

Above this heavy bed of drift, and at the distance of half a mile to the south, the conglomerates crop out and form the summit of a high table ridge, on examining which, the marks of the old water line of the sea were distinctly engraved upon its surface for a linear disiance of nearly three miles. These rocks extend north and south from this point, forming the summits of a set of similar table ridges, for a distance of 20 miles, beyond which they were not followed in this State.

The altitude of these marine beds above the level of the sea is less than 800 feet, and in three localities they were found to range between 900 and 1000 feet. I consider these as corresponding with equivalent beds at the distance of 150 miles farther north. In this section of the State we have another illustration of those periodical elevations which form so conspicuous a feature in almost every district which has been visited, and which will prove a constant attendant of the traveler wherever he may wend his way.

The most eastern limit at which these tertiaries have been met with, is upon a line running north and south and cutting through Mormon Island on the south branch of the American River. The fossils beds will be found in the immediate vicinity of the following localities, viz: Texas Flat, Half Way House, Volcano Ridge, and Mississippi Flats in the county of Placer. The conglomerates on these table ridges are the same as those which pass beneath the edge of the valley, and it is in this section of the State, that the thickness of those rocks can be ascertained with a precision, sufficiently accurate for any practical purpose.

By reference to my notes taken at the beds, I find the following to be the order and thickness of the deposits as they occur at the different localities above named, and which are known to reach the edge of the plains immediately to the west. This table includes the rocks only, and such as are known to pass beneath the eastern border of the valley, and may serve to direct those operations which were spoken of in the preceding article.

THICKNESS OF THE SEDIMENTARY ROCKS IN THE SIERRA NEVADA.

East of the border of the Valley.

	FEET.
Argillaceous Slates,	144
Conglomerates,	312
Clay, sands and gravels,	86
Total,	542

At the border of the Valley.

	FEET
Argillaceous Slates,	130
Conglomerates,	270
Sand, Clays, &c.,	56
Total,	456

The fossil drift beneath the conglomerate east of the plain is not perceptible to that extent which would guide us to any conclusion as to the depths to which it descends at the edge of the valley. Therefore no estimate is entered for this deposit in this table.

The survey of the U. S. Rail Road Expedition, for 1854, has demonstrated that the fossil deposits of this range of country, are continuous to the extreme southern portion of the Tulare plains. The fossils of Pose Creek appear identical with those of the counties of Placer and Sacramento, but I am unable to give their differences in altitude if any exist, as the observations which would determine that point, are not accessible at the present time.

Between the Tulare plains and the American River, there are some fou or five other localities in which the tertiary deposits have been observed, and which contain imbedded fossils closely allied to those found in the localities specified; and the evidences thus furnished in relation to this subject are very conclusive in their character, as pointing to that period when the Tertiary seas had their boundaries far to the east of their present limits. A recession of the waters of the Pacific Ocean has therefore taken place, to the distance of 140 miles, since the period at which those fossils lived. A suite of these specimens for the State collection has been secured, from this very interesting portion of the State, a list of which will be found appended to this report.

We have now a more practical and economical view to take of this subject, so far as relates to the positions of these beds, and as this will involve a pecuniary interest in which the mining community are directly concerned, I solicit their particular attention, as well as that of the State authority, to the subject.

In order that a better understanding of the position of these rocks may be obtained, the following table showing their natural and relative positions is inserted. It commences at a point due north of Beale's Bar and continues west to the ends of the plains:

Beale's Bar,
Texas Flat,
Slates,
Conglomerate,
Fossil Beds,
94 feet Shaft.
Alder Springs,
Conglomerates,
Fossil Beds,
Granite. Granite. Granite.
Plains

From the above table it will be seen that the 94 feet shaft which was sunk on what is familiarly known as volcano ridge in the county of Placer did not reach that point at which the drift deposit containing gold may be expected to occur.— This is proved by the fact that at Alder Springs, a short distance to the west, the basis rock is granitic, and the auriferous deposit is found lying upon it, and below the conglomerates and fossil beds to the east. The same fact is noticeable at two other mining localities to the south and west of Alder Springs, also in the flats some three miles to the north of Beale's Bar. There are then at least five different positions at which the fossil beds are known to lie above the auriferous drift, and the positions assigned to the beds under consideration in the table furnish the data on which to found the conclusion. They occupy the terraced positions as occurring at the points designated, denudation having caused the outliers to the west of Alder Springs. Similar peculiarities are also noticeable in some of the lower mining localities further to the south, where the workable placers are found to occupy a like position among the hills a few miles east of the plains.

The position of those beds as they are found to occur in the lower hills, and where also the best opportunities are offered for their study, leads us to the conclusion that during this portion of the tertiary era a submarine deposit of drift was formed and that subsequently the superior conglomcrates had their origin, and are now found superimposed upon the deposits above named. Should this doctrine be finally demonstrated by more extensive and well directed improvements in mining operations, and the facts before us at the present moment most certainly favor the presumption that it is probably correct, than a new and wider field for mining operations is soon to open in this district of the State, and we may reasonably expect to meet with deposits equally valuable beneath these rocks in other parts of the State, on the same line of elevation, as those which have already been developed in the counties of Placer and Sacramento.

In this State it is well known that numerous instances have occurred in the mining districts where the miners have passed through the sedimentary rocks, (slates,) and found the deposits of gravel drift beneath, the same containing gold in fully equal quantities with that found in the surface material above them, and which was thought the foundation stone below which no gold would be found. These suggestions are not made as bringing to light any new principle in relation to placer deposits, for facts of similar character have been known for three years past in different sections of the State. The present case relating to the placer deposits of the counties of Sacramento and Placer, may be regarded as corroborative testimony of our former knowledge, and the existence of a much more extensive range of this character, than has heretofore been discovered.

The position of these auriferous deposits in the counties above named, and the corresponding character of a large portion of country lying north and south of the above section is adverted to at the present moment for the purpose of directing attention to those districts near the foot-hills which present similar features, and which are as yet untouched. These districts on either hand having the same altitude above the plains present equal certainties of the existence of the same deposits as those met with in the county of Placer. Under the head of placer mining, I shall have occasion to allude to this subject again.

The other members of the tertiary group on the foot-hills of the Sierra Nevada, consists of sandstones and clays, the most important of which are found upon the Cosumnes and other rivers south of this stream. The sandstone beds as far as examined have every appearance of being much more recent than any member of the stratified rocks of which we have heretofore spoken, and their position is evidently unconformable with the latter, resting very evidently on rocks having a much higher degree of inclination. In favorable localities for their examination, I have found their depth to exceed 110 feet. An instance of this kind is afforded upon the banks of the Tuolumne River, at a distance of two miles east of Jackson's Ferry.

As a general rule, these rocks have been but little, if any, disturbed, having but a slight inclination from the horizontal, and it might be said none, except that which is found to correspond with the gradiency of the plains beyond, and seldom exceeding two or three degrees. Immediately east of these deposits, and as you enter the hills, the other sedimentary rocks are seen cropping out and assuming high angles of inclination which are found to increase as you travel in an easterly direction.

Sufficient opportunity did not offer for a more critical examination of the recent sandstones than that of a mere passing notice. It would be desirable that they should receive a closer investigation during the coming season, than was afforded, from want of time during the past summer. Their proper place in the tertiary formations must be deferred until that time shall arrive, when we shall be able to speak with more precision in relation to the peculiarities which they may present. The older tertiaries in the more elevated portions of the mountains are more or less auriferous in nearly every locality in which they have been examined.

The soft clays which are at times found between the slates and conglomerates, and the gravel beds which are also found beneath the latter, are of the same character in as marked a degree as the drift beds of the surface which are imposed upon them. So far as those beds have been opened there appears little or no exception to the rule.

Within the last year the older conglomerate rocks have been found to contain gold, but not to that extent which would warrant mining explorations. The fact, however, is sufficiently well established to require notice in this place.

The sedimentary rocks extend eastward in the more central mining counties to within twelve miles of the summit ridge of the chain. Here a few imperfect fossils have been found, but none of sufficient distinctness to determine either their geological position or character with any degree of certainty. It is proper to state however that there are some evidences of the cretaceous, or perhaps, the upper secondary rocks being found in those districts, though as yet it is a matter of much doubt, arising from the imperfect condition of the organic remains found imbedded within them.

The following table exhibits the approximate depths of the superficial coverings of the mountain mining districts, in which that department of industry is conducted. The table is intended to represent the more central line of country which corresponds with the trend of the chain, and is usually found at a distance (air line,) of about forty miles from the eastern border of the plains. It will include in its range the towns of Forest City, Nevada, Georgetown, Volcano, Mokelumne Hill, and Sonora.

TABLE.

Sierra.

Gravel drift	60 feet
Light gray and blue clays	15 "
Blue clays	15 "
Gravel and sands	30 "
Clays, with lignites	18 "
Blue clays	25 "
Clays, with leaves	8 "
Auriferous gravel	18 "
Slates	22 "
Primitive rocks.	
Total,	201 feet.

El Dorado.

Gravel drift	60 feet.
Blue and brown clays	20 "
Cemented drift, clays, and lignites	40 "
Sand clays	20 "
Clays, with leaves	10 "
Sandy clays and lignites	10 "
Coarse sand, pyritous	4 "
Auriferous gravel	25 "
Primitive rocks.	
Total,	189 feet.

Amador and Calaveras.

Gravel drift - - - - - - -	60 feet.
Clays and sands - - - - - -	40 "
Plastic clays - - - - - - -	50 "
White clays - - - - - -	30 "
Cemented gravel and clays - - - -	45 "
Clays, with silicified woods - - -	15 "
Auriferous drift - - - - - -	30 "
Primitive rocks.	
Total, - - - - -	270 feet.

Nevada.

Gravel drift - - - - - - -	80 feet.
Blue and yellow clays - - - -	20 "
Blue and gray sandy clays, with leaves - -	30 "
Gravel and light clays - - - - -	50 "
Gravel and brown clays - - - -	10 "
Sands, gravel, and petrifactions - - -	8 "
Auriferous drift - - - - - -	40 "
Primitive rocks.	
Total, - - - - -	238 feet.

There is much uniformity, it appears, in the general character of the superior coverings of the primitive rocks in the placer ranges, and no little coincidence in the material which makes up the great mass of these beds; as much, at least, as the different sources from which the detrital materials were derived would permit; the modifications that may be present in any of the beds being produced entirely from local circumstances.

There is one feature, however, that is deserving of notice, and which is strongly marked throughout the State; one of which will enable us to arrive at a much better conclusion relative to the age of these deposits, than any relations which their lithological characters present; this is the close similarity which is manifest among most of the lignites and dycotyledonous leaves found in every portion of this part of the State, as well also as in many parts of the coast mountains. The beds that produce these forms in the mining districts have been placed in the tables as they occur in nature, and we may thus see at a glance theposition which each of these beds hold to each other.

The peculiarities connected with the distribution of these remains, leads to the conclusion, that a great uniformity of climate, and other conditions, prevailed for a long period after the disturbance of the older tertiary slates; this is proved from the fact, that comparatively little if any disturbance is manifest during the age in which the drift beds were being deposited. Notwithstanding these beds are elevated considerably above the sea, they do, in most cases, preserve their conformability with each other, and are unconformable with the slates on which they at many points rest. This may be regarded as one of the evidences of a persistent elevatory action going on through all the periods of the latter, as well as some of the earlier portions of this epoch. It would be a difficult task for the observer to define, with any degree of accuracy, the differences of age between the one part of the state and that of any other, so far as these particular deposits are concerned.

The close similitude in most of the fossil vegetation found in the drift beds, would render it difficult to define from what portion of the State any one suite of those specimens may have been taken. I have the impressions of leaves from the counties of El Dorado, Tuolumne, and Trinity, (the two latter counties being two hundred and seventy-five miles distant from each other,) that a close observer would be very likely to declare as having all been taken from the same locality. These organic forms are now in the hands of gentlemen fully competent to define their generic and specific characters, and whenever their investigations shall have been completed, the same will be placed before you.

PLACER MINING.

This branch of industry in this State has been prosecuted with much vigor during the past year, and many new discoveries of placer deposits have been developed within the past season. Those who have engaged in the heavier operations of this department, have carried their workings to an extent heretofore unparalleled in the history of mining in this State, the details of which will be noticed more at length in the following pages.

In the present article I shall review, briefly, the history of this branch of industry, and adduce such testimony of their probable continuance as has fallen under my observation, and such as will be found supported by facts alone.

There has been much discussion abroad relative to the probable continuance of the placer deposits of California, and attending this discussion, a manifest disposition among Atlantic writers to underrate the capacities of the State for the production of gold. So far as the personal interests of such individuals are involved in this question we have nothing to do; but when the publication of such articles are carried to an extent that a public injury is sustained upon our shores as a consequence, then it becomes a duty we owe to ourselves to speak in defence of the State of our adoption, and place the question before our friends and relatives abroad upon that basis upon which alone it can stand.

We shall, therefore, confine ourselves to facts, as developed within the past year and the year preceding, which will define, to some extent, the areas of the placer ranges on the western slope of the mountains; and it is to be hoped that they may prove sufficient to convince such as may be seriously affected with melancholy for our future fate in this particular, that they are in no danger of sinking deeper into the slough of that insolvency which their over-heated imaginations have prepared, from any failure, on the part of this State, to produce even an increase on her past annual exports. The commercial circles of the East, have been saved from bankruptcy by our exports, and we shall still continue to exercise the same paternal care over their interests as formerly, provided they will relieve us from accepting the entire produce east of the Rocky Mountains. Since 1849, we have had but a reiteration, from year to year, of this doleful prognostic, and this in the face of a continual advance on each annual aggregate exported from our shores, until now the public mind has become less sensitive to the dismal moan, which greets the eye or ear from some portion of the Atlantic board on the arrival of almost every mail.

The failure of an arrival of the accustomed number of millions per month to the Atlantic cities, is found to create a feverish panic among our distant friends, which is to be regretted, as an injustice to the people of this State usually follows such a contingency, from some portion of the Atlantic board. This arises from the fact that parties abroad do not possess the local information of those causes which are productive of such a failure, neither could they properly appreciate the same, were it in their possession.

The only regret to which we must submit in this matter is that, as a State, we have exported too much; but the prospect is that in the future we shall export much less gold than formerly. The report of the Controller of State for this year shadows forth the long wished for advent of confidence in capital investments for home improvements, and is a true exhibit of our resources; showing that, notwithstanding we have an increase of one million above our exports of the preceding year, yet we still have added to our home capital, permanently invested, fourteen millions, within the same period.

In my report of last year, it was stated that the placer ranges were at that time known to extend nearly to the summit ridge of the mountains; but this year it has been ascertained that they pass beyond the ridge, and are now fonud on the eastern declivity, having nearly the same altitude as those occurring on the opposite side. Within the past season, many of these deposits have been examined, and thus far are found to be equally productive with those of similar ranges to the west, and, with a favorable season ensuing, they will be largely occupied.

This increases the breadth of the placers, in the more elevated districts, about nine miles, and the length between twenty-five and twenty-seven miles, on a line parallel with the trend of the mountains. This additional field is what may be denominated "dry diggings." Still they will prove available only during the summer season and early part of autumn, from their altitude and local position.

Since my last report, I have been enabled to trace the "Eastern Blue Range," for a distance of thirty miles south of the point at which it was left last year, and, as far as examined, it possesses most of the general characters that were mentioned in relation to this district at that time. Its line may be defined to a considerable degree of accuracy by the following localities:

South of the middle branch of the American River, it is found at what is known as Cement Hill, being part of the same range of the Mameluke Hill, a short distance south of the former. Extending in a southerly direction from the vicinity of Georgetown, it is next met with at White Rock, some sixteen miles distant, and about three miles east of Placerville. In this section of country, the outliers of the range are distinctly seen, forming level ridges for long distances, the latter surrounding small basins or forming the flanks of broad ravines, similar to that known as Coon Hollow, and other adjacent localities. From Placerville it extends in a southerly course for eight miles, and it is again met with some three miles east of the town of Ringold, forming a flat table, of small extent, on the side of a hill facing to the southwest. From this locality it assumes a more southeast course, and is again seen on the sides of the hills forming the banks of Indian Creek, in the county of El Dorado. This is the most southern limit to which these placers have been traced with any degree of certainty.

A course a little east of south would bring this line of deposits in the vicinity of the town of Volcano, in the County of Amador, but it is yet quite uncertain whether this mining town is absolutely upon this range of placers, or whether it passes to the east of the high ridge back of this locality. From what observations I was enabled to make at Mokelumne Hill, and also south of this point, I am inclined to the belief that if it passes through this section of the State it will be found to the east of these latter towns, at distances within eight or twelve miles. The high table ridge to the east of Chilian Gulch possesses many of the external features which mark this range in other parts of the State; but the conglomerate beds found adjacent to this section indicate this to be of much more recent origin than the placers under consideration. The absence of any fossil remains from this district renders it difficult to form any conclusion that would be satisfactory on this point; it will therefore be omitted until such times as farther investigation may be had upon this immediate vicinity.

We will now turn to the more particular consideration of the placer, as far as known, and examine its capacities for production, with other characteristics that mark it in its course.

The line of the deposit has now been traced distinctly for a distance of one hundred and thirty-six miles, in an almost continuous line, and upon it are now located many of the most valuable mining districts of the State, on which the heavier investments of capital have been made for its successful workings. From the nature of the ground and its location, being very remote from the plains, and in many cases difficult of access from its elevation even above the adjacent country, it necessarily has required a much greater outlay of capital to develop its treasures than any of the districts lying to the west of it and improved as mining ground, and thus far has yielded a proportionably greater amount of gold.

So far as these districts have been opened, they have fully sustained the character which they have heretofore acquired, and particularly noticed in the preceding report, viz: *that in no instance, up to the present time, has this placer failed to reimburse the money expended in opening the ground, reaching the lead and returning a handsome profit to the adventurer.* This cannot be said of any other range of placers in this State.

Up to the month of November last, there had not been an abandoned claim upon the range where the works had been conducted with the view of reaching the lower lodes of the range, and no failure has occurred in striking the lode where the adits have been driven at any sufficiently low point.

From these facts alone, it will be seen that placer mining is not altogether a game of chance when conducted with skill, well-directed and practical judgment, and it teaches, also, another valuable lesson, which is, that segregated labor and capital is not sufficient to cope with the heavier branches of placer mining, neither is it as profitable in its results as when otherwise and judiciously directed. This branch of industry in this State has taken that place at the present time, which strictly entitles it to the appellation of a science, and he that would fully appreciate it should witness it. Placer mining to California is what coal mining is to Pennsylvania, and the great coal districts east of the Rocky Mountains, and we are fast approximating that day when its subterranean operations will equal, and in many instances exceed the latter. Should there be those who foster doubt on this point, and doubtless there are many such abroad, I would respectfully suggest to such a visit to the upper portions of the counties of Placer and El Dorado, with those of Amador and Calaveras on the south, and those of Nevada and Sierra on the north. In these counties they will find an ample field of operations, on which they will find but little difficulty in forming an opinion of the character and extent of the workings beneath the surface and the means employed to consummate the end. They will find the engineer with his levels as carefully adjusted and applied as though his survey was instituted for the leveling of a rail track, and the necessities of accuracy in the selection of the most feasible point to tap the heart of the mountain is equally as great in the one case as in the other.

The placer miner of the present day in this section of the State, estimates the costs of the operation on which he is about to enter with all that care and attention that would be bestowed upon any other enterprise where the sum of ten to thirty thousand dollars is the sum to be invested, and where his interests are involved to that extent. It is not uncommon to find amounts equal to the above, invested in our larger operations now in progress of working, and a few instances among many, may serve to illustrate the fact. I will mention but two or three in connection with this part of our subject.

The cost of opening the Mameluke Hill, near Georgetown, by the parties interested, exceeded forty thousand dollars, while the receipts from the same during the period of little more than one year, has exceeded five hundred thousand. Another case is that of Jones's Hill, the opening of which has already risen above thirty-four thousand dollars, the receipts being above two hundred and eighty-four thousand dollars; and still another in the County of Nevada, (Laird's Hill) the expense of opening was nearly forty thousand dollars, while the receipts from the latter in June last, had reached the sum of one hundred and fifty thousand—the resonrces of either are as yet in any thing but an exhausted condition The above are mentioned only for the purpose of conveying a better idea of the expenses and profits of what is denominated deep mining, in this State, and the localities named form but a small proportion to the aggregate of similar workings.

In the counties of Nevada, Sierra, Placer, El Dorado, Amador and Calaveras, there are scores of adits and other workings of smaller dimensions, which have already cost sums varying in amount from ten thousand dollars upward to the figures given above, and from which proportional profits have been derived. The mining districts abound with evidences of wealth like those above, and they possess equally as strong evidences ot permanency of chatacter, and it would be no difficult matter for the incredulous to banish his incredulity, if he will but take the trouble to investigate the facts which nature and individual enterprize have placed before him.

An idea of the necessary expenses that must be incurred in conducting these branches of placer mining, can be obtained only by an examination of the adits which have been driven in prosecuting these labors. There are but few which are less than three hundred feet in length, and many that range from ten to twelve hundred feet, and of a size sufficient to use a horse within for the purpose of delivering the earth to be washed at the sluice or the attle to the end of the tram-road. These adits are driven in some cases hundreds of feet through solid rocks, and when thus conducted they often penetrate the very centre of a mountain, or as in the case of the high ridge south of Placerville, they have not only reached the center, but have passed entirely through the ridge.

In other parts of the State, the heavier placer operations are conducted in a different manner. In place of the adit, a broad ditch is carried through the hill, and the entire hills removed to their base by hydraulic washings. This system of working, as conducted in this State at present, will compare very favorably in magnitude with any system of mining operations of the Atlantic States, or even in many parts of the older continent, and from the success which has thus far attended it, it bids fair to advance much beyond the limits to which it is now confined. Five years have elapsed since the mines of this State were worked to any considerable extent. The area that is now known to contain valuable deposits of gold, is believed to be at least six times greater than that which was developed during the years of 1848 and 1849, while the number of miners actually engaged in the extraction of gold is less than those of 1852, yet the export of the year last past exceeds by nine millions the total exports of the former year. Under these circumstances, it is rather a forced conclusion to arrive at, that the mines of the State are in any way likely to recede from their former productions; and we would suggest to our friends abroad, that it is time they had divested themselves of the idea too long prevalent, that our placers will soon become exhausted, or that the workings consist in mere surface scratching, without depth or probable continuance. We have evidences that should prove satisfactory to reasonable beings, that they are something more than an ephemeral show, as all known facts in this State are opposed to that position, and they are abundant for two hundred miles of the length of the eastern mountain chain.

In order to convey a better idea of the mining districts they will be divided into three distinct ranges, denominated the Upper or Eastern Range, the Middle Placers, and the Valley Mines. This has now become necessary from the fact that the characteristics of these districts are as distinctly marked as are the northern, middle, and southern portions of the State. It separates also three evidently distinct periods of the geological history of this part of the continent, in which marked changes are apparent upon the surfaces that had emerged above the ocean during that epoch.

EASTERN RANGE.

This district extends from near the summit ridge of the mountains to within about twenty-five miles of the edge of the plains. It maintains a very uniform breadth of about twenty miles, and a length of one hundred and thirty, as far as known. It covers an area equal to about three thousand square miles, a large proportion of which is available as mining grounds.

In this district is situated the major part of what is known as the "dry diggings" which includes the towns of Forest City on the north and Placerville on the south. At the present time there is but a comparatively small portion of this district occupied and improved. Admitting, that of the area included within the lines of this district, but one-third of the same may be considered as containing placer deposits, we shall have for the immediately available purposes of mining an area equal to one thousand square miles.

A glance at the entire area which is now in actual occupancy on this range, and employed as mines in active operation, will convince those acquainted with the district that but a very small fraction of the available territory is as yet opened or in any manner improved. It is estimated that twenty square miles will cover that area and even this may be considered a large figure for the grounds so improved; amounting to two per cent. only, of the lowest aggregate that can be placed upon the unoccupied district of the range. It is doubtful whether there are men enough in this State (aside from those required for the transaction of other departments of business,) to occupy and improve even one half of the available mining lands that lie in the four middle mining counties of the State which at the present time is untouched, for it is pretty well ascertained that the absolute amount of ground in fourteen of the mining counties, now under improvement for those purposes, does not exceed five hundred square miles. The amount of territory in each county which is unoccupied forms a heavy aggregate against the other.

Of the eastern range of placers there are wide districts intervening between the settlements on the range, and an approximate idea may be obtained, of the extent of these placers, by citing districts that are well known, which will convey at the same time a better conception of the proportions occupied and the reverse.

The counties of Placer and El Dorado are fair examples of this district; they lie adjoining each other and are situated nearly in the middle of the State, and of the range. The deep workings of the above counties extend north and south for a distance (air line,) of thirty-three miles, the north fork of the American being one boundary, and the mountains and its tributaries being the other on the south; the breadth included in the above line and extending east and west is about fourteen miles. The mining towns within this district are Iowa Hill, Michigan Bluffs, Georgetown, Spanish Flat, Placerville, and other smaller settlements situated between the above and to the east of the line as given.

The area of the eastern range in these counties alone, amounts to four hundred and sixty-two miles, nearly one half of the aggregate amount for the State as belonging to this particular range of deposits; and when we recollect that

10

there are four additional counties through which their placers are found, the estimate of one thousand square miles will not be considered as excessive.

To those who are acquainted with the section alluded to, I have no hesitancy of submitting the above figures, for there is no object to be attained in presenting a fancy sketch of our available resources. We may draw upon facts for many years to come in regard to matters of this character, for the mining districts are possessed of an ample fund for that purpose.

It must not be understood that the "deep diggings" of this district are the only resources obtainable, or that they constitute the only deposits of gold in the range, for it is far otherwise. The entire surfaces of this range are productive of this metal; it was from the surface washings of portions belonging to this district of the State that a large proportion of the gold was obtained during the earlier periods of mining. These placers still continue to yield profitable returns for labor, though long since they were among the old workings which were considerrd exhausted. The returns from these old placers at the present time are attributable to the improved methods of mining that have been introduced subsequent to their first becoming abandoned, and the greater care which is now bestowed in washing the earth.

The placer miner of the present day will not exhaust the same quantity of ground that he would have done in 1850 or 1851, and at the same time obtain an equal and, in some instances, a greater amount of gold from one of these exhausted placers. We may, therefore, regard the surface deposits of these sections as prolific sources of wealth for years to come. This conclusion is based on the facts which past experiment has demonstrated, and which are acknowledged throughout the State by those who have given any attention to the subject.

In selecting the Counties of Placer and El Dorado as illustrative of the character of the eastern range of deposits, I would not be understood as expressing any preferences, of productive capacity or of a better defined range of these deposits; they were selected from the fact that they held a more central position in relation to the above than for any other purpose, and they do not, to my knowledge, afford any better illustration of the characteristics of this district, than the Counties of Sierra, on the North, or that of Amador or Calaveras on the South; in fact, this range is much better exemplified in the County of Sierra than at any point south of the latter.

MIDDLE PLACERS.

By this term is expressed that range of country which is situated at an average distance of about twenty miles from the line of the higher foothills, or having its western border within about four miles of the edge of the plains, comprising a district of country of twenty miles in width and three hundred in length, having a trend parallel with that of the mountain chain in which it is situated; it covers an area equal to about six thousand square miles.

On this range is situated what is denominated the surface workings, although there are some instances in which the deposits of drift containing gold lie nearly as deep as those alluded to in the preceding article. This, however, is not the general fact relative to these districts, and the labor and expense of extracting the métal, consequently, is not as heavy. The ordinary depth of the placer drift in this district, ranges between twelve and forty feet; it is composed of a more heterogenous collection of stones than the deposits of the higher range; in the latter the pebbles and boulders have but few varieties, while those of the middle placers are composed of many; so much so is this the case, that it is often difficult to distinguish what rocks predominate.

The "bed rock" of these districts is composed mostly of slates elevated to high angles of inclination, or the same rocks changed by heat, in some cases to that extent as nearly to obliterate their former structure; their transition has been so complete that they have assumed the character of true porphyries; this must have occurred prior to the deposition of the drift as these deposits bear no marks of igneous action since they were deposited. In some localities the drift beds are found resting upon the granite direct, the latter rock often presenting evident marks of the action of water.

In examining the gravel from this district, we will often find the stones which are peculiar to the eastern range mingled with those of more recent date, and which are often found in closer proximity *in situ*; with the above is also found more or less of the smaller gold of the upper districts commingled with that which is incident to the middle sections of the State.

These facts naturally lead us to the conclusion that at the period in which the gravel drift of the middle placers were deposited that the country to the east was subjected to the action of floods which must have been somewhat violent in their character. I am not prepared to say at this time, that the deposits of this district of the State, were formed during the period of the NORTHERN DRIFT, for there are some features wanting to establish that point conclusively. Should the above fact be ultimately established, there are attendant circumstances that will prove the eastern range to have preceded that period, and which has been alluded to in former reports.

The economical value and extent of the middle placers, is the principal object of their notice in this place, and we will therefore direct our attention to that particular point. It is upon this range of country that the g eater proportion of the mining community of the State are located, and more particularly upon the central and eastern portions of the same. The cause of this is obvious, for from the nature of the ground to be operated upon, segregated labor is more prosperous, and small companies with limited means can prosecute mining with better success and profit than in the heavier workings of the eastern range of placers. The labor and incidental expenses for facilities in the extraction of gold, are much less and more easily obtained as a general rule than in the former case; hence men who are possessed of limited means usually occupy the middle sections before entering the field of the more lengthy operations that are conducted in other districts.

This district of the State is but sparsely settled, at the best; and like many other portions of the mineral and agricultural sections, there is but here and there a few scattering cabins or small settlements, often for many miles. The placers that are spread far and wide throughout this section, are scarcely touched, or if so, they are marked by a few small shafts only, which have been sunk by some prospecting miners, in their rambles over the State in search for richer fields than those they left. It is often the case that these shafts have remained for two or three years after they were driven, when they have again become occupied by others, yielding profitable returns for small amounts of labor. It is from these very partial examinations of traveling miners made in preceding years, that some of the most valuable placer deposits have been developed; the hints thus given in the former case have been adopted by those who have subsequently followed, and have thus led to pleasing results.

The introduction of water by artificial canals into regions lying remote from natural streams has had the effect to develop further the fact, that but limited sections exist in this district in which the staple product of the State does not abound. From the above facts we should be led to infer that a much larger population than that at present found in these districts should follow under the circumstances: it should be thus, but there are causes which at present operate to prevent such a result, the principal of which, is the want of a sufficient supply of water to conduct mining operations to that extent which the character of the country require. The natural supply of this material seldom exceeds four months of the year, in amounts that would be equivalent to subserve the above purposes, in the greater proportion of the mining localities of this range, and this too at that season when labor is nearly suspended from inclemency of the weather. In order therefore that an extensive population should be found upon the unoccupied portions of this part of the mineral district, the introduction of water by artificial means becomes an essential requisite.

An increase of our mining population in any district of the State, has no tendency whatever to excite any fear of the exhaustion of the mines of that locality to which they may chance to wend their way; for it is now admitted that sufficient room for labor abounds in any of the mining settlements, for a much greater number than those who now occupy them. The introduction of water by canals through an unoccupied portion of the State, is as certain to bring in an active population along its line, as the fact that such an agent is known to exist, as it is well known that nearly the entire surface contains a sufficiency to largely pay for labor in its extraction.

So far as the middle placers have been opened, they have thus far proved productive to an eminent degree, and the new placers which had been developed within this range have, as far as known, proved fully equivalent to those which have preceded them, and there is no good reason that can be advanced for the untenable position that has been assumed, that the present theatre of operations is the *finale*, any more than for a similar opinion which was entertained four years since in relation to those localities at that time occupied, and which are still yielding their annual quota nearly the same as before.

VALLEY MINING.

We come now to the consideration of the lower and most western districts in which deposits of gold have been found, and which constitute the third and last in the order of arrangement.

The valley mines are those districts which are situated among the lower foot-hills of the mountains, and extend westward from thence into the eastern edge of the plains of the San Joaquin and Sacramento to the extent of three to five miles. These mines are distinctly traceable from Chico Creek in the County of Butte on the north, nearly to Snelling's ranch on the Merced River to the south, having a linear distance of about two hundred and fifty miles. The position which they maintain, or whether they exist at any point north of the first named boundary, and south of Fort Reading on Cow Creek, in the County of Shasta, I am at present unable to state, not having passed over that particular district during the past season. But the opinion may be safely entertained, that they are continued through the latter district, and that the placers of the Upper Sacramento Valley alluded to in the preceding pages of this report are but the northern termini of this belt. The valley mines are situated on what has been spoken of as constituting the higher terraces of the plains, and are composed of alluvial drift mostly, which have been derived from the lower hills adjacent to their borders. The gravel of the lower beds is usually small and composed of the pebbles found in the conglomerates commingled with the smaller stones which have been conveyed by the agency of water from the approximate portions of the middle districts. The gravel is usually much discolored by the ferruginous materials with which they are intimately commingled, and all the beds containing gold, from the surface to their greatest depth partake in a high degree of the same peculiar characteristic. The deposits are found to extend to depths varying from three to eight feet, and rests on sandstone, slates or clay beds above the latter, and are the most shallow of any of the placer ranges as yet discovered in the State, and at the same time the most easily worked. In my report of 1853, the attention ot the Legislature was directed to the peculiarities of this district of the country under the head of mineral resources, and which will be found on pages 21 and 22, cf Assmbly, Doc., session 1853. I recur to this subject again at the present time, trusting that this district may attract that attention to which it is entitled, hoping that some measure may be adopted that will have the effect of preventing those collisions which must ultimately ensue between the agriculturists and miners in regard to the occupancy of the lands.

It is incumbent upon me to define, as nearly as possible, the probable extent and local position, both of the agricultural and mineral lands, so far as the same comes within my knowledge; and for this purpose, this subject is again introduced, so that in sectionizing, hereafter, these districts may be distinctly marked, and their boundaries thus known.

It has been generally supposed that the entire valley lands skirting the foot-hills, possessed but limited amounts of the precious metals, and that when such lands containing gold were thus known, the deposits have been regarded as purely accidental. Such is not the case, however, and if it were, the same rule would be equally applicable to every other portion of the mining districts of the State. Since the days when that opinion prevailed, there have been circumstances occurring, at different times, respecting the true characteristics of these lands, which have had a tendency to modify the views then entertained respecting them, to that extent that those views have now become entirely obsolete, and the valley mines are now considered nearly co-extensive with the middle or upper districts, and they probably fall but little short of the latter.

So well defined is the mineral district of the plains, that, at the present time, there are not less than eight water companies who have extended their works to the foot-hills, and three of this number were distributing water four miles beyond the hills, into the plains, during the month of December last. In the central and more northern portions of this range, the extension of these canals is being prosecuted as fast as the nature of attending circumstances will permit, and from what is now in process of being completed beyond the line of the lower mountains, there will not be less than twenty-three of these canals discharging water on to the surface of the valley within the current year. In seven of the principal mining counties of the State, there are one hundred and nine companies engaged in the conveyance of water for mining purposes, and with this amount, even, there is not sufficient to supply the demand. We may therefore conclude that the small quantity which twenty-three flumes will convey to the valley mines will not probably amount to over eighteen per cent. of that which will be requisite for their operations.

Should an ample supply of water be furnished to open this entire range of placers, we have not a population sufficient to occupy and improve it, aside from those engaged in similar occupations in other parts of the State. A large proportion of these mines will, therefore, remain untouched for many years to come, and improved only in isolated portions, where the conveniences of water are easily obtained.

Most of those who are at present engaged in this district, are men who have formerly occupied themselves in the older and mountain districts since 1850, and are, therefore, capable of judging of the comparative value of a placer of this kind, with those of other sections. Their experimental knowledge is, therefore, of some value, as a criterion, to judge of the prospects of these mines, as being remunerative for labor, if no other more conclusive considerations presented themselves.

We will not stand upon the basis of individual opinions alone, in this matter, but will present an outline of the settlements upon this range of country. They will present the best argument of the capacities, progress and development of the mines, from the date of their discovery to the present time, and the character of these valley sections.

The localities situated along the line of these mines are well known in the State, and as a consequence, their comparative products will be easily estimated by those who have even but a slight acquaintance with the mineral products of the country.

Commencing in the county of Butte, the first mining locality is on what is known as Neal's Flat; following a southerly direction to Butte Creek, they are again found at Rich and Reeve's Bars, on that stream, and a few miles further south the mines are occupied in and about the vicinity of Spring Valley, and thence to the banks of the main Feather River; crossing this stream they again occur in the vicinity of Iowa Ranch, nine miles southwest of the town of Bidwell. Following the line of the foot hills to the Honcut Creek, miners are engaged on both sides of this stream, and but twelve miles distant from the town of Veazie.

From the Honcut south, the next placers which are improved, are those upon the banks of the Yuba, in the vicinity of Ousley's Bar, being but fourteen miles east of Marysville. There are two mining camps near the edge of the plains between the south banks of the Yuba, before reaching Camp Far West, on Bear River, which is the next locality of any note. From this place to the American River, there are four localities in which these mines have peen opened, and which run west of a line cutting through Massachusetts Bar, the lowest on the latter stream.

From the latter locality, we pass through placers three miles from Alder Springs, and in a southerly course from thence to the west of Prarie City. On the Consumnes they are again found at Michigan Flat and Cook's Bar, and following the plains they again occur four miles west of Ione Valley. South of the latter and along the western lines of the county of Calaveras to Jackson Ferry, on the Tuolumne River, and between that stream and the Merced, there are ten locations, known as mining camps or towns, the inhabitants of which will equal those of some of the more inland districts. The number of settlements on this range, at this time, amounts to thirty-one, several of which have been occupied for the past two years. This fact alone is sufficient to establish its character as a mining district, and it is one also that many hundred thousands in gold has been extracted from during 1854.

I have been thus particular in noting the localities situated upon this range, for the purpose of quieting if possible, some few of those periodic effusions which flow from the over-anxious conservators of the public good both at home and abroad, by exhibiting what may be considered an approximate outline of the area of our mineral resources so far as known, and to contradict plainly by statistical facts, (the bolder enunciation which too often appears in the columns of those who should be possessed of better information) that the mines of this State are in a depreciating condition, to that extent that either confidence or capital investment in either branch, may be considered a hazardous enterprize.

Another reason for the local details respecting the valley mines, as given, is for the purpose of eliciting that attention to the location of lands for agricultural purposes, which the statutes of this State and the United States prescribe in relation thereto, and to define as near as possible, the western limits to which the mineral lands in all probability extend; and due care in selecting lands for the purposes of agriculture along the eastern borders of these plains will ultimately save much expensive litigation and trouble.

The western limits of the mineral lands are generally well defined, and so distinctly marked that even the stranger may readily recognize them in passing across them. The following are the characteristics that will designate these grounds, from those in which no gold has as yet been found, and which latter approximate and form in some few instances the eastern borders of the plains.

I will here quote from my report of 1853, the original description of this section of the State. I have seen no reason to change the opinion then entertained, but believe that all subsequent events to the present time are fully corroborative of that position.

"This district of country is situated in the lower foot-hills and immediately on the eastern edge of the valley. It maintains a very uniform breadth of about four miles, (from the base of the hills,) and is almost uninterrupted throughout the valleys adjoining the foot-hills to the east. A large part of the mining district of the county of Sacramento is a true example of these lands, though the principal range alluded to is situated a short distance west of those points in which mining operations are conducted at the present time."

This district is strongly marked throughout its entire extent, and in passing over it either from the mountains or from the valley to the mineral districts proper, the transition is so marked that it cannot fail to attract the attention of the most careless traveler. It will recur to the mind of almost every person who has passed from the valleys into the interior, that at the distance of some fourteen miles east of the Sacramento River, that he enters very suddenly a district of the plains thickly strewed with small *angular* pebbles of quartz, the belt is scarcely less than two miles in width at any point and in some places much broader, (extending often to four miles.) On reaching the eastern verge of the plains, the transition is equally marked and sudden as in the first instance; the *angular* pebbles disappear and a few round pebbles mixed with alluvium, replace them for a short distance, when these are immediately succeeded by the outcrop of the slates."

"From what the writer has seen of this district, I feel no hesitancy in saying that it must in a few years become the busy field of active and extensive mining operations, and I think this opinion will meet the concurrence of those persons who are intimately acquainted with the localities and are engaged in mining operations, at the present time, within the limits prescribed."

"It is not to be understood that this section of country will prove as highly productive in a short space of time as the superficial deposits of the interior sections, nor can it with any degree of propriety be expected, but as a compensatory principle, they will possess the double advantage of being readily accessible and though yielding a lower, they will render a more continued remuneration for labor and a surer prospect of success"

In quoting the first part of the last paragraph I would not be understood as entertaining the same opinion at this time, for the development of these placers since that day has furnished grounds for a change of opinion in that particular, and I take this opportunity to recall it.

Within the past year, where the advantages of water in sufficient quantity existed to conduct operations in mining, these districts have yielded as fair average returns for labor as any district of the State. And though situated so far to the west and into the plains, where we should have expected to have found little else than fine "drift gold," it is proved that in the majority of those localities which have been opened, that metal equally coarse with much found in the more elevated districts has been taken from the valley mines. This fact is sufficient to do away with the idea that the deposits of the plains are merely accidental, as they have been termed; they have evidently been derived in a great measure from the breaking down of the adjacent sedimentary rocks, which contain veins of auriferous quartz, the disintegration of which has furnished the material which we now find distributed throughout the range, and from that cause we may expect that these placers will prove equally advantageous for operation on an extended scale as many of the more ancient beds of the Sierra Nevada.

The limits of that district, containing gold upon the plains, I should estimate as carrying a line parallel with the foothills and at a distance of four miles west of the latter, and which should be considered mineral lands in the strictest sense in which that term is applied, and they should be subjected to the same jurisdiction that now obtains in the mountain sections. Such lands under our present system of laws are not subject to entry, and the fact is thus mentioned that their position may be better understood.

From the best information obtainable from all parts of the State, it is believed that the amount of ground in actual occupancy and under improvement for mining purposes does not probably exceed four hundred square miles, one fourth of which area may be included in what are known as old placers, and which are still productive. During the year 1852 it was estimated that one hundred thousand men were engaged in the extraction of gold, (this is probably a close figure) a much greater number than has been employed since that time, and whose aggregate product for that year amounted to the sum of forty-five millions of dollars. Taking as a basis the returns of the last census from which we find that the total number of inhabitants in the mining counties for that year amounted to one hundred and forty-three thousand (allowing thirty thousand for El Dorado not returned) of sixty per cent. of which number were probably engaged in the actual process of mining or a total of about eighty-six thousand thus employed for 1853.

This is probably above the actual number employed during 1853 and 1854, as a very large number of those formerly engaged in mining have employed their time, since 1852, in agricultural pursuits. These estimates may be considered approximations only, but taking the highest possible figure that can be given for those employed for the years 1853 and 1854, (eighty thousand) the following proportional results for labor will be found; the actual working time, in this branch of employment, in this State, being about eight months of the year. The figures below comprise those only which have appeared in manifests, with the exception of those of 1854, in which the deposits at the Mint for coinage and bars during the months of November and December are included with that known to have remained on deposit in different parts of the State, and which was the product of the year last past. The two latter sums make up an aggregate of little more than eleven millions, which, with the exports of 1854, amounts to the sum of sixty-one millions that is known as the product for that year:

TABLE OF EXPORTS, PRODUCT, AND AVERAGE WAGES.

	Exports and Product.	Miners.	Average Per Annum.
1852,	$45,000,000	100,000	$450
1853,	56,000,000	86,000	670
1854,	61,000,000	86,000	700

The above is certainly a much better remuneration for labor than can be found in any other State of the Union, and is fully corroborative of the fact long since stated, that our mines are absolutely yielding a higher income at present, than at any former period, with a less amount of work expended. There are no pretensions to accuracy in the above figures, as no fractional amounts are included, which would have swelled the amounts given, to a material degree. They are intended to convey but a general idea of what labor will command in the mines of the State, from one portion of the mining sections to any other extremes thus far known.

From what has been said of the areas comprised within the lines of the different ranges, as given in the preceding pages, it will be seen that we have still enough and to spare for all who are present, and for all that may hereafter arrive, for at least the next half century. There need be but little fear of their failing to yield their annual crop of gold, as long, perhaps, as our valleys will yield their crops of grain.

The aggregate areas amount to about eleven thousand square miles, that is known to contain gold; and, when this is compared with the area actually occupied, the latter will be found to comprise but a mere mite of our available resources. With our present population of the mining districts, and the broad expanse of territory over which they are spread, they appear like mere specks, dotting the surface of an inland sea, so indistinct as scarcely to be appreciable on the broad expanse by which they are surrounded.

QUARTZ VEINS.

In my report of last year, it will be seen that the quartz veins of the State were divided into separate groups denominated the older and recent groups, each having a different age and apparently belonging to different geological periods. These were again separated into three divisions, each occupying certain districts of the State, and the divisions of the older group were found running in lines nearly parallel with each other.

It will be necessary briefly to allude to the relative disposition of these veins among their investing rocks in order to obtain a better idea of the positions and relations of other veins which have been developed with the year that has passed.

That group which was denominated the "older," and which includes the eastern and more central line of dikes that traverse the inland districts of the State pursue a strike which is nearly north and south. This intrusion occurred evidently during the period immediately preceding the upheaval of the rocks belonging to the tertiary epoch, the proofs of which are found in the part that in no instance are they known to have disturbed the rocks of that date, though often found closely adjoining the latter, and which in some instances are found to overlie the dikes themselves.

The uniformity which these rocks present in their latitudes with the rocks by which they are invested, compels us to admit that they must be regarded as a distinct group, equally as marked in feature as are any of the different beds which go to make up any series found in the sedimentary rocks of any portion of the State.

To the west of this suite of veins, are found the more recent dikes, and which were called the "recent group." These extend from the edge of the plain eastward for about fifteen miles, and in some few instances have been found intruded among the rocks of the preceding period.

The peculiarities that remove these veins from the former, is found in the fact that they have disturbed not only the primitive but also the most recent of the tertiary rocks of these districts, and as late as the *pliocene* group in other parts of the State, abundant evidences of which are met with in many parts of the coast mountains.

The course of the recent dikes diverges from those of the older at an angle of about twenty-four degrees, their mean trend being south twenty-four degrees east, and north twenty-four degrees west. Were these peculiarities merely local, we might with some degree of reason assign to the entire series a cotemporaneous age, the characteristics noticed pervade so great an extent of country that we should find some difficulty in demonstrating that they made their appearance among the other rocks during one and the same period.

In addition to the preceding series we have now to consider another and distinct set of veins which have been developed and clearly defined during the past eighteen months. These are the east and west veins, which often cut former dikes at nearly right angles, and when first seen were regarded as branches of the north and south lodes ; but subsequent observation has established the fact that they are an entirely independent group.

At present there are eight localities in the State at which these veins are known to occur, four of which are found to cut the older veins, and the others are located among the slates of the tertiaries. We have no means as yet of determining the fact with any degree of certainty, whether the east and west veins are older or nearer than the tertiary dikes, but what evidences there are existing leads to the inference that they preceeded the latter. This presumption is based upon the fact that where the east and west veins are noticed among these rocks, there is not the same evidences of disruptive agency as at those points where they are found in contact with the older veins. The information in our possession relative to these dikes throughout the State, is such at present that we are enabled to arrange them in somewhat a more systematic order than has heretofore been presented.

The table below will present at one view the different systems that are at present known, and which are beyond all question ; but it is not to be supposed that those presented comprise all that will ultimately be developed among the metalliferous lodes of the State. Others might be added to the present list were we to adopt the plan of arranging a system from surface features alone, but we prefer waiting until those lodes which present indistinct evidences of being unconnected with the others shall have been definitely settled by subterranean openings, for nothing can be lost by the delay.

SYSTEMS OF VEINS

No. 1—North and South Veins.
No. 2—East and West Veins.
No. 3—Northeast and Southwest Veins.

The above are the only lodes yet known, and the former division of the groups will still be retained until such time as the effects of the east and west veins on the recent or tertiary dikes shall have been ascertained. The rocks disturbed by each system will be found as follows :

SYSTEMS.	GROUPS.	ROCKS DISTURBED.
North and South Veins.	Older.	Primitive.
East and West Veins.	Median.	Primitive.
Southeast and Northwest Veins.	Recent.	Tertiary Slates and Sandstone.

The dissimilarity in the metallic constituents of these systems is worthy of remark, as well also as the peculiar dispositions of the metal itself. In the first and second cases we find but little disposition to the crystalline form in any of the veins yet explored, while in the other, the metal more frequently assumes this character, and the percentage of silver is also much greater.

The constituents of the veins are equally well marked, the ores of lead are far more common in the east and west lodes than that usually found in either of the others. As a general fact, it may be stated that the metal from the placers in the immediate vicinity of these veins often bears but little analogy to to that found in *situ* among the rocks of the district in which the latter are situated. It is not uncommon to find gold of a very low carat in a placer, while that of a metallic lode adjoining would be correspondingly high, and the reverse of this is also true.

The gold of the North and South veins is usually destitute of any crystalline form with the exception of one or two instances, while that from the east and west veins possesses this character in a much higher degree These lodes also contain the largest amount of other metallic compounds, as lead and copper, the first of which is frequently productive of silver; I have seen gold from one of these veins producing five per cent of that metal; the assay was made at the United States Mint of this State.

These points lead to interesting inquiries relative to placer gold, and when fully understood, will settle many of the discrepancies that now obtain in relation to the variable character of the metal produced from these districts; and will ultimately be the means of determining the relative ages of such deposits.

From mining explorations we are constantly acquiring information of the distribution of the metallic lodes of the State, and the day is not far distant when all the different systems of productive veins will be fully understood and their peculiarities noted with that precision which the necessities of this department of business demands, and an intimate acquaintance with the changes that occur in these lodes is now being understood as necessary in prosecuting this business with advantage.

There is a manifest disposition in the veins below the surface to produce silver, and as before remarked that tendency is much the strongest in the Median set of veins. Associated with the galena of those lodes, molybdenum and tellurium are common attendants throughout, and when these veins shall have been carried to near those depths to which similar operations have been conducted in other countries, we may confidently look for a supply of this metal that will be but little inferior to the present product of gold.

QUARTZ MINES.

The operations in this department have continued active during the past season, and the number of mines is on the increase. So far as the workings have been conducted on the lodes during the past year, there are no farther evidences of pinching out than was presented in my former report. But to the contrary, the majority of the veins have increased a little in power, or have maintained fully that to which they had arrived last year. The greater proportion of the mines have been carried to more depth than before attained.

Of the total number of mines reported in active operation during the year, there are thirty-one still engaged, nine of the number having suspended during 1854. Of the total number suspended, five can be considered but temporary, as two are erecting new reduction works, the other three have ceased to reduce ores from the inefficiency of their machinery, and it is not probable that they will again resume operations until the means of transportation is such that heavy freights can be conveyed to near the districts in which the latter are located. At present the only transportation to these sections is upon the backs of mules and horses, and those acquainted with the requisites of machinery for the reduction of ores will readily perceive the inadequacy of such material as could be conveyed over rugged mountain trails by the latter process.

The parties owning these mines have not abandoned the enterprise on which they entered, but will await the time when the avenues of communication afford advantages superior to those at present in use, and which will undoubtedly be opened during the present year.

The remaining four companies that have stopped their operations, I am unable to give any cause for, as the parties who had the control of affairs were absent at the time I visited the districts. The report of those in the vicinity of these mines, in relation to the cause of their suspension, was not of a favorable character for their early resumption, but I should be unwilling to say that a mine was valueless upon such evidence, as private interests often exaggerate unfavorable circumstances above their true color The four last are in reality all that can be considered as permanently suspended, and the five preceding are at the best but temporary, as three of the number will resume work about the beginning of June, and the remaining two probably as early as September next.

In the immature state of this branch of industry, and the inefficiency of machinery, with the difficulty of commanding often the necessary amount of capital to conduct these operations to a successful termination, the ratio of ten per cent. of those who fail cannot by any means be considered as very large. And when it is compared with similar transactions in this State little more than two years since, the above sinks into insignificance. Or, if we look to more distant regions, it will not be difficult to find more than a parallel in the operations that transpired in the early days of the Lake Superior mines. The history of mining, either in the United States or Great Britain, when carefully examined, will not present a broader margin of successes than is to be found in the gold mines of this State since it became what might be considered a settled business, and the position which they hold as sources of profit, with an increasing confidence, is the best proof of their value. As we are situated in this State, these mines are subjected to the most severe test which it is in the power of man to inflict upon a business of this character. It is the test of intrinsic merit, and though invidious clamors are at times uttered, and often by those who have never taken the pains to inform themselves as to their native richness, still these even grow fainter as each succeeding month brings to light new evidences of success.

Had we the same facilities of exhibiting the characters which our gold mines present, through the agency of mining journals and jobbing boards, like those in New-York, Boston, and the English Metropolis, we have no fear but that the mines of this State would take their position in the front rank of those operations. But unlike the mines abroad, they do not require at home the prestige which fancy paper throws around the many faltering institutions of our distant neighbors.

That our mines have thus withstood the violent assaults that have been made upon them by those who stand behind the scenes of a foreign press, and thus attempt to give a fatal thrust unseen, is one strong evidence that they inherit a vitality which it is beyond the powers of those in this State still thus employed to deprive them of. We have passed that day when either British *skill* or capital is required to foster these operations, and the evidences are strong, that under the circumstances, as they have proved themselves, we should have been far better conditioned had their attention been directed to other, and probably to them more congenial channels.

We had expected to have received instruction in the mysterious art of mining from a people who boast the knowledge of centuries of experience in that profession; but to their own astonishment, American miners in California have become their tutors. I would not be guilty of casting envious reproaches upon foreign friends, but justice to ourselves demands that the FACTS should come out.

Another argument which in itself carries weight in regard to the integrity of these mines, is the fact, that none of those at present engaged exhibit the slightest hesitancy in embarking in additional enterprises. This is proved from the fact of a constant addition of new reduction works in different parts of the State, and more particularly in those counties where the mines have been opened to the greatest extent. It is hardly a supposable case, to believe that men would thus coolly invest in speculations that require sums varying from fifteen to fifty thousand dollars, which three years experience before them has demonstrated to be a failing and unprofitable business. We might torture the fact into such a conclusion, but the exercise of a little reason would be likely to dictate otherwise.

At the present time we find parties entering the field with new and increased facilities at their command, (and who, from mismanagement, in times gone by, have lost heavily) and are now realizing their most sanguine expectations from a judicious management of those operations in which they formerly failed to succeed.

The greater proportion of those who have embarked in this business within the past year, are men who have heretofore lost heavily in the same business. Their experience of former days taught them somewhat a severe lesson, but at the same time, they learned enough of the value of these metallic veins to inspire that confidence in ultimate success which they are now realizing in an eminent degree. This proves that their confidence was not misplaced, and the only error committed in the premises was too hasty and inconsiderate action, and the use of means inadequate to secure the desired end.

Gold mining in this State has arrived at such a point, that it is now looked upon by those in the least conversant with the business, as one of the principal and best employments for capital and labor; yielding a higher rate of profit for the means employed than any one branch of mercantile pursuits at present known in this country; and as an evidence of this it will be but necessary to state that several of the mercantile men of the larger cities have withdrawn their capital from their former pursuits and invested the same in the latter. It is a rare thing to find one of these mines doing a losing business, for it has become a settled principle, that the lodes will pay the expenses of opening the mine, and there are but few that do not do it.

Numerous instances of this character are found in the State, and so well has this been demonstrated that those who engage in this business seldom fail to realize that result. One of the best examples of this is the case of one of the mines in the county of Amador, the aggregate expenses of which, in opening their mine and the erection of their reduction works, amounted to seventy-one thousand dollars, while the receipts from the mine, consisting of ore removed from the shafts and gallerys in opening, amounted to sixty-two thousand, the engine of the mill costing over twenty-two thousand. In this case the opening of the mine paid nearly the entire expenses of the concern. This is not an isolated instance, it is mentioned as illustrating what we have formerly said on this subject, and is stated as a fact which speaks louder than words.

Such is a brief history of the general phases which are presented in this branch of employment at the present time in this State, and with what has been said relating to this subject in my former reports, may serve, perhaps, to correct some of the erroneous impressions that still attach themselves to this important source of wealth, and which are as groundless as the wind. The sun of that day has set, when it will again be in the power of any man, or set of men, to again wreck that confidence which now reposes in the value of the gold mines of this State; their results have placed them beyond the reach of cavil, and beyond the shade of doubt.

In what follows I shall confine myself to such statistics of mines as are at the present time in my possession, with a catalogue of such new mines as have been opened during the past year, and also a notice of such mines as were in operation and unknown to me at the time of the publication of my former report.

LAFAYETTE AND HELVETIA MINE.

This mine is located in Grass Valley, and the diagram of their workings is taken from the lode on Lafayette Hill, one and a half miles southwest of the town. In this mine is found a heavy east and west vein, having a dip of about thirty-eight degrees, with a power of four feet at eight fathoms. The lodes of this hill have been fairly opened, and thus far present a somewhat envious feature to neighbors. The present depth of the workings are about eleven fathoms at the deepest point, the lode in the greenstone, with the above power and a tendency to advance from the latter. The underlie of the vein for about one hundred feet and immediately adjoining the walls, is a bed of hydrosilicate of magnesia of an extremely fine texture. containing gold. And the adit level of the mine, exclusive of the team-road for conveying the cattle to the mine-yard, is in its total length 1200 feet. Not increased from last year, it will be seen, in consequence of the change in the course in which they have been driving during the past year on the east and west lode. The working on the latter is near one hundred and forty feet, and thus far proved a fine quality of ore.

During the past season the company have erected a new mill directly upon the last lode. This is a most judicious movement on their part, as it will be the means of saving the neat sum of eleven thousand dollars each year which has been heretofore paid out for teaming. The arsenical ores do not increase much from last year, and the sulphuret of iron containing and investing the metal, is more abundant than formerly. The reduction works are carried by a twenty-five horse-engine, with a double battery of nine stamps each, and when in full operation is capable of reducing about thirty tons of ore per day. This mine employs twelve miners on the lode, day and night, while the aggregate of the other laborers amounts to twelve more; making a total of twenty-four.

The use of Cram's cylinder and Berdan's amalgamating apparatus, have been thrown aside as of little use, and inferior to the more simple and far less expensive methods that have been suggested from practical experience in this district.

OSBORN HILL MINE.

This mine is located two miles east of Grass Valley, on the above hill, and the Lawrence Hill adjacent. Vein has a strike north and south, with an easterly dip of forty degrees. The workings of 1853 have been abandoned for the purpose of attacking the lode at a lower point, some six hundred feet to the north of the latter, and thus drain the southern part of the lode. This has been accomplished by the sinking of their water-shaft to the depth of one hundred and sixteen feet, and which is fifty-one feet deeper than their former shafts of the old workings, and cuts the lode about 80 feet below the greatest depth reached at any former period. The amount of levels driven on Osborn Hill, and principally south of the deep shaft, exclusive of the extreme south workings, is four hundred and fifty feet, and upon Lawrence Hill three hundred feet; making a total of seven hundred and fifty feet thus exposing a heavy bed of good ore. The amount of shafting on both hills is near that of the levels; the mine is thus well ventilated. The power of the vein is three and one half feet, at the depth of twenty feet into the solid greenstone. Arsenical pyrites are plentiful among the ores of this mine. The full complement of laborers at this mine engaged in the lode, is thirty-two.

EMPIRE MINE.

Situated in Grass Valley, near the southern extremity of the town. This mine has been in active operation for two years, and their works have been uninterrupted during the greater part of that time.

Their principal lode is situated at Ophir Hill, one and a half miles to the east of their reduction works. The superior portion of the lode is situated in a decomposed granitic rock, and enters the greenstone at the depth of 103 feet, at the engine shaft A. The accompanying diagram is a general plan of their tower workings which is on a level with the bottom of the above shaft. The entire lode is very much decomposed, and the quartz matrix heavily charged with peroxide of iron; it is very seldom that gold is easily discoverable with the naked eye in any of the ores from this hill, yet is found to yield remarkably high in the reducing process. At the main shaft, A, is an eight inch lifting-pump, driven by steam to free the mine from water and also for bringing ores to the surface from level, B, and gallery, C, the same being conveyed from the latter down to the level through the winzes, 1, 2, 3, 4. The ores from the galleries, D, are delivered at the whim shafts, E, E.

The ground plan exhibits the extent of the workings in December, 1854, and from it may be gleaned some idea of the amount of ore immediately available, as well also as the very judicious manner in which the mine is conducted, both for convenience and economy. The ores from the lode, like all the other mines of this section, are breasted out, giving ample and convenient room for the disposition of the attle. The strike of the lode is north eighteen degrees west, with a dip of twenty degrees, and power of three and a half feet.

The complement of laborers at the mine is thirty-four, and including the reduction works it amounts to about forty men actively engaged.

JONES' AND DAVIS' MINE, AMADOR COUNTY.

The mine and reduction works are situated on the east side of a small tributary of the Amador Creek, the latter passing through the town of Amador one mile north of this mine. The top of the whim shaft C is one hundred and forty-five feet above the level of the creek, and ninety feet below the outcrop of the vein to the south. The shaft 4 on the vein is three hundred and sixty-four feet above the town of Amador. The design of the company in the working of their mine, as mentioned in the report of last year, has been carried out, the connection of the lower level throughont having been completed but a few days before I visited the mine this year. The mine, as now opened, presents the following arrangement: whim shaft C, 100 feet; south shaft, 140 feet; upper level, 280 feet; middle galleries, 150 feet; bottom levels, 180 feet. The amount of work completed within the past year is indicated by the dotted lines, and the total amount of excavation on the lode is exhibited in the dark shades of the accompanying diagram. The characteristics of the mine and the investing rocks, and reduction works, are seen by reference to the latter.

This company have erected a thirty-horse water-wheel and double-battery of eighteen stamps, their power is sufficient to reduce 25 tons of ore per day. They have discontinued the use of steam.

The full complement of laborers for this mine during the ensuing year, will amount to twenty-three; they have formerly employed thirty-four doing the opening of the lode.

KEY-STONE MINE.

Situated about three-fourths of a mile south of the former, and on the same tributary of the Amador. It is evidently a parallel lode with that of Spring Hill, and Jones' and Davis's mines, and is situated about twenty-five feet above the level of the Creek. The adit runs nearly east and west for the distance of one hundred and ten feet, at which point the lode is cut with a power of three feet, at nine fathoms from the surface. At the end of the adit, a shaft has been sunk through the lode for seven fathoms; its diameter is four and a half feet. This shaft is heavily timbered, and well ceiled, the planking and frame snugly jointed. It is one of those operations that partakes strongly of the character of permanency in its design and construction, like most other of the workings of 1854 in this branch of business. The diagram presents the work on the lode as now progressing. The old gallery at the end of the adit has been driven to 100 feet on the south, and 90 feet on the north. The gallery 18 feet above the end of the adit, has been carried 100 feet in each direction. The level at the bottom of the seven-fathom shaft is 94 feet, with a power in the lode of five feet.

This company have also abandoned the use of steam for power, and have erected a forty horse water wheel, and heavy battery at the old reduction works. They have also built another large mill south of the former, of equal capacity, in order to work their mine at distant points to better advantage.

The complement of laborers at this mine for the present is sixteen, but on opening the southern workings they will employ about thirty-five. Many important and valuable improvements have been made during the past year on this mine.

MIDIAN MINE (Lea & Johnson's.)

This mine is beginning to show its true character, a handsome lode and much decomposed at the bottom of the nine fathom shaft. At the bottom of this shaft, two short levels of forty feet each have been driven, which shows a power of three feet in the lode at those places. On the south end of the vein an adit has been driven sixty-six feet, at the end of which the lode was struck with a power of four feet, on this one level has been driven of fifty-six feet. The vein shows a fair prospect.

The company have erected their reduction works this year, but were not in operation at the time I visited the mine.

EUREKA MINE.

Situated near the town of Sutter, county of Amador. The whin shaft A, has been carried from seven to sixteen fathoms during the past year. The adit enters from the west, and is about one hundred feet in length. The upper gallery has been carried south of the adit a distance of one hundred and fourteen feet, and north seventy-five feet. The middle gallery is thirty feet below the preceding, and opens at the whin shaft, being driven on the north sixty feet, and south eighty-five feet. The level at the bottom of the sixteen fathom shaft, is one hundred and forty-four feet in length. The tramroad which was commenced last year has been completed for nine hundred feet, and is now within some eighty feet of the lode. The rocks are a graphic slate, very firm, and often charged with pyritic crystals.

The rich thread which commenced at the surface, and for fifty feet in depth, was highly piritiferous; is found at the bottom of the main shaft much more productive. The pyrites have ceased entirely at this depth, and the hilo is composed of metalic gold, not disseminated, but forming a true vein, at times exceeding three-eighths of an inch in thickness. The vein has been struck in an adjoining mine, about one thousand feet to the south. This is the only instance of a true vein of metalic gold having been found in this State.

The compliment of laborers in this vein is sixteen, and the capacity for reduction of ores about ten tons per day.

STATISTICS OF MINES.

During the past year I have obtained statistics from fourteen of the gold mines of the State. These consist of mines located in the counties of Shasta, Nevada, El Dorado, and Amador. The statistics consist of all general and incidental expenses, the number of operatives employed as miners, engineers, tenders, &c., with their wages per month; expenses of fuel, teaming, dead work, quantity of ore reduced per day, average product of the same, with monthly and annual receipts. These statistics were taken from the books of the companies, and may, therefore, be entitled to confidence as a fair exhibit of the character of this branch of mining.

To save time, and at the same moment render the subject more comprehensive, the aggregates of these statistics will be given:

Capital invested, - - - - -	$ 793,000
Net receipts, - - - - - -	1,483,000
Expenditures, - - - - -	507,000

In addition to the above fourteen mines, there are thirty others which have continued in operation during 1854, and which, from the known investments of the preceding year, will give an additional investment of $334,000. From the net proceeds of the fourteen mines above known, and their expenses, it would be safe to assume that the thirty not heard from, have yielded fully fifty per cent. on their capital invested. This, it will be seen, is much below the proportion of the first. This then would give for the total number of mines, an amount of capital actively employed, as follows:

Investments, - - -	$1,127,000
Gross receipts, - - -	2,157,510
Total capital and products, - -	$3,284,510 for 1854.

From the above it appears that the aggregate product of these mines is about four per cent. of the product of the State, as far as the latter is known with any degree of certainty.

The aggregate number of persons actively employed in extracting the ores, and in reducing the same, amounts to six hundred and ten, bearing a very small proportion to the great mass engaged in the other branch of mining in the State.

In regard to the above figures, I would state that they represent rather the minimum than the maximum of investments and receipts, and it has been a leading object in collating these statistics, to avoid those extravagant estimates, heretofore indulged in, with relation to this subject.

The above list of additional mines, with the number still actively engaged from last year, swells the aggregate number for 1855, to fifty-three mines in actual operation, and a net increase of thirteen from the preceding year over all that have suspended for any considerable length of time.

WATER COMPANIES.

The table below will give an approximate idea of the value and extent of our artificial water courses, constructed for the purpose of facilitating mining operations The valuation in the aggregate of the counties are placed at those figures on which they are known to yield a profit of five per cent. per month. The estimates are based on a careful examination of the aggregate receipts of eighty-three of one hundred and nine companies included, and our list comprises but seven of the principal mining counties of the State. Much interesting local details was obtained, which the want of time this year prevents from appearing in these pages:

TABLE.

Counties.	No. Companies.	No. Miles.	Valuation.
Amador, - - - - -	15	129	$298,000
Calaveras, - - - - -	12	165	397,000
El Dorado, - - - - -	10	173	380,000
Nevada, - - - - - -	27	210	412,000
Placer, - - - - -	11	160	369,000
Sierra, - - - - - -	14	137	180,000
Tuolumne, - - - - -	20	185	446,000
Total, - - - -	109	1,159	$2,480,000

LIST OF NEW AND RESUMED MINES EOR 1854–5.

The following is a list of those mines that have gone into operation within the year 1854, comprising those which have erected works for the reduction of their ores.

Name of Mine.			Location and County.	
Crœsus,	-	-	Auburn, Placer county.	
Canada Hill,	-	-	Canada Hill, Nevada county.	
Van Ammon,	-	-	Wolf Creek,	Do.
Orleans,	-	-	Grass Valley,	Do.
Whitesides & Co.,		-	Wolf Creek,	Do.
Rocky Bar,	-	-	Grass Valley,	Do.
Mount George,		-	Mount George,	Do.
Pacific,	-	-	Placerville, El Dorado County.	
Maryland,	-	-	Do.	Do.
Whitlock's,	-	-	Logtown,	Do.
Bryant's,	-	-	Do.	Do.
Fort John,	-	-	Drytown, Amidor County.	
Badger's,	-	-	Sutter,	Do.
Tuolumne,	-	-	Sonora, Tuolumne County.	
Orleans,	-	-	Do.	Do.
Experimental,		-	Columbia,	Do.
San Juan,	-	-	Mokelumne river, Calaveras County.	
Burleigh,	-	-	Do.	Do.

Mines omitted in report of last year, and still in operation.

Mount Pleasant,		-	Grizzly Flat, El Dorado County.	
Sierra Nevada,		-	Do.	Do.
Eagle,	-	-	Do.	Do.
Pocahontas,	-	-	Logtown,	Do.

ALTITUDES,

AS OBSERVED BY ANEROID BAROMETER.

County.	Locality.	Position.	Feet above tide level.
Sacramento,	Lexington House,	House,	141
El Dorado,	Smith's Exchange,	Natoma Valley,	325
Do.	Salmon Falls,	Bridge,	325
Do.	Indian Springs,	Top of Hill,	1,327
Do.	Pilot Hill,	Base,	1,288
Do.	Oak Valley,	Road,	1,240
Do.	Greenwood Valley,	Do.	1,511
Do.	Georgetown,	Main street,	2,484
Do.	Spanish Flat,	Hotel,	2,444
Do.	Kelsey's Flat,	Road,	2,486
Do.	Chile Bar,	South Fork American,	980
Do.	Placerville,	Main street,	2,058
Do.	Coloma,	River,	857
Do.	White Rock,	Top of Hill,	2,300
Monterey,	Infusorial beds,	Do.	310
Shasta,	Shasta city,	Main street,	912
Do.	Red Bluffs,	River,	184
Do.	Mt Washington Mine,	Mill,	2,028
Do.	Mt. Washington,	French Gulch,	3,028
Do.	French Town,	Clear Creek,	1,754
Do.	Mountain House,	Do.	2,0 0
Do.	Tower's Bridge,	Do.	1,112
Do.	Mountain House,	McLaughlin's Ranch,	3,154
Trinity,	Brown's Mountain,	Summit,	3,361
Do.	Trinity Do.	Do.	3,980
Do.	Weaverville,	Main street,	2,116
Do	Lewis's Bridge,	Trinity river,	1,668
Los Angeles,	Los Angeles City,	Main street,	257
Santa Barbara,	Santa Barbara,	Mission,	188

INDEX.

NOTE.

During the tour for 1854 a large collection of Marine Secondary and Tertiary Fossils has been made, with a variety of other mineral specimens, and as soon as arranged will be deposited in the office of the Secretary of State, with those of the preceding year.

JOHN B. TRASK.

www.ingramcontent.com/pod-product-compliance
Lightning Source LLC
LaVergne TN
LVHW011226110826
845150LV00006B/1559

* 9 7 8 1 4 2 5 5 1 5 4 7 8 *